SUPERMAN BATMAN

VENGEANCE

D1077502

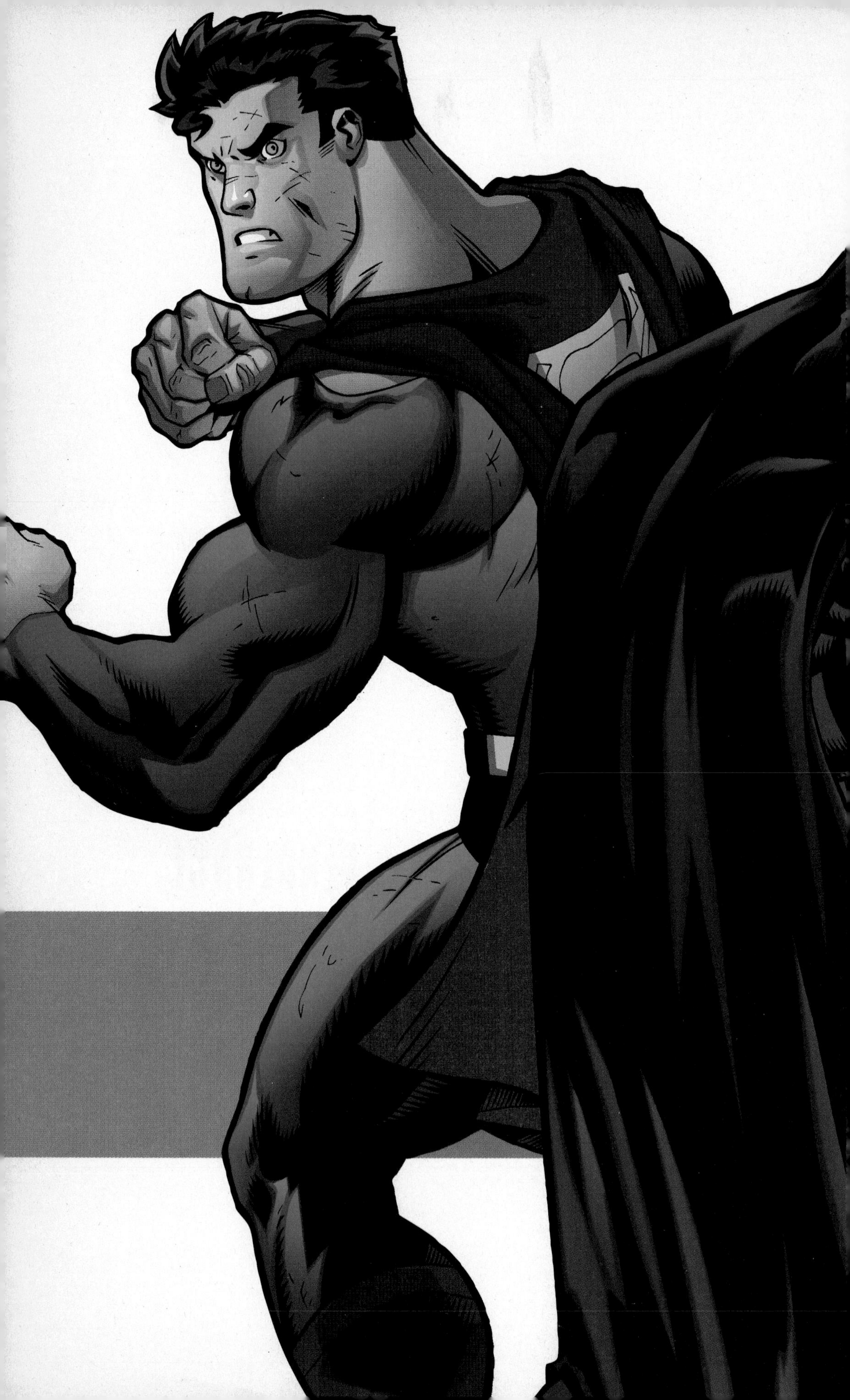

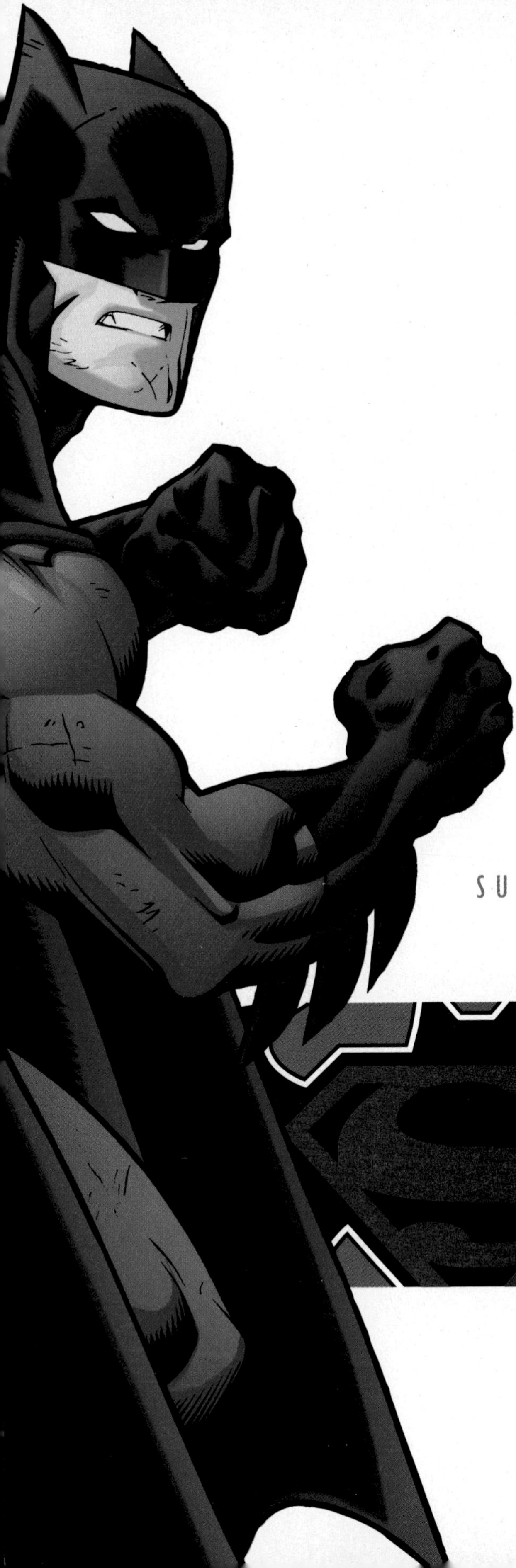

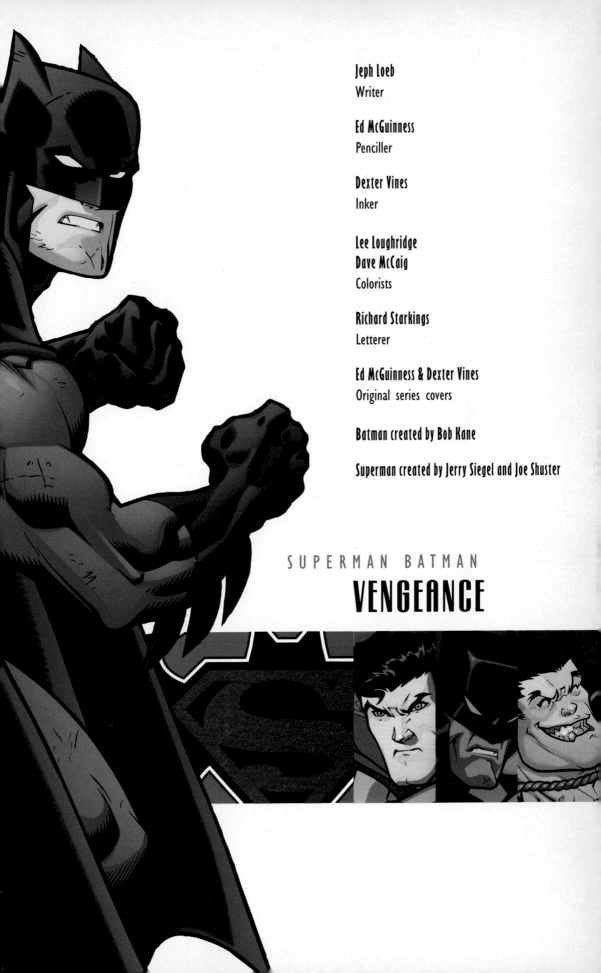

Jeph Loeb
Writer

Ed McGuinness
Penciller

Dexter Vines
Inker

Lee Loughridge
Dave McCaig
Colorists

Richard Starkings
Letterer

Ed McGuinness & Dexter Vines
Original series covers

Batman created by Bob Kane

Superman created by Jerry Siegel and Joe Shuster

SUPERMAN BATMAN

VENGEANCE

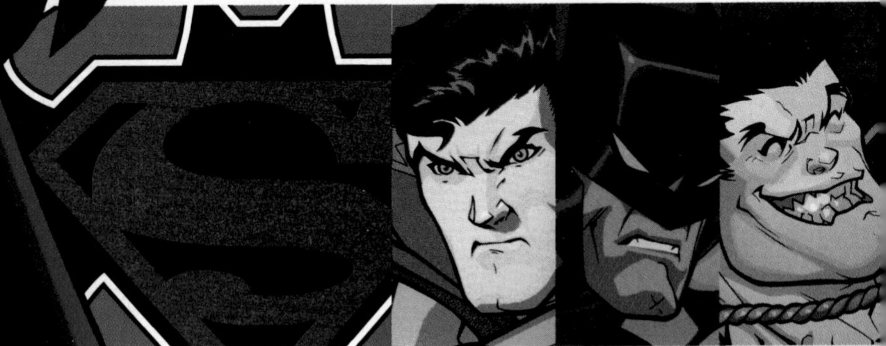

DAN DIDIO Senior VP-Executive Editor   EDDIE BERGANZA Editor-original series   TOM PALMER, JR. Associate Editor-original series   BOB JOY Editor-collected edition
ROBBIN BROSTERMAN Senior Art Director   PAUL LEVITZ President & Publisher   GEORG BREWER VP-Design & DC Direct Creative   RICHARD BRUNING Senior VP-Creative Director
PATRICK CALDON Executive VP-Finance & Operations   CHRIS CARAMALIS VP-Finance   JOHN CUNNINGHAM VP-Marketing   TERRI CUNNINGHAM VP-Managing Editor
STEPHANIE FIERMAN Senior VP-Sales & Marketing   ALISON GILL VP-Manufacturing   RICH JOHNSON VP-Book Trade Sales   HANK KANALZ VP-General Manager, WildStorm
LILLIAN LASERSON Senior VP & General Counsel   JIM LEE Editorial Director-WildStorm   PAULA LOWITT Senior VP-Business & Legal Affairs
DAVID MCKILLIPS VP-Advertising & Custom Publishing   JOHN NEE VP-Business Development   GREGORY NOVECK Senior VP-Creative Affairs
CHERYL RUBIN Senior VP-Brand Management   JEFF TROJAN VP-Business Development, DC Direct   BOB WAYNE VP-Sales

SUPERMAN/BATMAN: VENGEANCE
Published by DC Comics. Cover, sketch gallery and compilation copyright © 2006 DC Comics. All Rights Reserved.
Originally published in single magazine form in SUPERMAN/BATMAN #20-25. Copyright © 2005, 2006 DC Comics. All Rights Reserved. All characters, their distinctive
likenesses and related elements featured in this publication are trademarks of DC Comics. The stories, characters and incidents featured in this publication are entirely fictional.
DC Comics does not read or accept unsolicited submissions of ideas, stories or artwork.
DC Comics, 1700 Broadway, New York, NY 10019. A Warner Bros. Entertainment Company. Printed in Canada. First Printing.
Hardcover ISBN: 1-4012-0921-1. Hardcover ISBN 13: 978-1-4012-0921-6. Softcover ISBN: 1-4012-1043-0. Softcover ISBN 13: 978-1-4012-1043-4.
Cover art by Ed McGuinness and Dexter Vines. All covers colored by Dave McCaig.

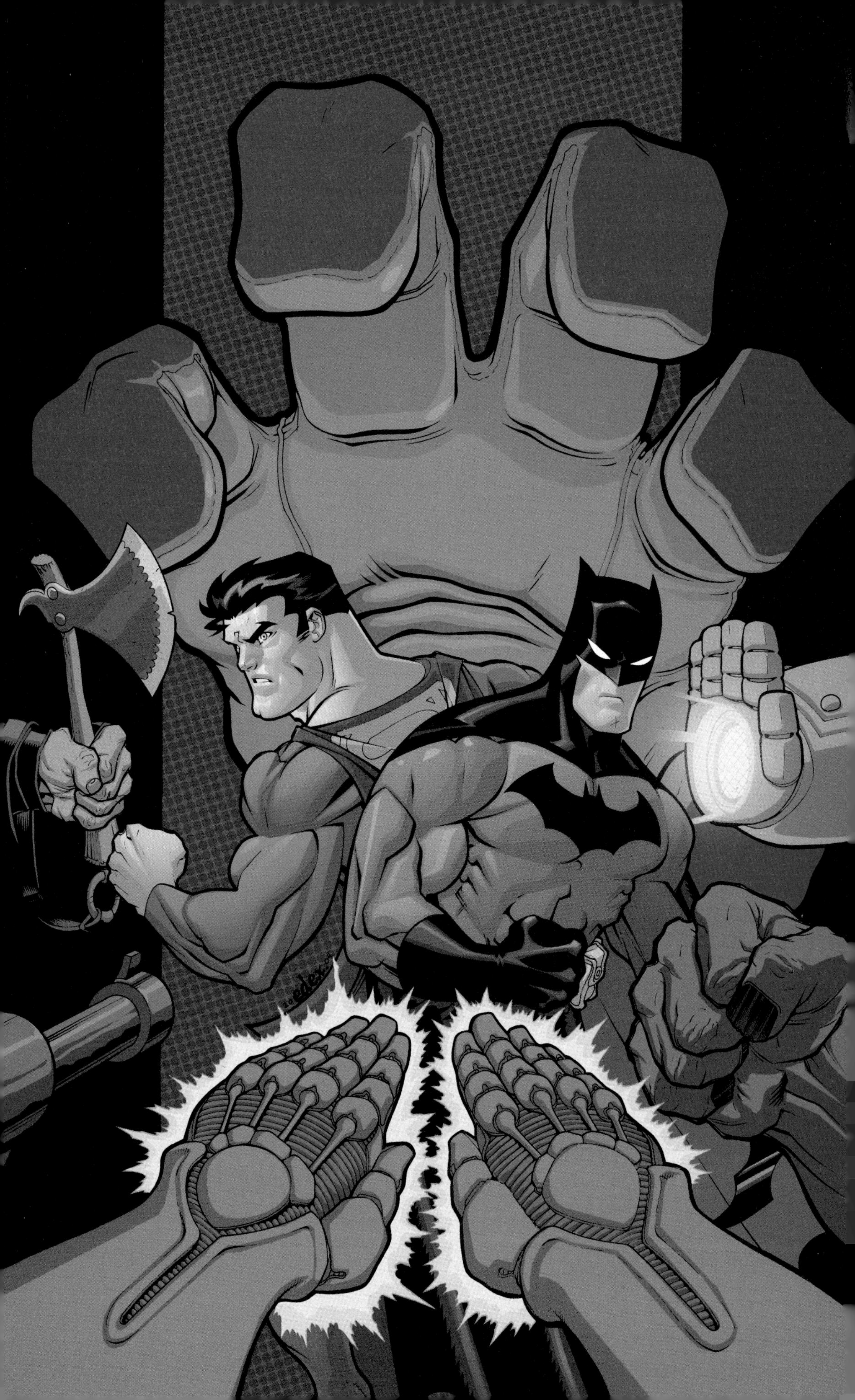

"HERE COME THE MAXIMUMS"

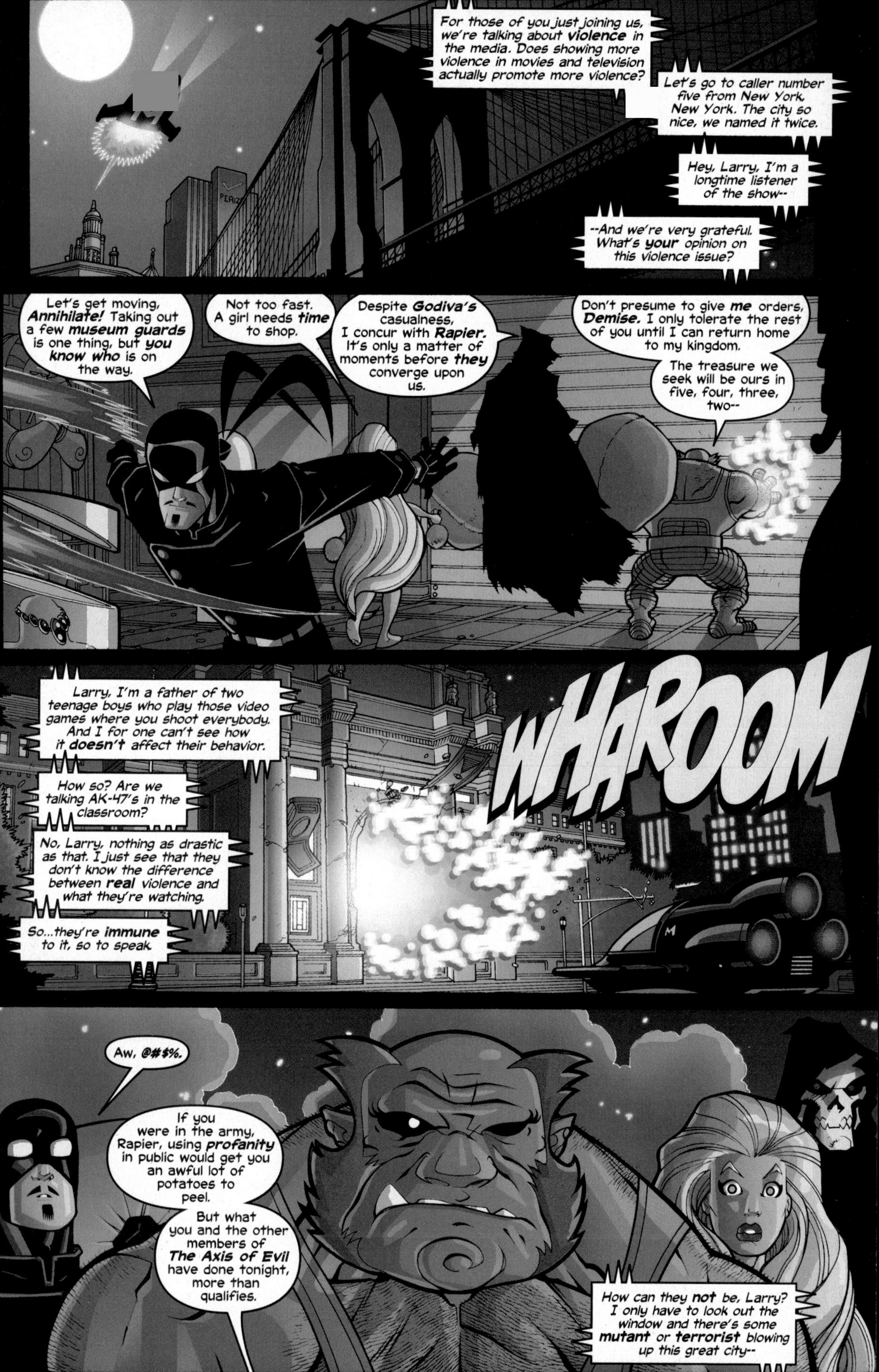

For those of you just joining us, we're talking about violence in the media. Does showing more violence in movies and television actually promote more violence?
Let's go to caller number five from New York, New York. The city so nice, we named it twice.
Hey, Larry, I'm a longtime listener of the show--
--And we're very grateful. What's your opinion on this violence issue?
Let's get moving, Annihilate! Taking out a few museum guards is one thing, but you know who is on the way.
Not too fast. A girl needs time to shop.
Despite Godiva's casualness, I concur with Rapier. It's only a matter of moments before they converge upon us.
Don't presume to give me orders, Demise. I only tolerate the rest of you until I can return home to my kingdom.
The treasure we seek will be ours in five, four, three, two--
Larry, I'm a father of two teenage boys who play those video games where you shoot everybody. And I for one can't see how it doesn't affect their behavior.
WHAROOM
How so? Are we talking AK-47's in the classroom?
No, Larry, nothing as drastic as that. I just see that they don't know the difference between real violence and what they're watching.
So...they're immune to it, so to speak.
Aw, @#$%.
If you were in the army, Rapier, using profanity in public would get you an awful lot of potatoes to peel.
But what you and the other members of The Axis of Evil have done tonight, more than qualifies.
How can they not be, Larry? I only have to look out the window and there's some mutant or terrorist blowing up this great city--

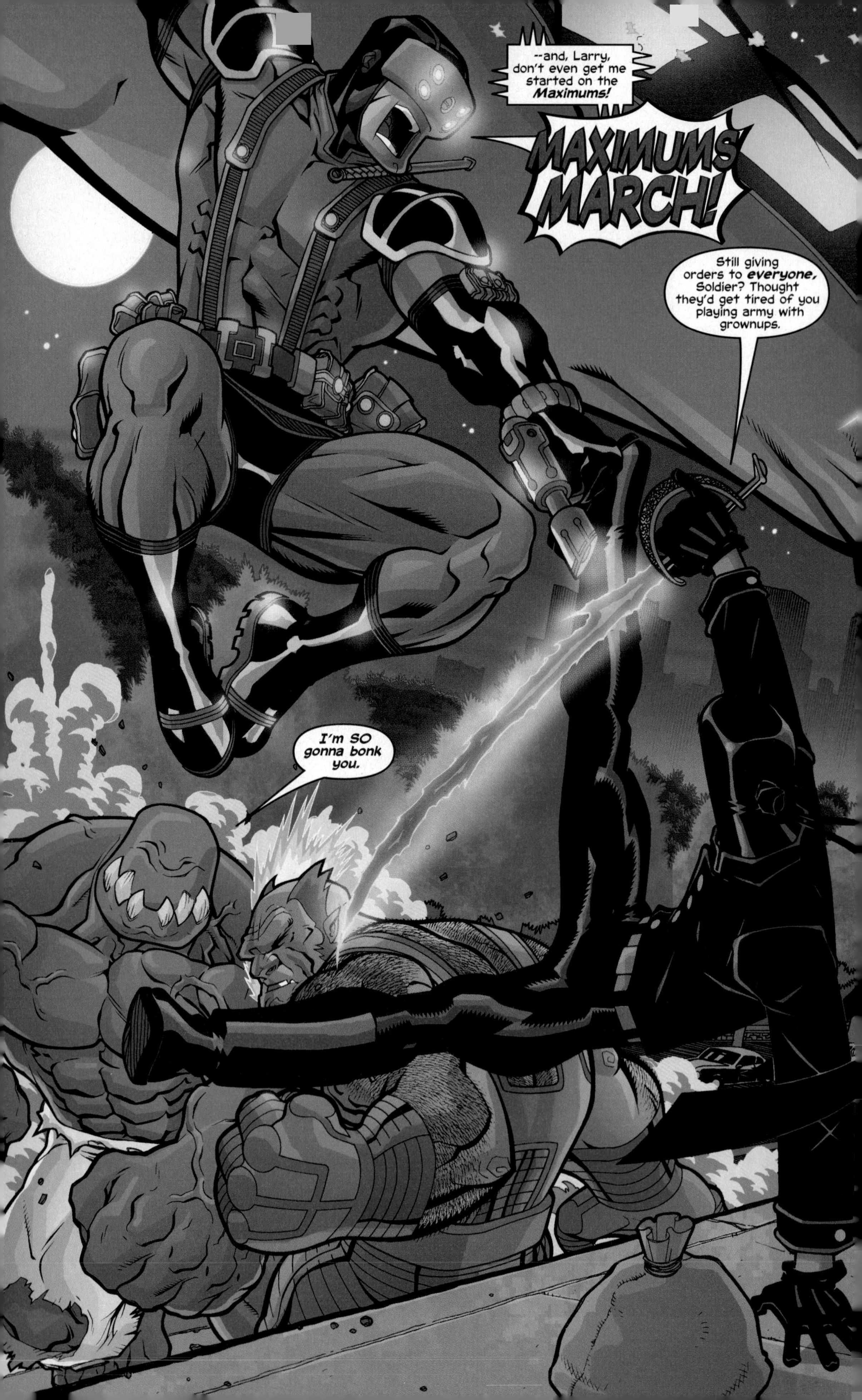
--and, Larry, don't even get me started on the *Maximums!*
MAXIMUMS MARCH!
Still giving orders to *everyone,* Soldier? Thought they'd get tired of you playing army with grownups.
I'm SO gonna bonk you.

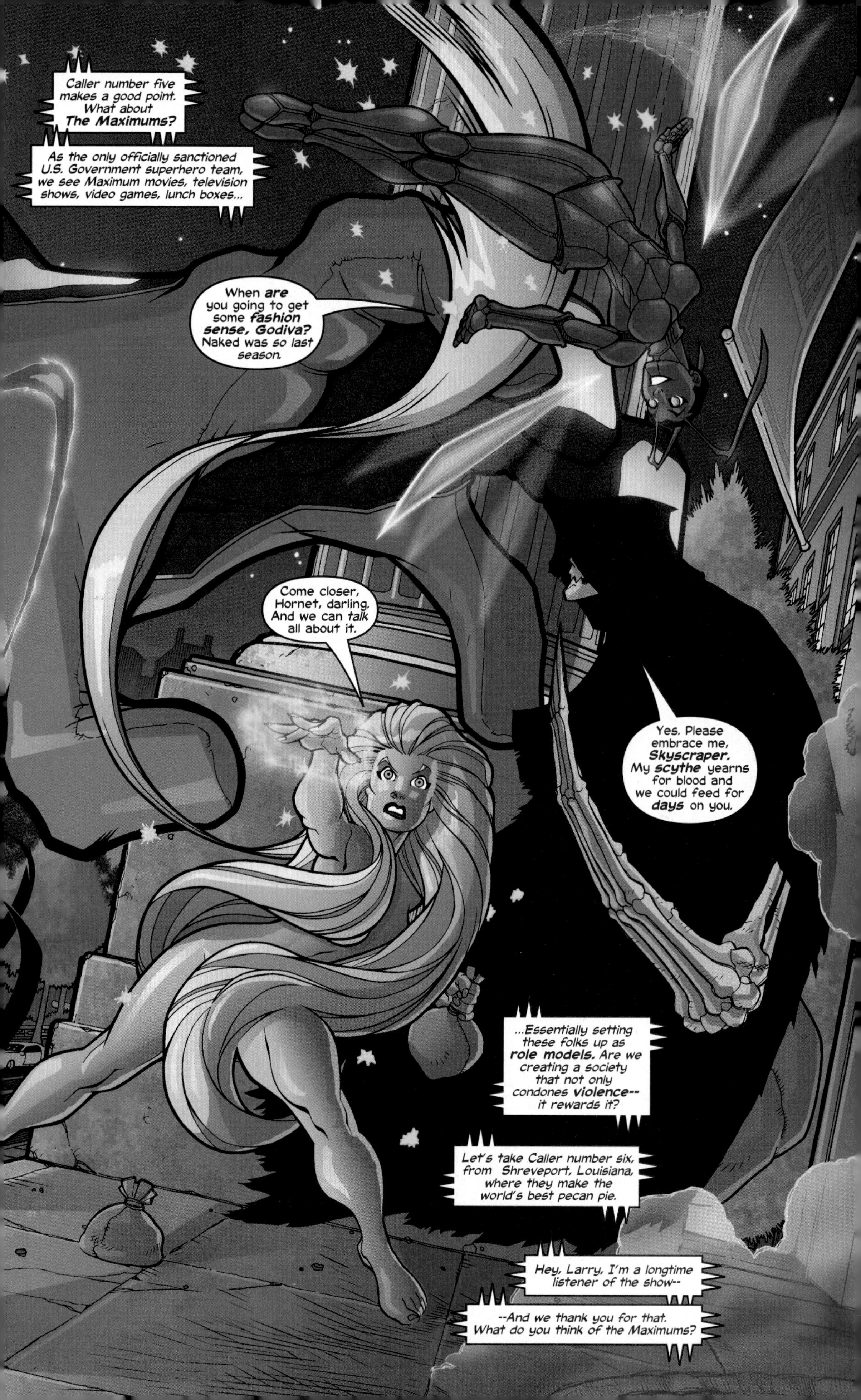

Caller number five makes a good point. What about **The Maximums?**
As the only officially sanctioned U.S. Government superhero team, we see Maximum movies, television shows, video games, lunch boxes...
When **are** you going to get some **fashion sense, Godiva?** Naked was so last season.
Come closer, Hornet, darling. And we can *talk* all about it.
Yes. Please embrace me, **Skyscraper.** My **scythe** yearns for blood and we could feed for **days** on you.
...Essentially setting these folks up as **role models.** Are we creating a society that not only condones **violence--** it rewards it?
Let's take Caller number six, from Shreveport, Louisiana, where they make the world's best pecan pie.
Hey, Larry, I'm a longtime listener of the show--
--And we thank you for that. What do you think of the Maximums?

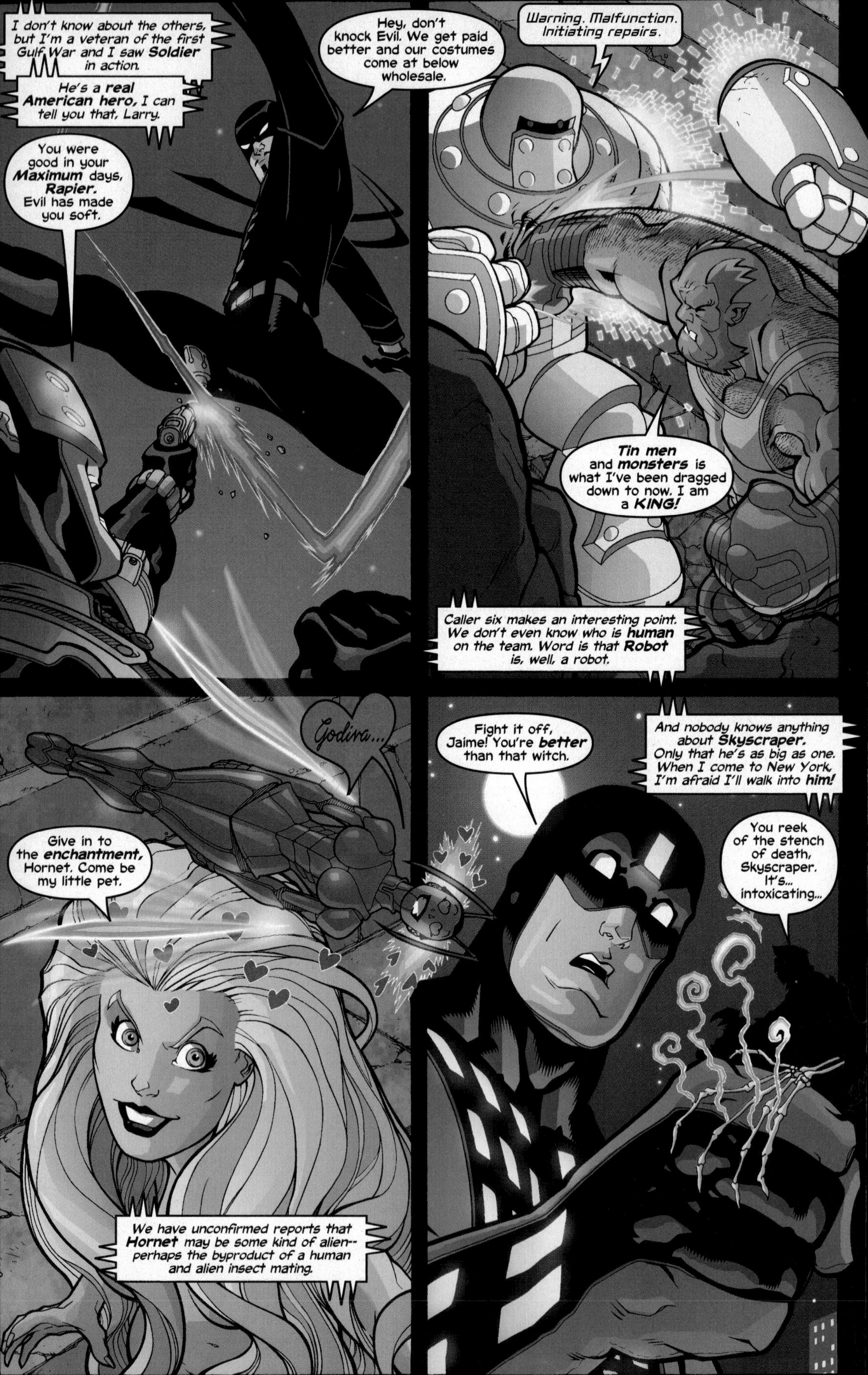

I don't know about the others, but I'm a veteran of the first Gulf War and I saw Soldier in action.
He's a real American hero, I can tell you that, Larry.
Hey, don't knock Evil. We get paid better and our costumes come at below wholesale.
You were good in your Maximum days, Rapier. Evil has made you soft.
Warning. Malfunction. Initiating repairs.
Tin men and monsters is what I've been dragged down to now. I am a KING!
Caller six makes an interesting point. We don't even know who is human on the team. Word is that Robot is, well, a robot.
Godiva...
Give in to the enchantment, Hornet. Come be my little pet.
We have unconfirmed reports that Hornet may be some kind of alien-- perhaps the byproduct of a human and alien insect mating.
Fight it off, Jaime! You're better than that witch.
And nobody knows anything about Skyscraper. Only that he's as big as one. When I come to New York, I'm afraid I'll walk into him!
You reek of the stench of death, Skyscraper. It's... intoxicating...

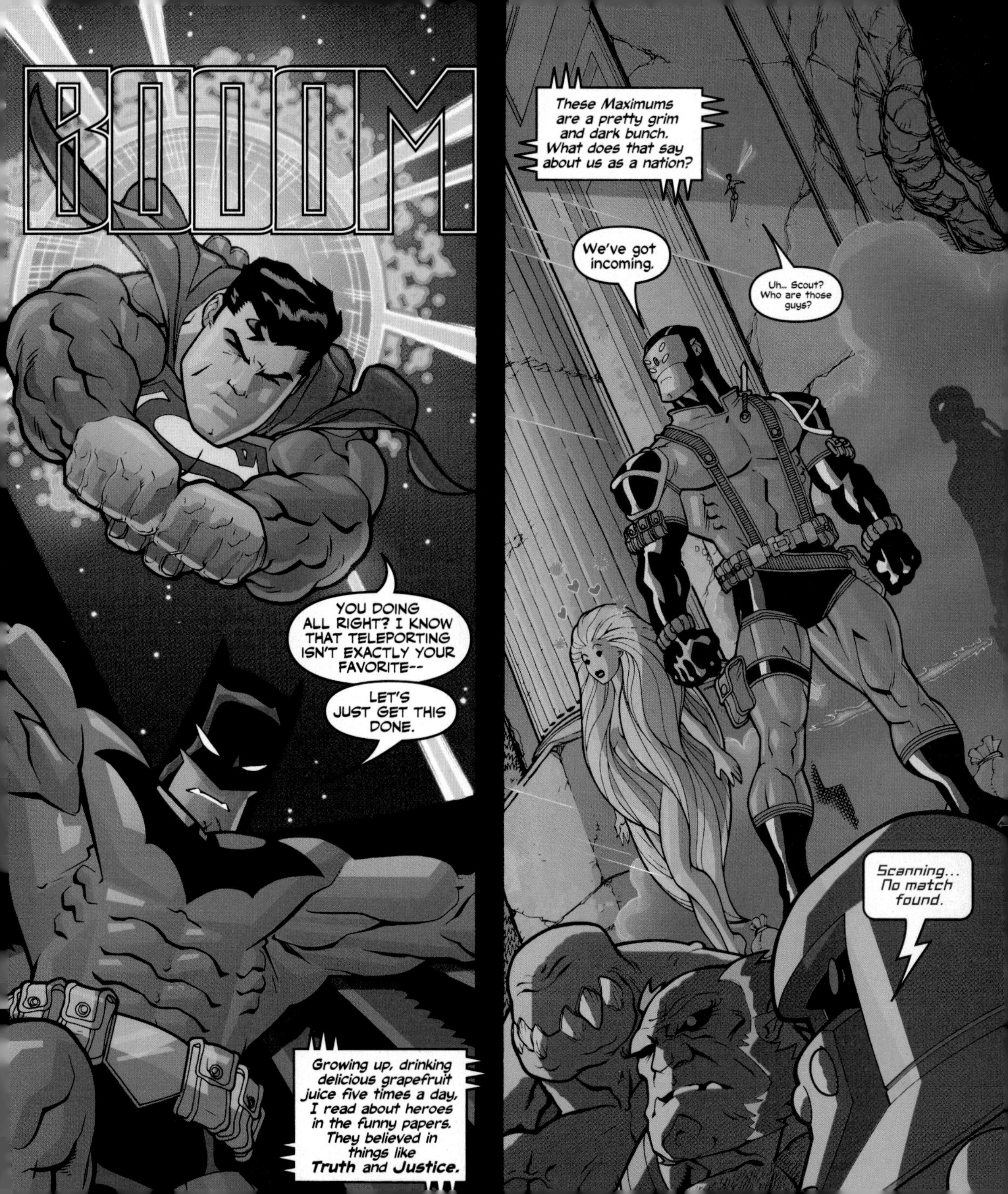
BOOOM
YOU DOING ALL RIGHT? I KNOW THAT TELEPORTING ISN'T EXACTLY YOUR FAVORITE--
LET'S JUST GET THIS DONE.
Growing up, drinking delicious grapefruit juice five times a day, I read about heroes in the funny papers. They believed in things like **Truth** and **Justice.**
These Maximums are a pretty grim and dark bunch. What does that say about us as a nation?
We've got incoming.
Uh... Scout? Who are those guys?
Scanning... No match found.

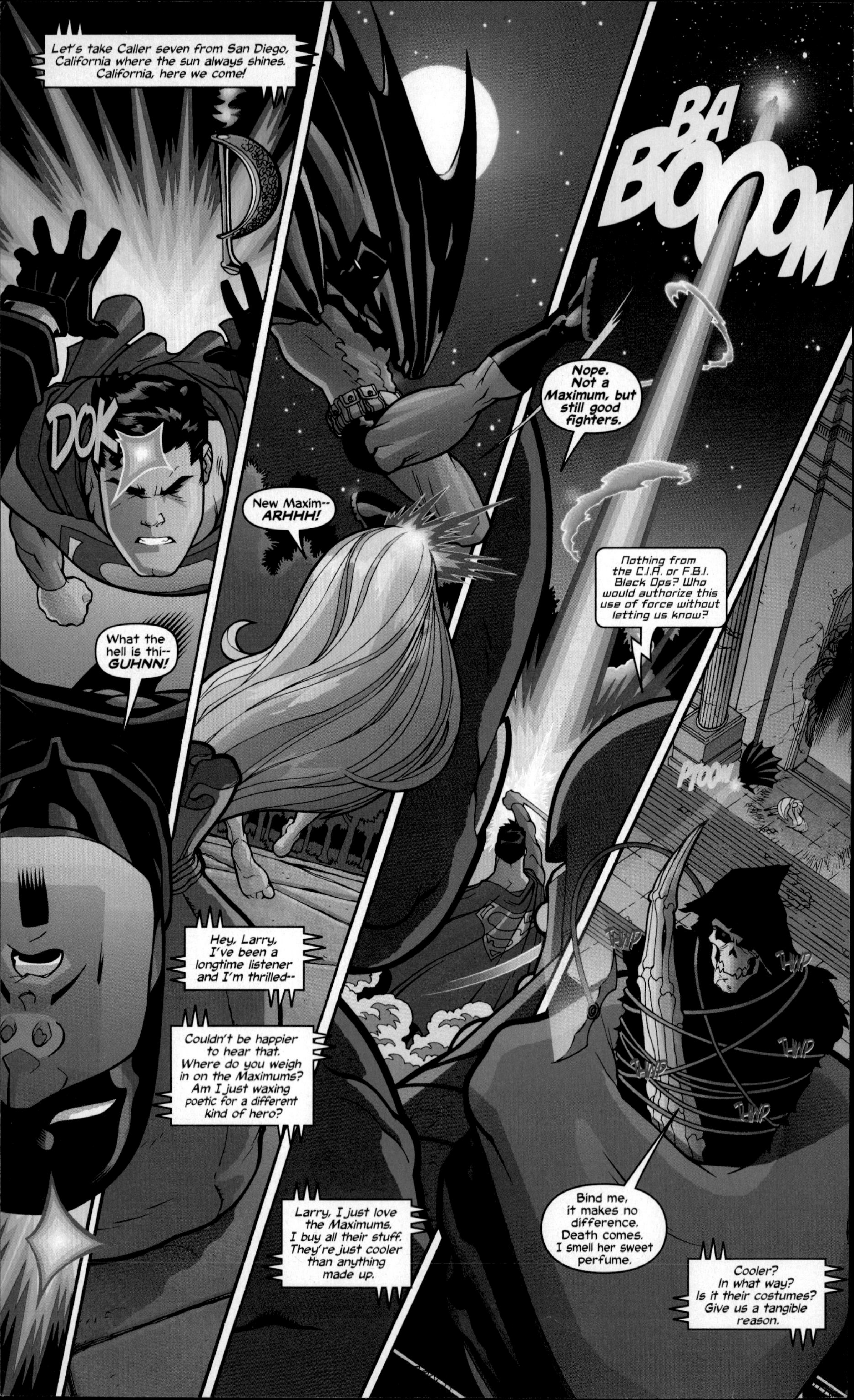

Let's take Caller seven from San Diego, California where the sun always shines. California, here we come!
DOK
What the hell is thi-- GUHNN!
BA BOOOM
Nope. Not a Maximum, but still good fighters.
New Maxim-- ARHHH!
Nothing from the C.I.A. or F.B.I. Black Ops? Who would authorize this use of force without letting us know?
PTOOM
Hey, Larry, I've been a longtime listener and I'm thrilled--
Couldn't be happier to hear that. Where do you weigh in on the Maximums? Am I just waxing poetic for a different kind of hero?
THWP
THWP
THWP
THWP
THWP
Larry, I just love the Maximums. I buy all their stuff. They're just cooler than anything made up.
Bind me, it makes no difference. Death comes. I smell her sweet perfume.
Cooler? In what way? Is it their costumes? Give us a tangible reason.

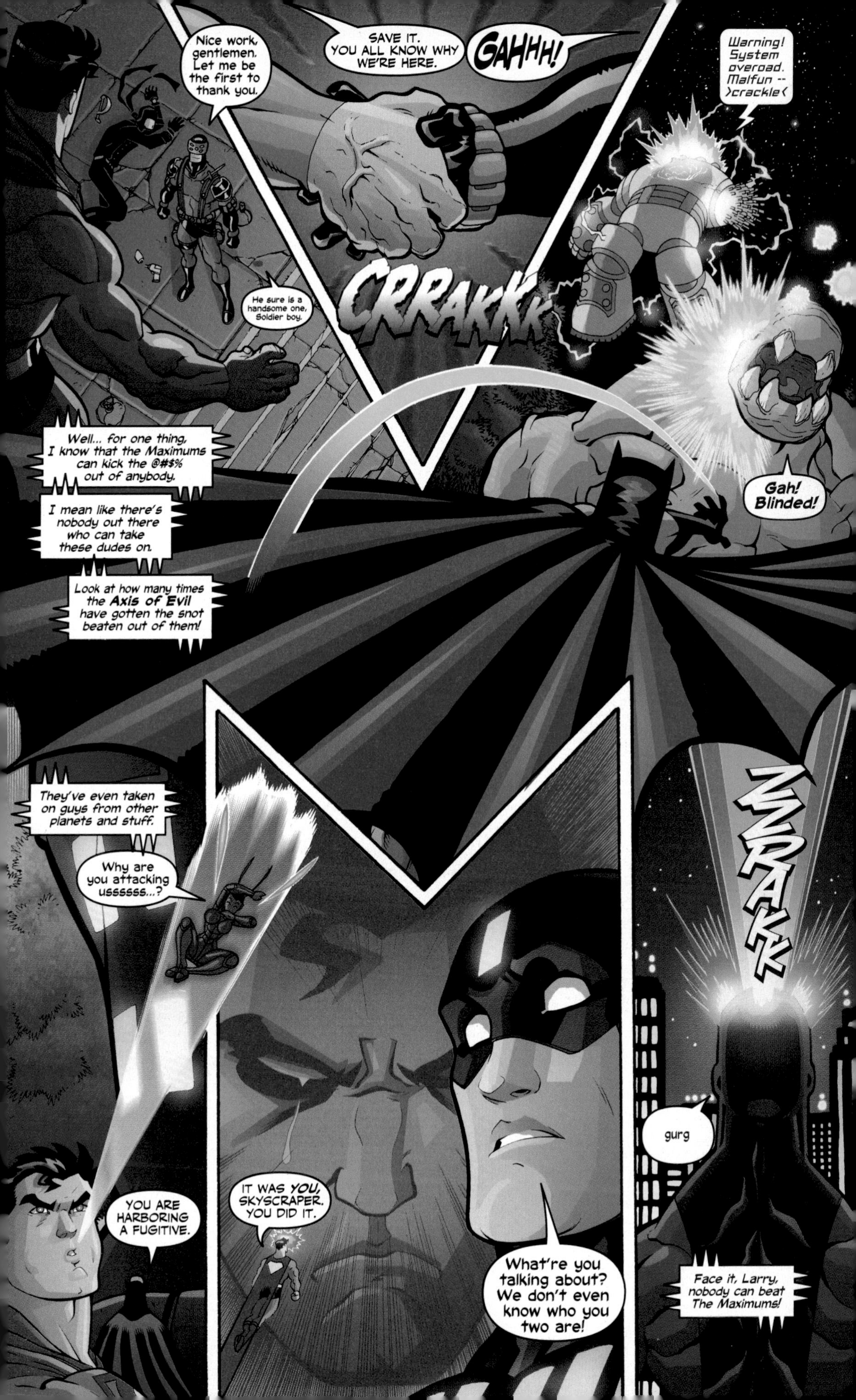
Nice work, gentlemen. Let me be the first to thank you.
SAVE IT. YOU ALL KNOW WHY WE'RE HERE.
GAHHH!
Warning! System overoad. Malfun -- >crackle<
He sure is a handsome one, Soldier boy.
CRRAKKK
Well... for one thing, I know that the Maximums can kick the @#$% out of anybody.
I mean like there's nobody out there who can take these dudes on.
Look at how many times the Axis of Evil have gotten the snot beaten out of them!
Gah! Blinded!
They've even taken on guys from other planets and stuff.
Why are you attacking ussssss...?
ZZRAKK
gurg
YOU ARE HARBORING A FUGITIVE.
IT WAS YOU, SKYSCRAPER. YOU DID IT.
What're you talking about? We don't even know who you two are!
Face it, Larry, nobody can beat The Maximums!

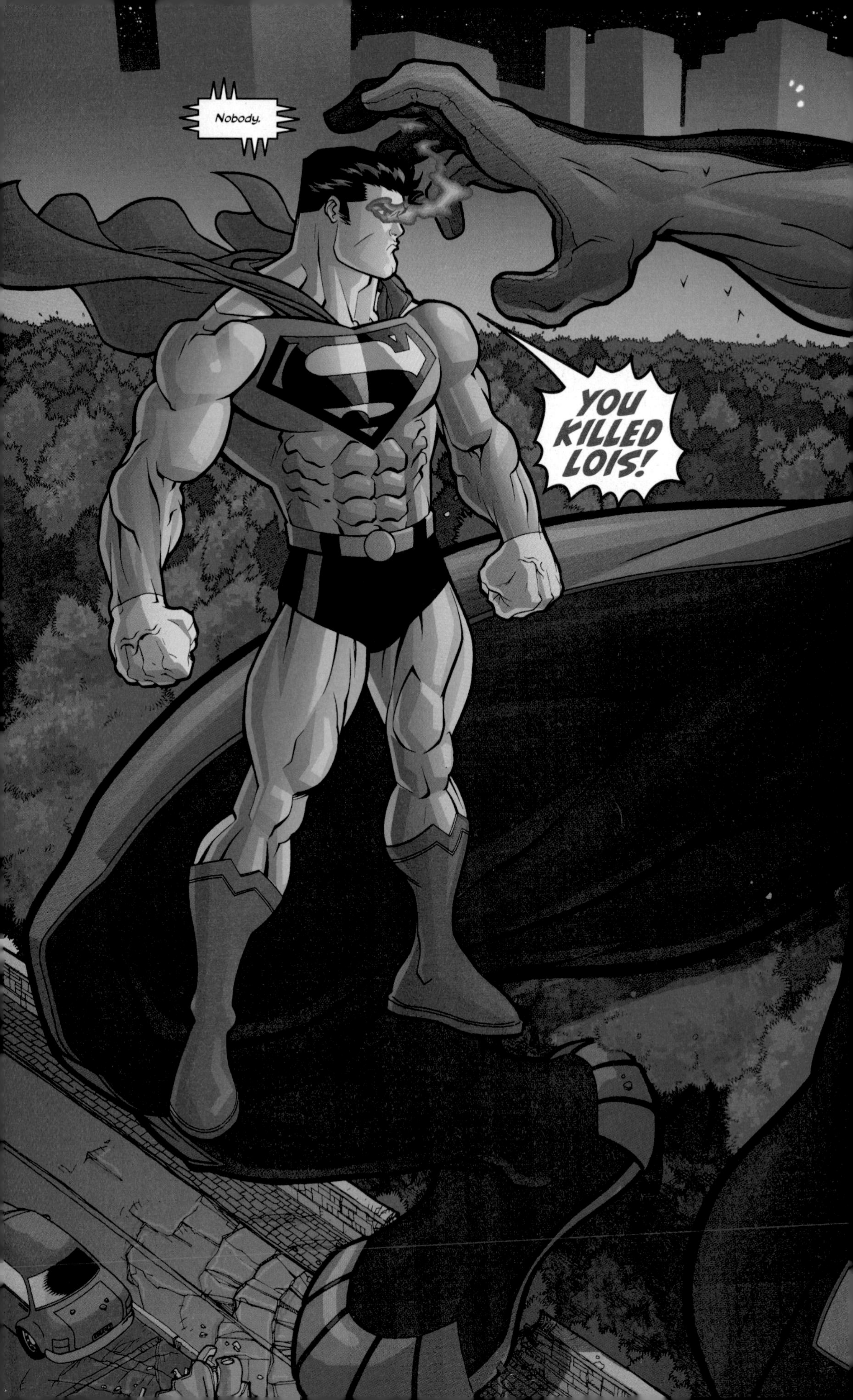
Nobody.
YOU KILLED LOIS!

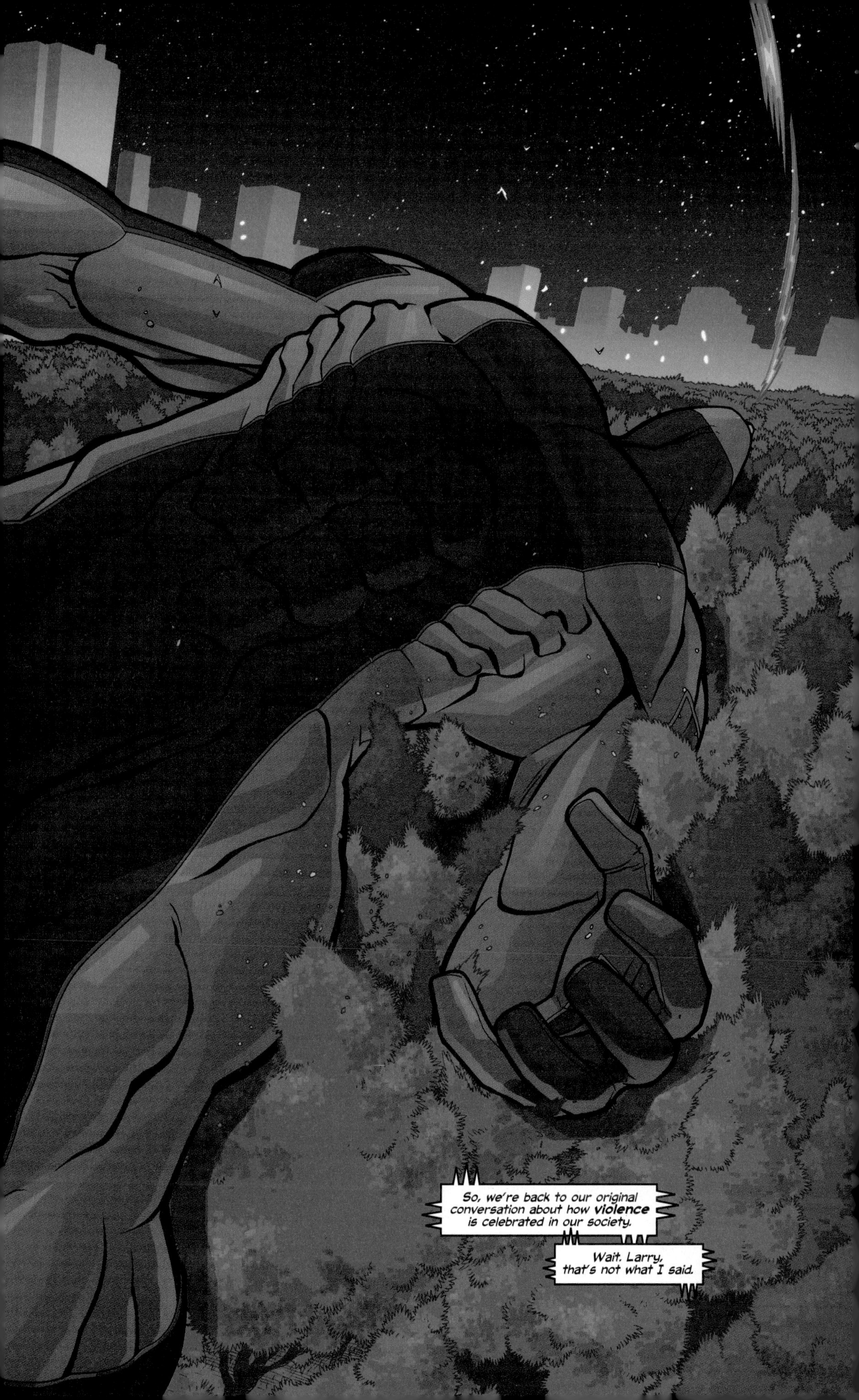
So, we're back to our original conversation about how **violence** is celebrated in our society.
Wait. Larry, that's not what I said.

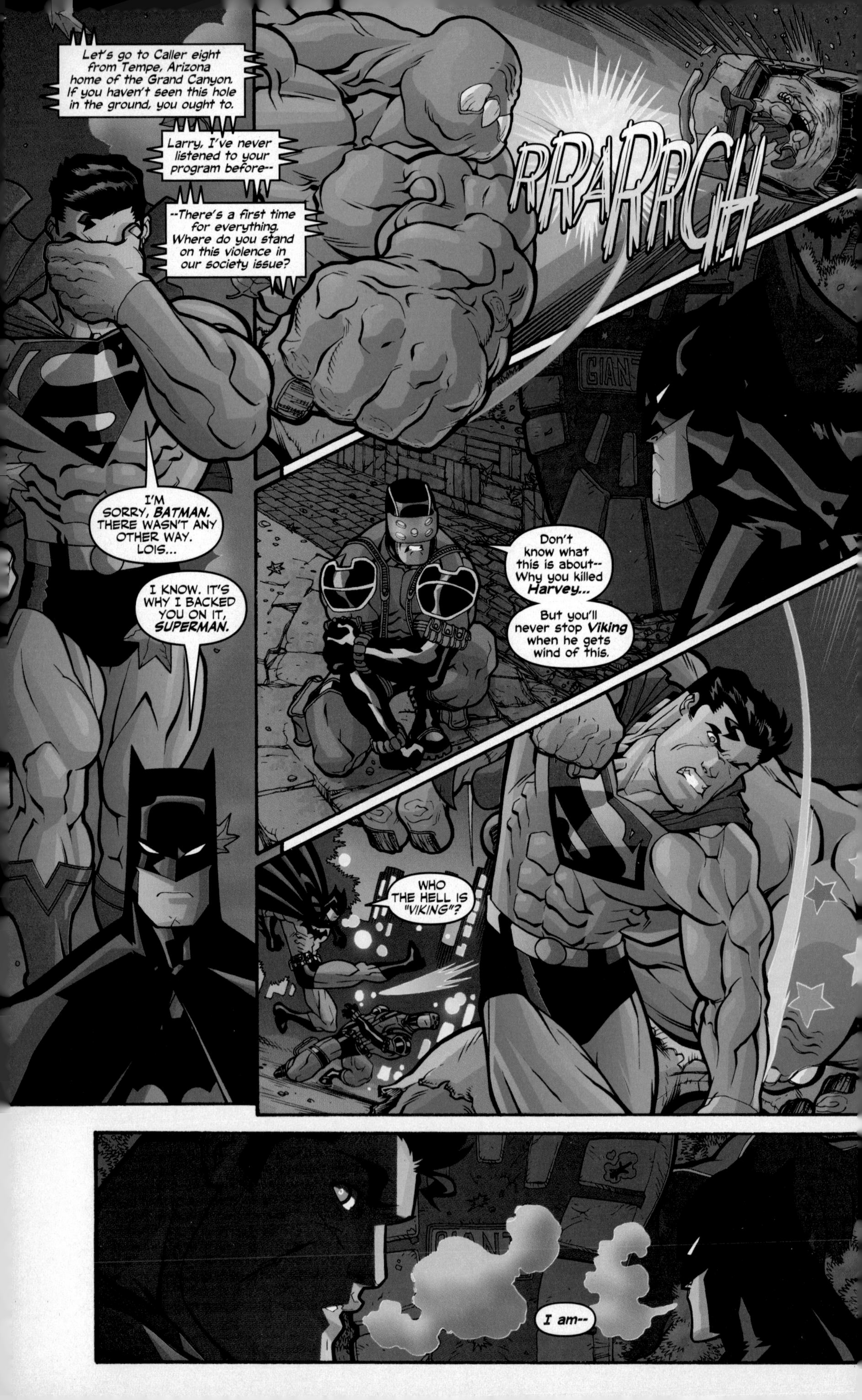

Let's go to Caller eight from Tempe, Arizona home of the Grand Canyon. If you haven't seen this hole in the ground, you ought to.
Larry, I've never listened to your program before--
--There's a first time for everything. Where do you stand on this violence in our society issue?
RRARRGH
I'M SORRY, BATMAN. THERE WASN'T ANY OTHER WAY. LOIS...
I KNOW. IT'S WHY I BACKED YOU ON IT, SUPERMAN.
Don't know what this is about-- Why you killed Harvey...
But you'll never stop Viking when he gets wind of this.
WHO THE HELL IS "VIKING"?
I am--

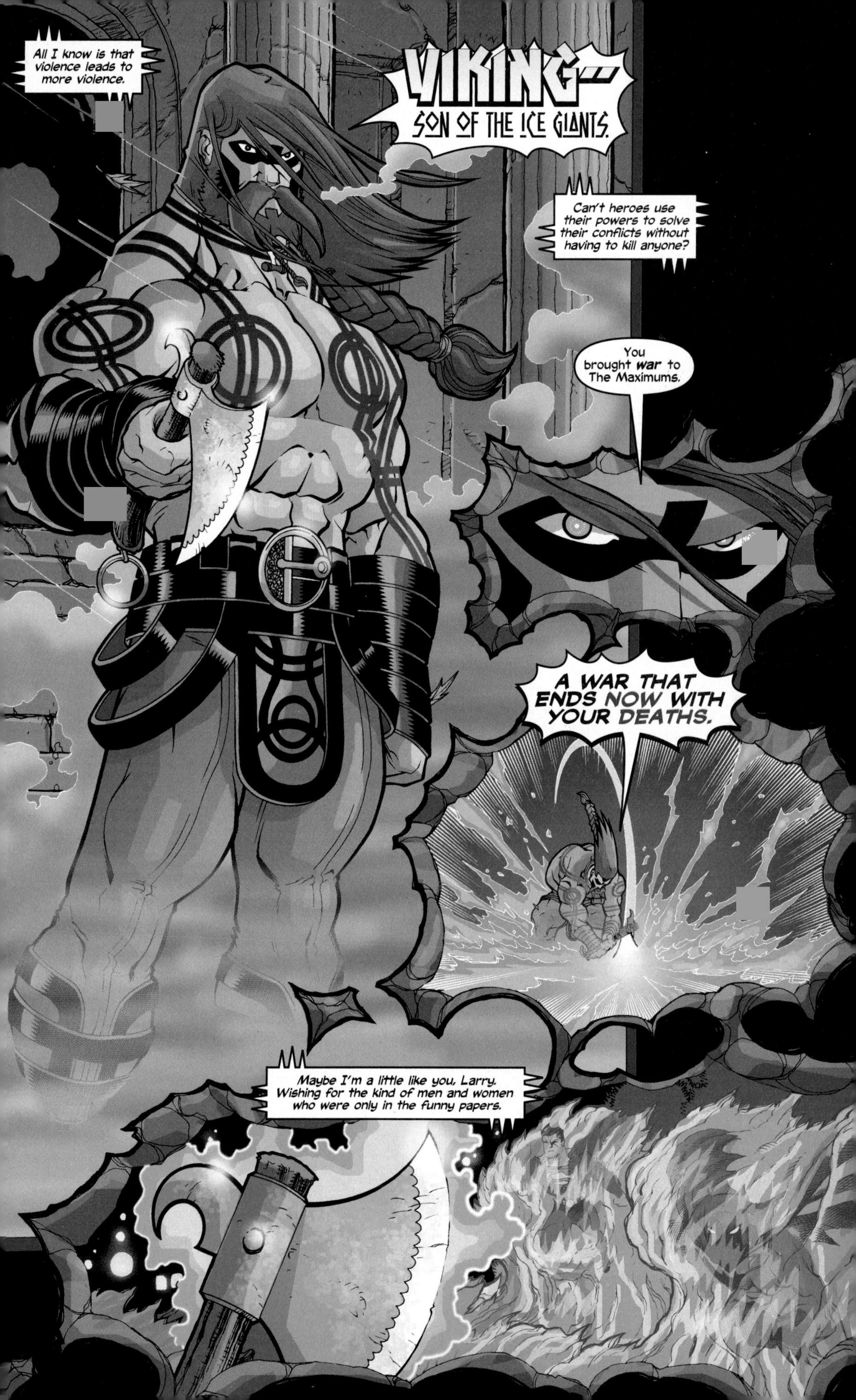
All I know is that violence leads to more violence.
VIKING -- SON OF THE ICE GIANTS.
Can't heroes use their powers to solve their conflicts without having to kill anyone?
You brought war to The Maximums.
A WAR THAT ENDS NOW WITH YOUR DEATHS.
Maybe I'm a little like you, Larry. Wishing for the kind of men and women who were only in the funny papers.

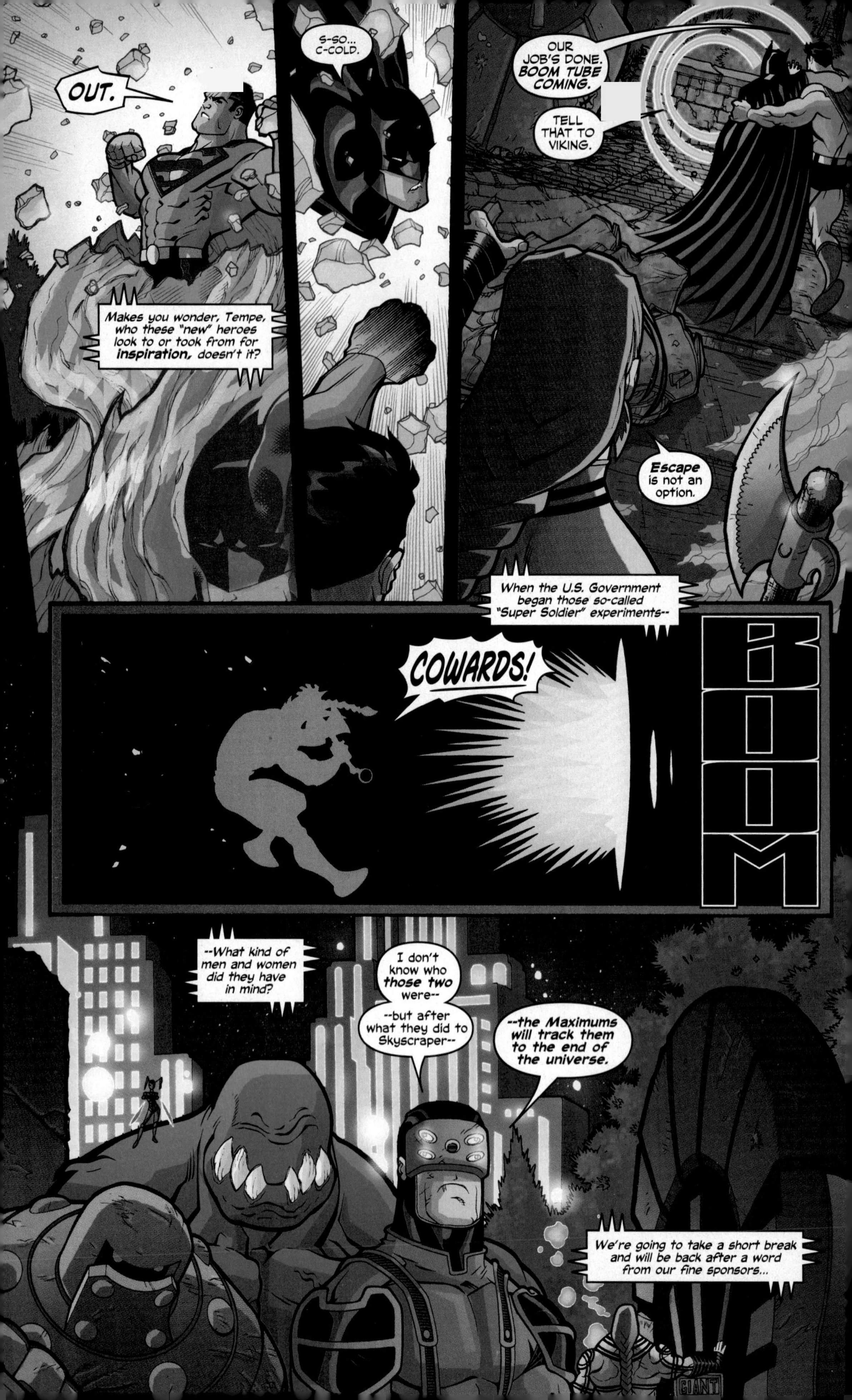
OUT.
S-SO... C-COLD.
Makes you wonder, Tempe, who these "new" heroes look to or took from for inspiration, doesn't it?
OUR JOB'S DONE. BOOM TUBE COMING.
TELL THAT TO VIKING.
Escape is not an option.
When the U.S. Government began those so-called "Super Soldier" experiments--
COWARDS!
BOOM
--What kind of men and women did they have in mind?
I don't know who those two were--
--but after what they did to Skyscraper--
--the Maximums will track them to the end of the universe.
We're going to take a short break and will be back after a word from our fine sponsors...
GIANT

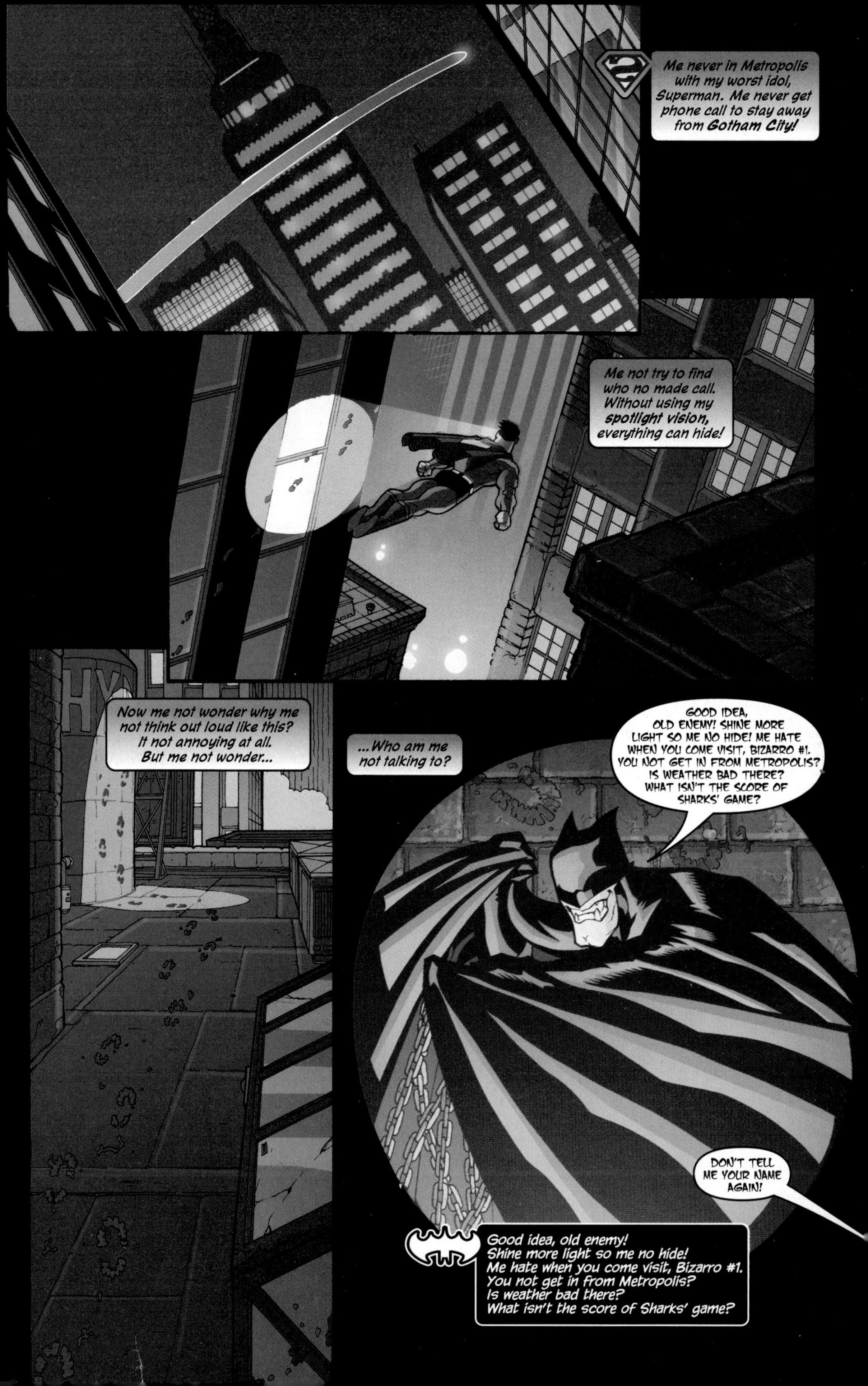
Me never in Metropolis with my worst idol, Superman. Me never get phone call to stay away from Gotham City!
Me not try to find who no made call. Without using my spotlight vision, everything can hide!
Now me not wonder why me not think out loud like this? It not annoying at all. But me not wonder...
...Who am me not talking to?
GOOD IDEA, OLD ENEMY! SHINE MORE LIGHT SO ME NO HIDE! ME HATE WHEN YOU COME VISIT, BIZARRO #1. YOU NOT GET IN FROM METROPOLIS? IS WEATHER BAD THERE? WHAT ISN'T THE SCORE OF SHARKS' GAME?
DON'T TELL ME YOUR NAME AGAIN!
Good idea, old enemy! Shine more light so me no hide! Me hate when you come visit, Bizarro #1. You not get in from Metropolis? Is weather bad there? What isn't the score of Sharks' game?

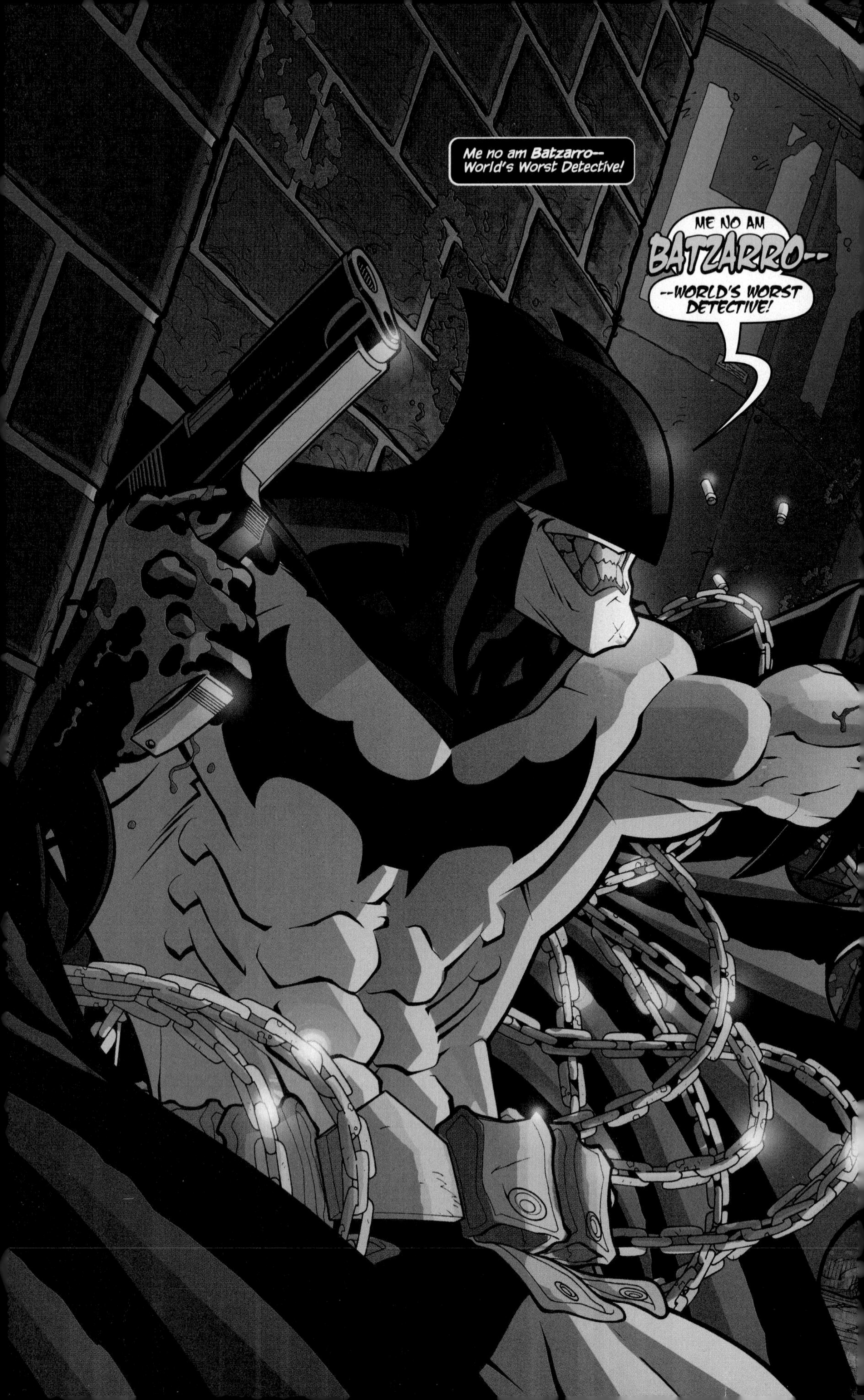
Me no am Batzarro--
World's Worst Detective!
ME NO AM
BATZARRO--
--WORLD'S WORST
DETECTIVE!

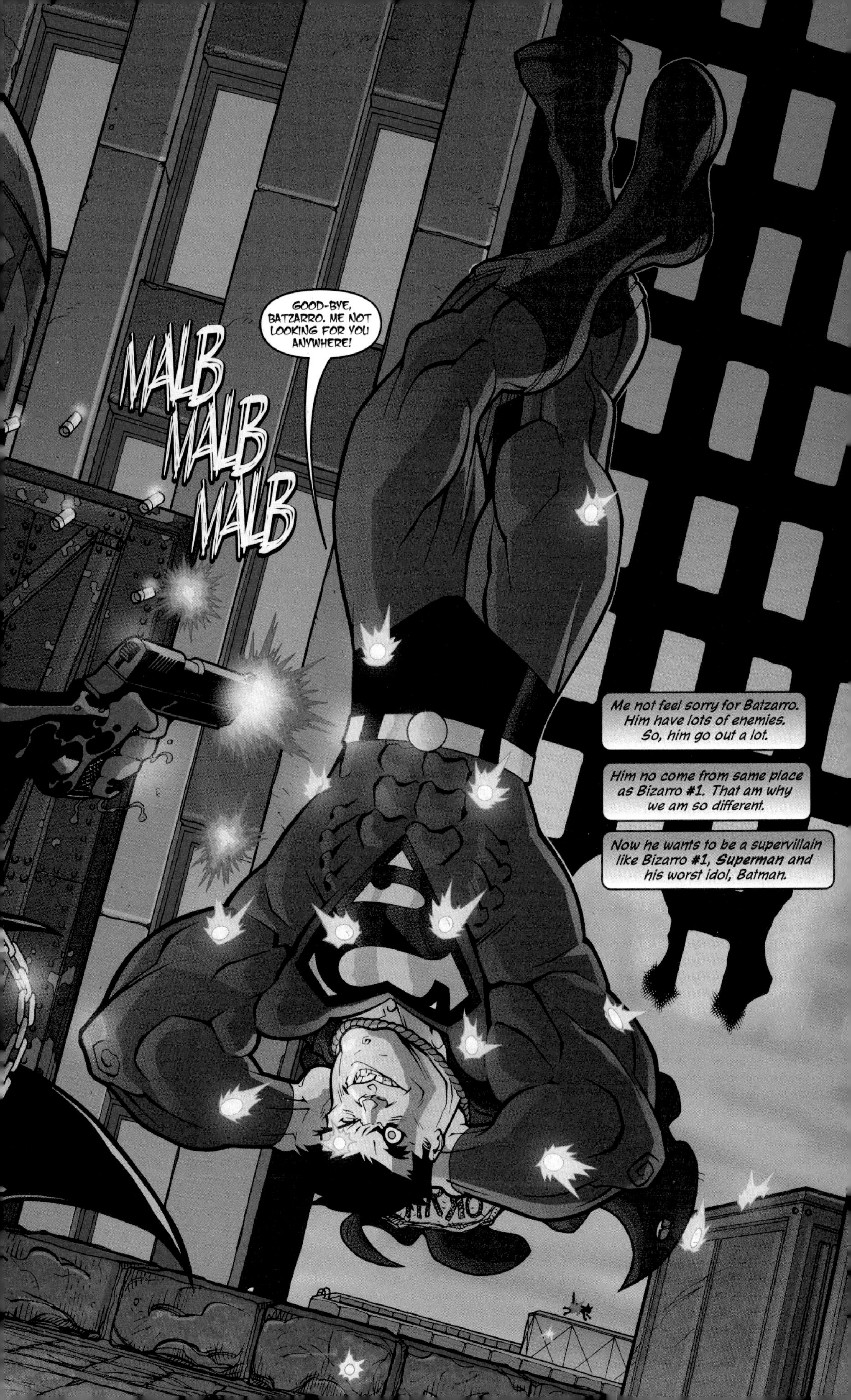
MALB MALB MALB
GOOD-BYE, BATZARRO. ME NOT LOOKING FOR YOU ANYWHERE!
Me not feel sorry for Batzarro. Him have lots of enemies. So, him go out a lot.
Him no come from same place as Bizarro #1. That am why we am so different.
Now he wants to be a supervillain like Bizarro #1, *Superman* and his worst idol, Batman.

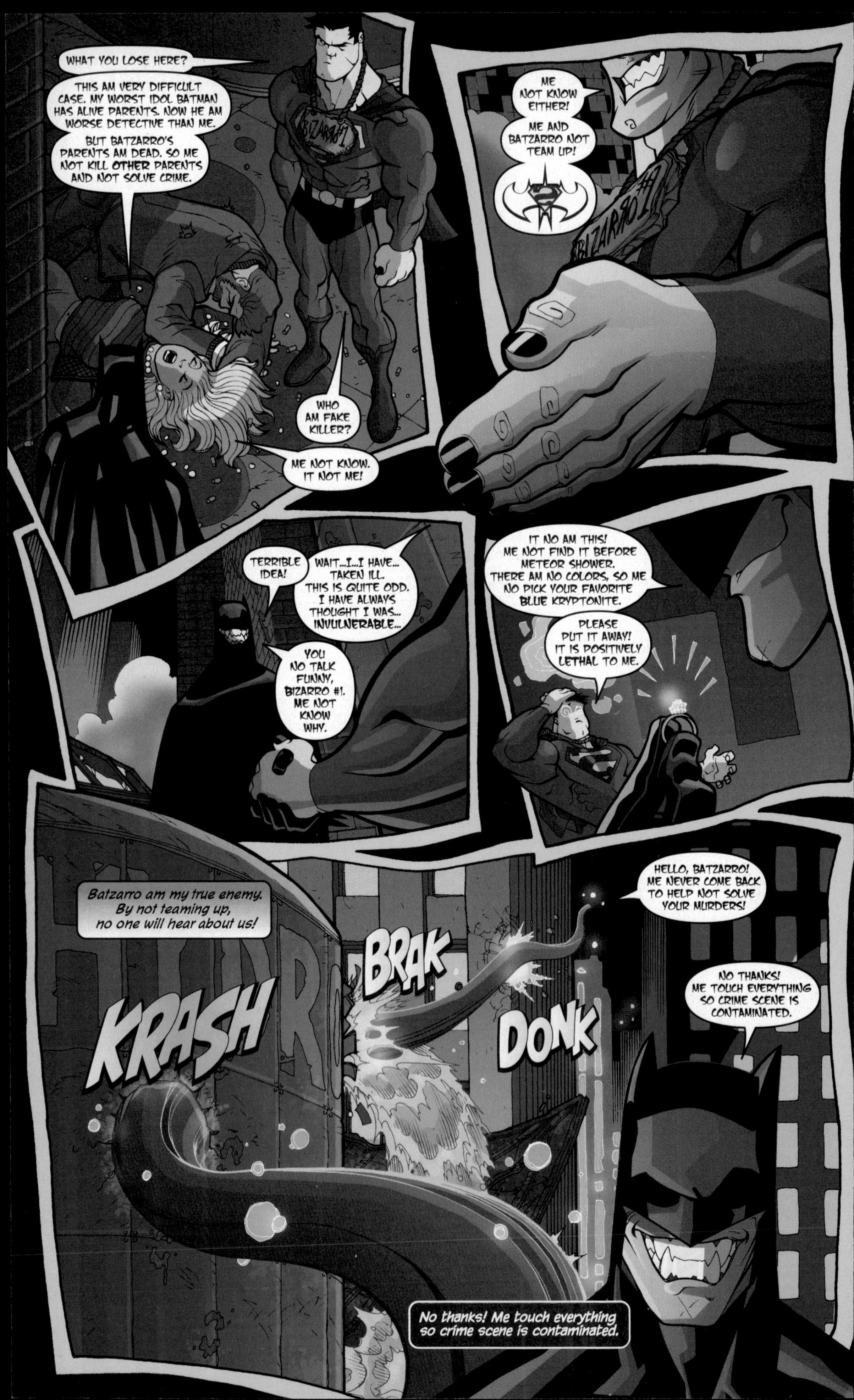
WHAT YOU LOSE HERE?
THIS AM VERY DIFFICULT CASE. MY WORST IDOL BATMAN HAS ALIVE PARENTS. NOW HE AM WORSE DETECTIVE THAN ME.
BUT BATZARRO'S PARENTS AM DEAD. SO ME NOT KILL OTHER PARENTS AND NOT SOLVE CRIME.
WHO AM FAKE KILLER?
ME NOT KNOW. IT NOT ME!
ME NOT KNOW EITHER!
ME AND BATZARRO NOT TEAM UP!
BIZARRO #1
TERRIBLE IDEA!
WAIT...I...I HAVE... TAKEN ILL. THIS IS QUITE ODD. I HAVE ALWAYS THOUGHT I WAS... INVULNERABLE...
YOU NO TALK FUNNY, BIZARRO #1. ME NOT KNOW WHY.
IT NO AM THIS! ME NOT FIND IT BEFORE METEOR SHOWER. THERE AM NO COLORS, SO ME NO PICK YOUR FAVORITE BLUE KRYPTONITE.
PLEASE PUT IT AWAY! IT IS POSITIVELY LETHAL TO ME.
Batzarro am my true enemy. By not teaming up, no one will hear about us!
HELLO, BATZARRO! ME NEVER COME BACK TO HELP NOT SOLVE YOUR MURDERS!
BRAK
KRASH
DONK
NO THANKS! ME TOUCH EVERYTHING SO CRIME SCENE IS CONTAMINATED.
No thanks! Me touch everything so crime scene is contaminated.

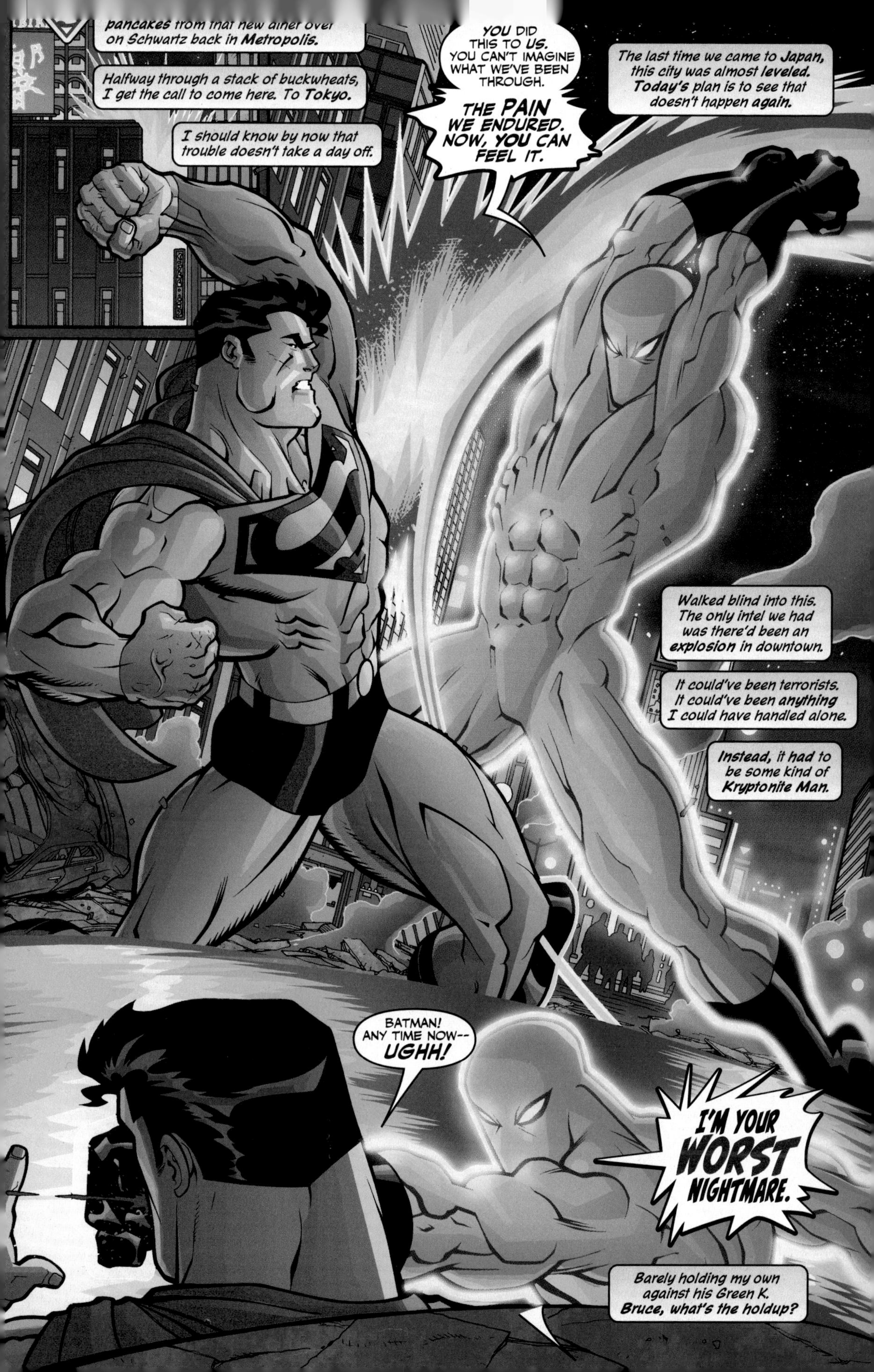

pancakes from that new diner over on Schwartz back in Metropolis.
Halfway through a stack of buckwheats, I get the call to come here. To Tokyo.
I should know by now that trouble doesn't take a day off.
YOU DID THIS TO US. YOU CAN'T IMAGINE WHAT WE'VE BEEN THROUGH.
THE PAIN WE ENDURED. NOW, YOU CAN FEEL IT.
The last time we came to Japan, this city was almost leveled. Today's plan is to see that doesn't happen again.
Walked blind into this. The only intel we had was there'd been an explosion in downtown.
It could've been terrorists. It could've been anything I could have handled alone.
Instead, it had to be some kind of Kryptonite Man.
BATMAN! ANY TIME NOW-- UGHH!
I'M YOUR WORST NIGHTMARE.
Barely holding my own against his Green K. Bruce, what's the holdup?

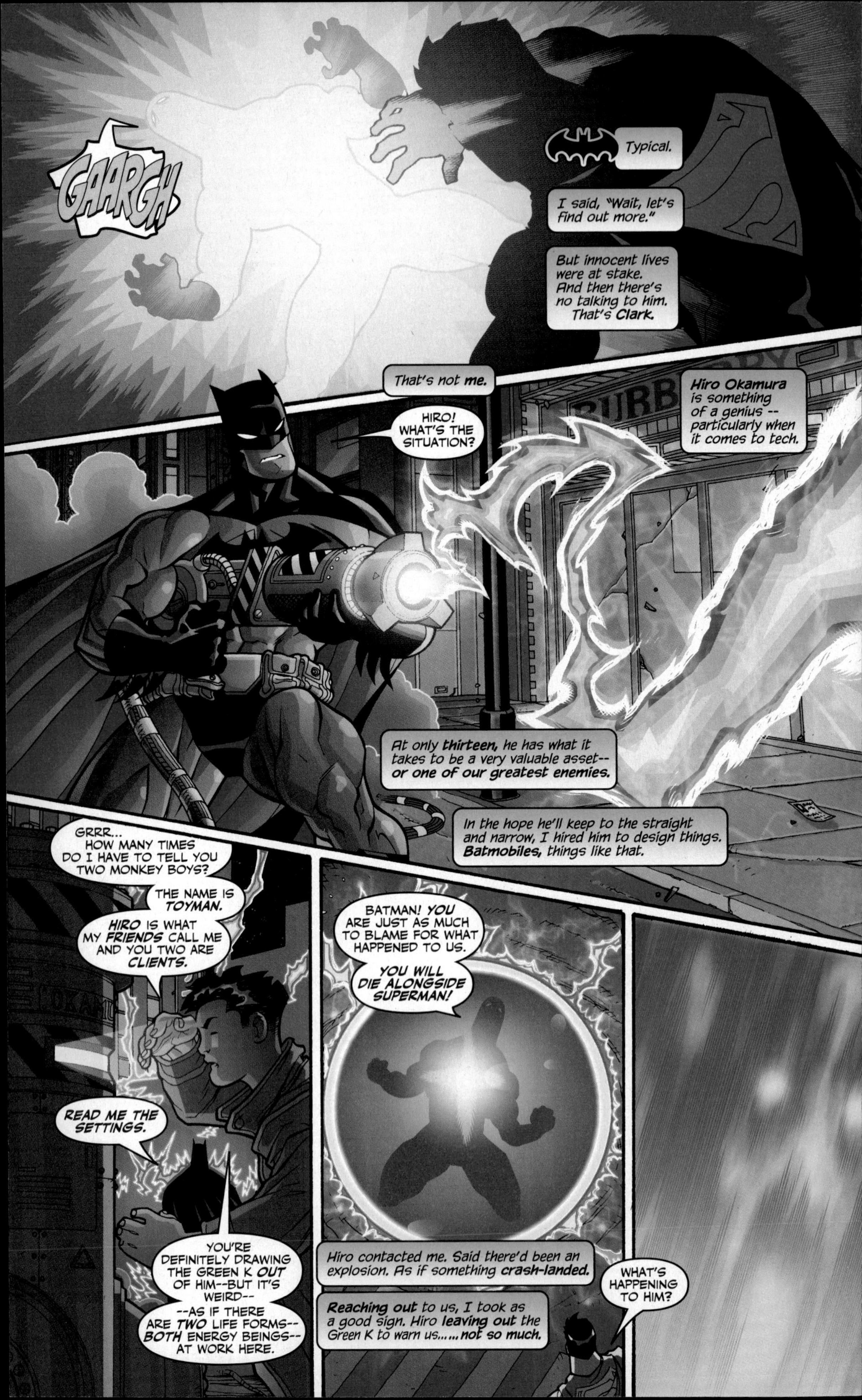

GAARGH
Typical.
I said, "Wait, let's find out more."
But innocent lives were at stake. And then there's no talking to him. That's Clark.
That's not me.
HIRO! WHAT'S THE SITUATION?
Hiro Okamura is something of a genius -- particularly when it comes to tech.
At only thirteen, he has what it takes to be a very valuable asset-- or one of our greatest enemies.
In the hope he'll keep to the straight and narrow, I hired him to design things. Batmobiles, things like that.
GRRR... HOW MANY TIMES DO I HAVE TO TELL YOU TWO MONKEY BOYS?
THE NAME IS TOYMAN.
HIRO IS WHAT MY FRIENDS CALL ME AND YOU TWO ARE CLIENTS.
READ ME THE SETTINGS.
YOU'RE DEFINITELY DRAWING THE GREEN K OUT OF HIM--BUT IT'S WEIRD--
--AS IF THERE ARE TWO LIFE FORMS-- BOTH ENERGY BEINGS-- AT WORK HERE.
BATMAN! YOU ARE JUST AS MUCH TO BLAME FOR WHAT HAPPENED TO US.
YOU WILL DIE ALONGSIDE SUPERMAN!
Hiro contacted me. Said there'd been an explosion. As if something crash-landed.
Reaching out to us, I took as a good sign. Hiro leaving out the Green K to warn us...... not so much.
WHAT'S HAPPENING TO HIM?

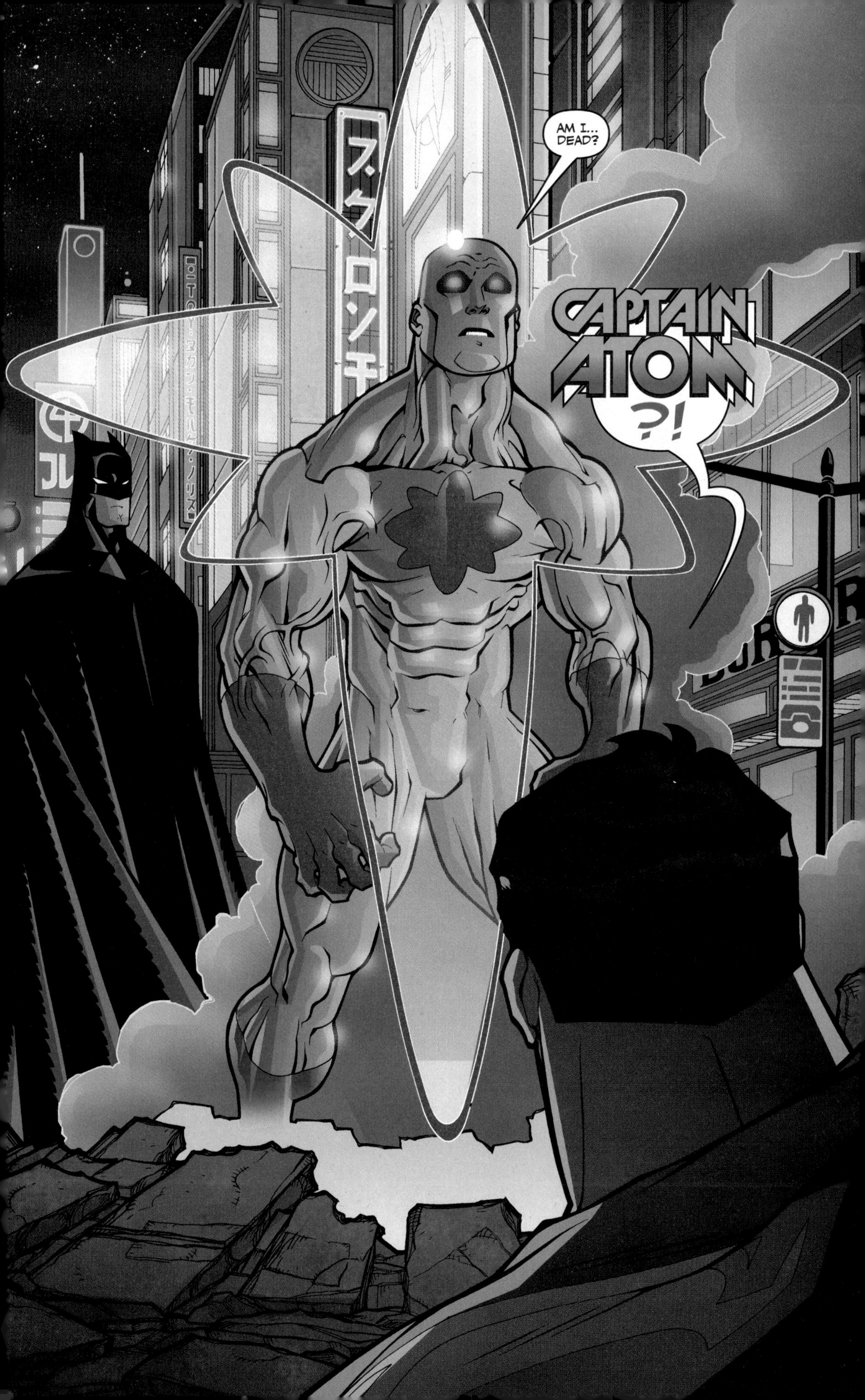
AM I... DEAD?
CAPTAIN ATOM ?!

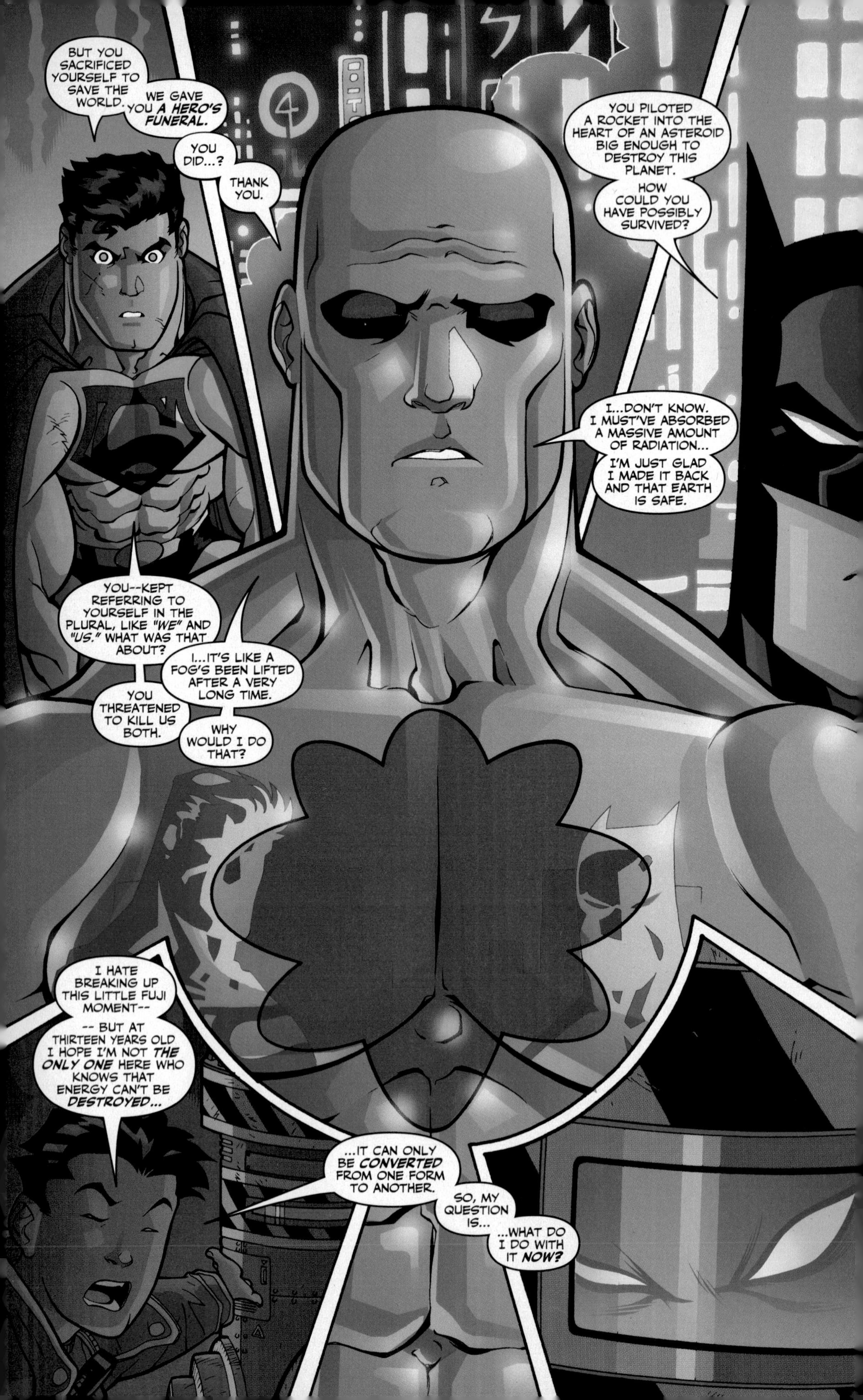
BUT YOU SACRIFICED YOURSELF TO SAVE THE WORLD.
WE GAVE YOU ***A HERO'S FUNERAL.***
YOU DID...?
THANK YOU.
YOU PILOTED A ROCKET INTO THE HEART OF AN ASTEROID BIG ENOUGH TO DESTROY THIS PLANET.
HOW COULD YOU HAVE POSSIBLY SURVIVED?
I...DON'T KNOW. I MUST'VE ABSORBED A MASSIVE AMOUNT OF RADIATION...
I'M JUST GLAD I MADE IT BACK AND THAT EARTH IS SAFE.
YOU--KEPT REFERRING TO YOURSELF IN THE PLURAL, LIKE *"WE"* AND *"US."* WHAT WAS THAT ABOUT?
YOU THREATENED TO KILL US BOTH.
I...IT'S LIKE A FOG'S BEEN LIFTED AFTER A VERY LONG TIME.
WHY WOULD I DO THAT?
I HATE BREAKING UP THIS LITTLE FUJI MOMENT--
-- BUT AT THIRTEEN YEARS OLD I HOPE I'M NOT ***THE ONLY ONE*** HERE WHO KNOWS THAT ENERGY CAN'T BE ***DESTROYED...***
...IT CAN ONLY BE ***CONVERTED*** FROM ONE FORM TO ANOTHER.
SO, MY QUESTION IS...
...WHAT DO I DO WITH IT ***NOW?***

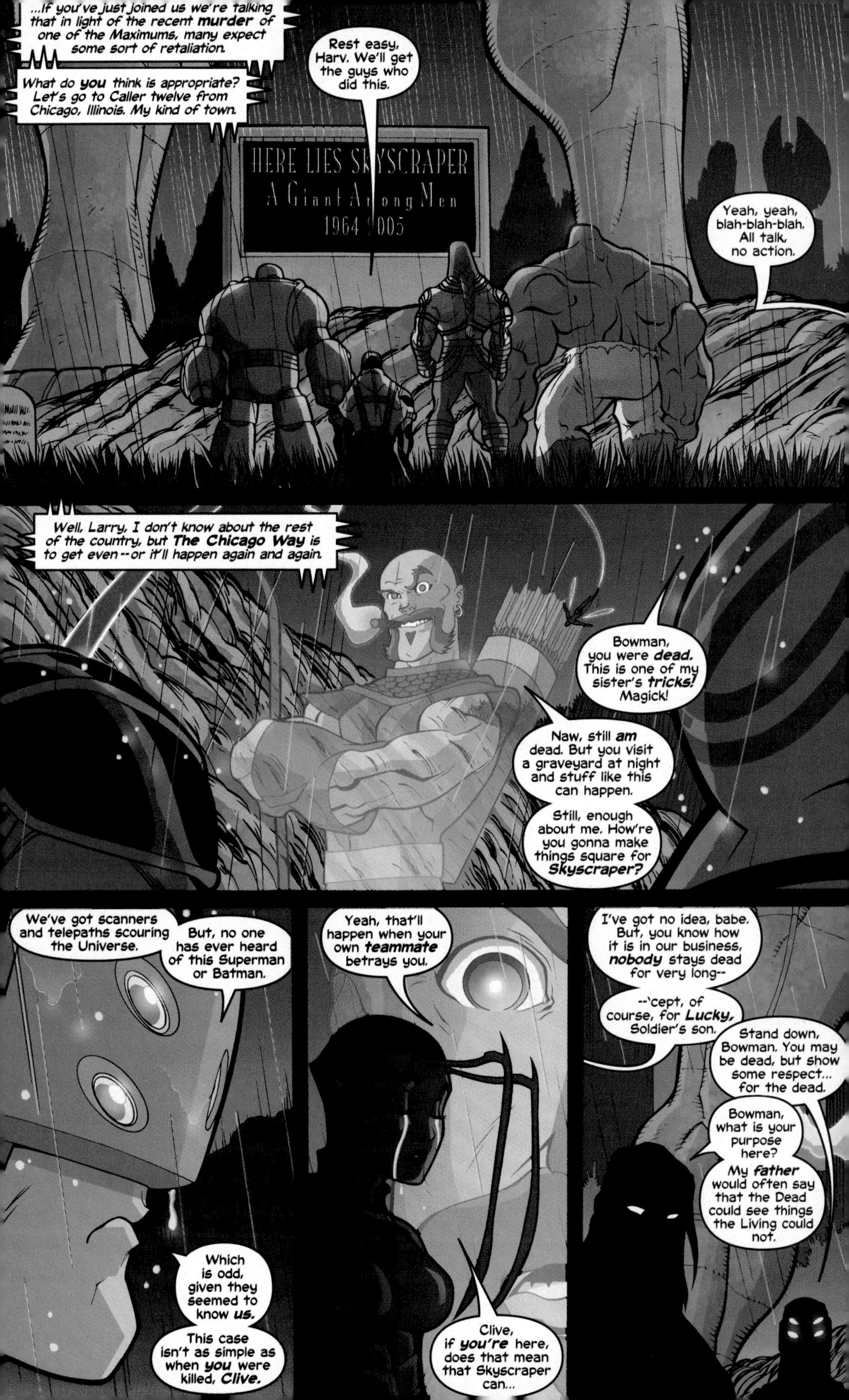

...If you've just joined us we're talking that in light of the recent murder of one of the Maximums, many expect some sort of retaliation.
What do you think is appropriate? Let's go to Caller twelve from Chicago, Illinois. My kind of town.
Rest easy, Harv. We'll get the guys who did this.
HERE LIES SKYSCRAPER
A Giant Among Men
1964 2005
Yeah, yeah, blah-blah-blah. All talk, no action.
Well, Larry, I don't know about the rest of the country, but The Chicago Way is to get even--or it'll happen again and again.
Bowman, you were dead. This is one of my sister's tricks! Magick!
Naw, still am dead. But you visit a graveyard at night and stuff like this can happen.
Still, enough about me. How're you gonna make things square for Skyscraper?
We've got scanners and telepaths scouring the Universe.
But, no one has ever heard of this Superman or Batman.
Which is odd, given they seemed to know us.
This case isn't as simple as when you were killed, Clive.
Yeah, that'll happen when your own teammate betrays you.
Clive, if you're here, does that mean that Skyscraper can...
I've got no idea, babe. But, you know how it is in our business, nobody stays dead for very long--
--'cept, of course, for Lucky, Soldier's son.
Stand down, Bowman. You may be dead, but show some respect... for the dead.
Bowman, what is your purpose here?
My father would often say that the Dead could see things the Living could not.

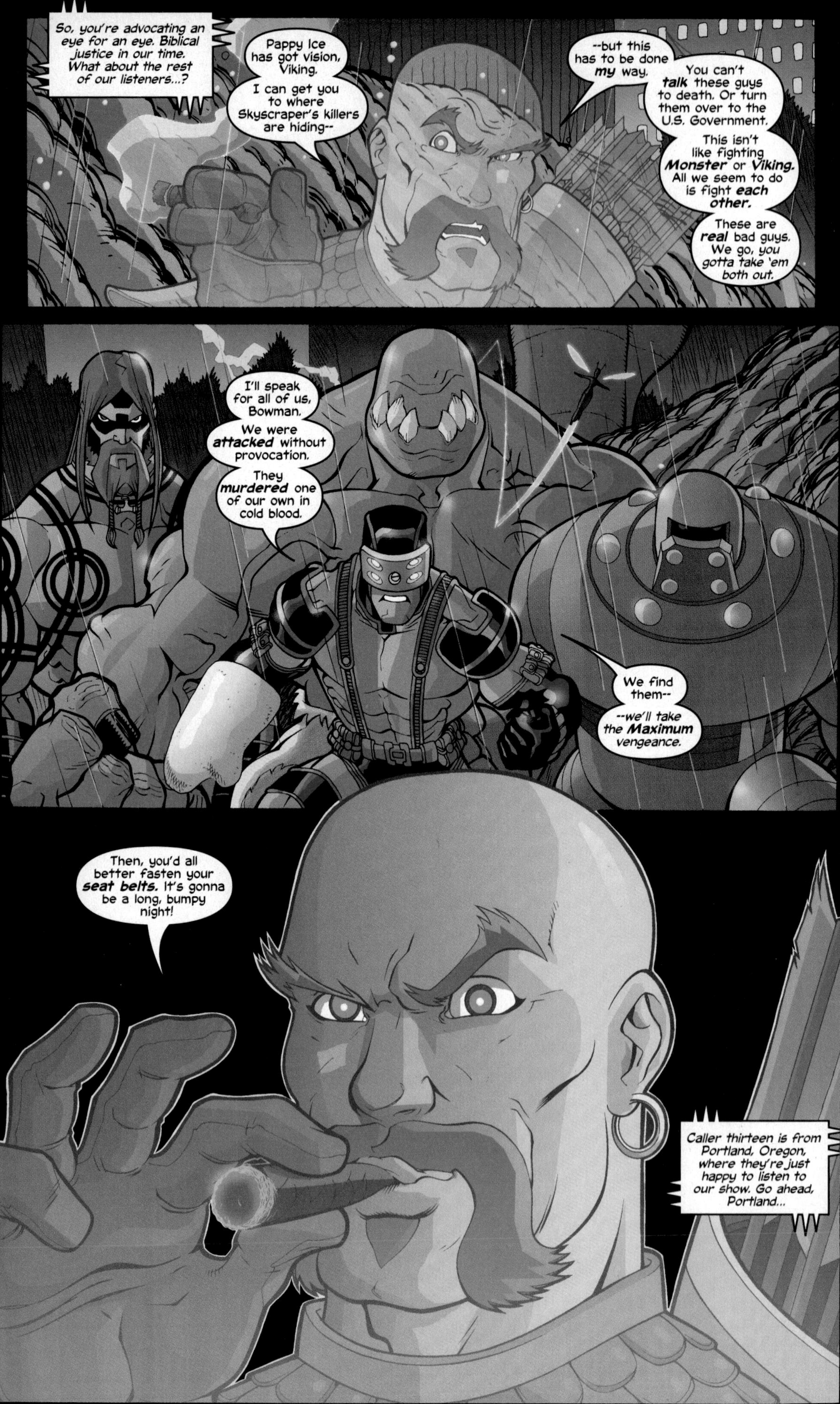
So, you're advocating an eye for an eye. Biblical justice in our time. What about the rest of our listeners...?
Pappy Ice has got vision, Viking.
I can get you to where Skyscraper's killers are hiding--
--but this has to be done my way.
You can't talk these guys to death. Or turn them over to the U.S. Government.
This isn't like fighting Monster or Viking. All we seem to do is fight each other.
These are real bad guys. We go, you gotta take 'em both out.
I'll speak for all of us, Bowman.
We were attacked without provocation.
They murdered one of our own in cold blood.
We find them--
--we'll take the Maximum vengeance.
Then, you'd all better fasten your seat belts. It's gonna be a long, bumpy night!
Caller thirteen is from Portland, Oregon, where they're just happy to listen to our show. Go ahead, Portland...

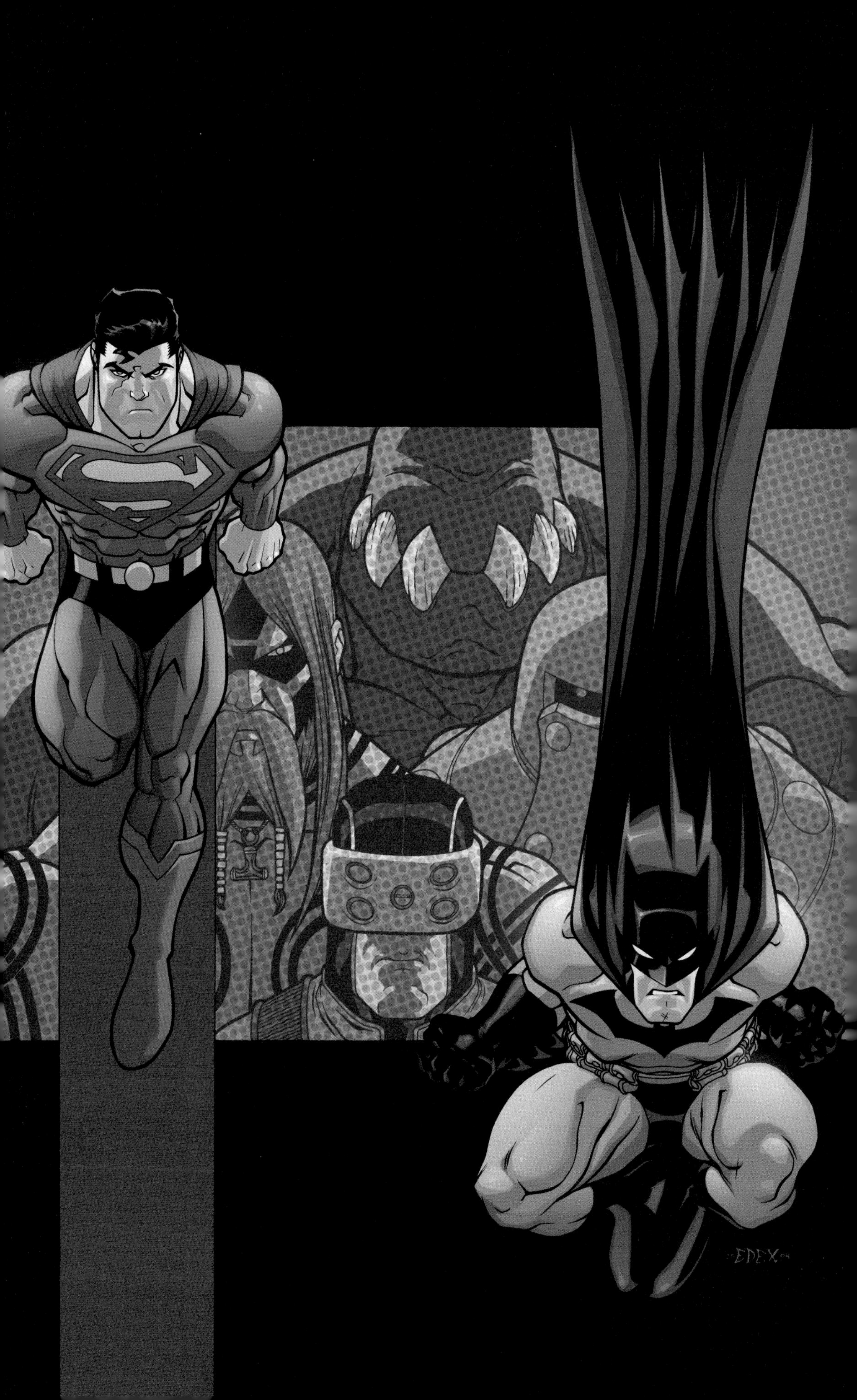

"MISTAKEN IDENTITY CRISIS"

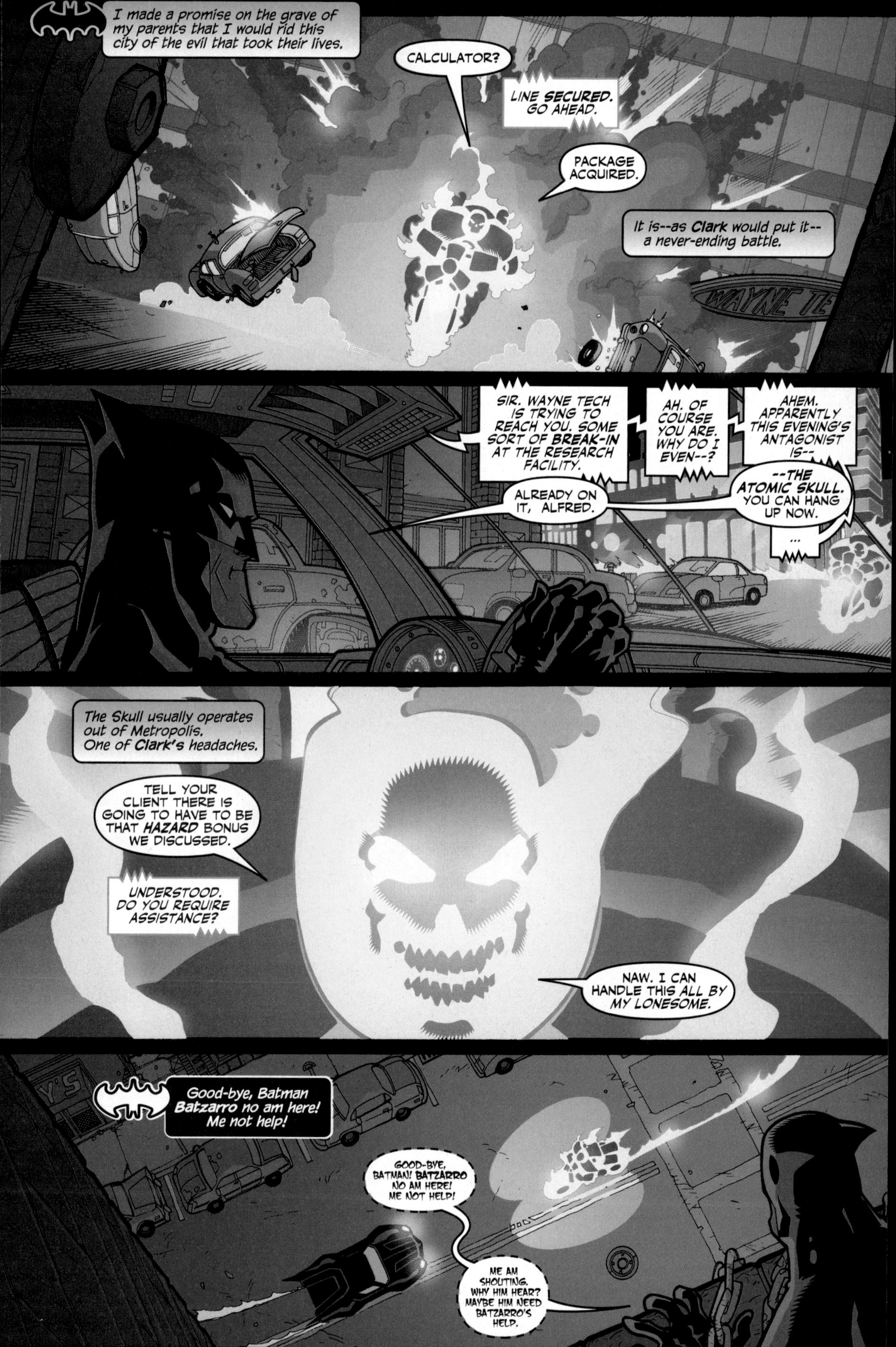
I made a promise on the grave of my parents that I would rid this city of the evil that took their lives.
CALCULATOR?
LINE SECURED. GO AHEAD.
PACKAGE ACQUIRED.
It is--as Clark would put it--a never-ending battle.
WAYNE TE
SIR. WAYNE TECH IS TRYING TO REACH YOU. SOME SORT OF BREAK-IN AT THE RESEARCH FACILITY.
ALREADY ON IT, ALFRED.
AH. OF COURSE YOU ARE. WHY DO I EVEN--?
AHEM. APPARENTLY THIS EVENING'S ANTAGONIST IS--
--THE ATOMIC SKULL. YOU CAN HANG UP NOW.
...
The Skull usually operates out of Metropolis. One of Clark's headaches.
TELL YOUR CLIENT THERE IS GOING TO HAVE TO BE THAT HAZARD BONUS WE DISCUSSED.
UNDERSTOOD. DO YOU REQUIRE ASSISTANCE?
NAW. I CAN HANDLE THIS ALL BY MY LONESOME.
Good-bye, Batman Batzarro no am here! Me not help!
GOOD-BYE, BATMAN! BATZARRO NO AM HERE! ME NOT HELP!
ME AM SHOUTING. WHY HIM HEAR? MAYBE HIM NEED BATZARRO'S HELP.

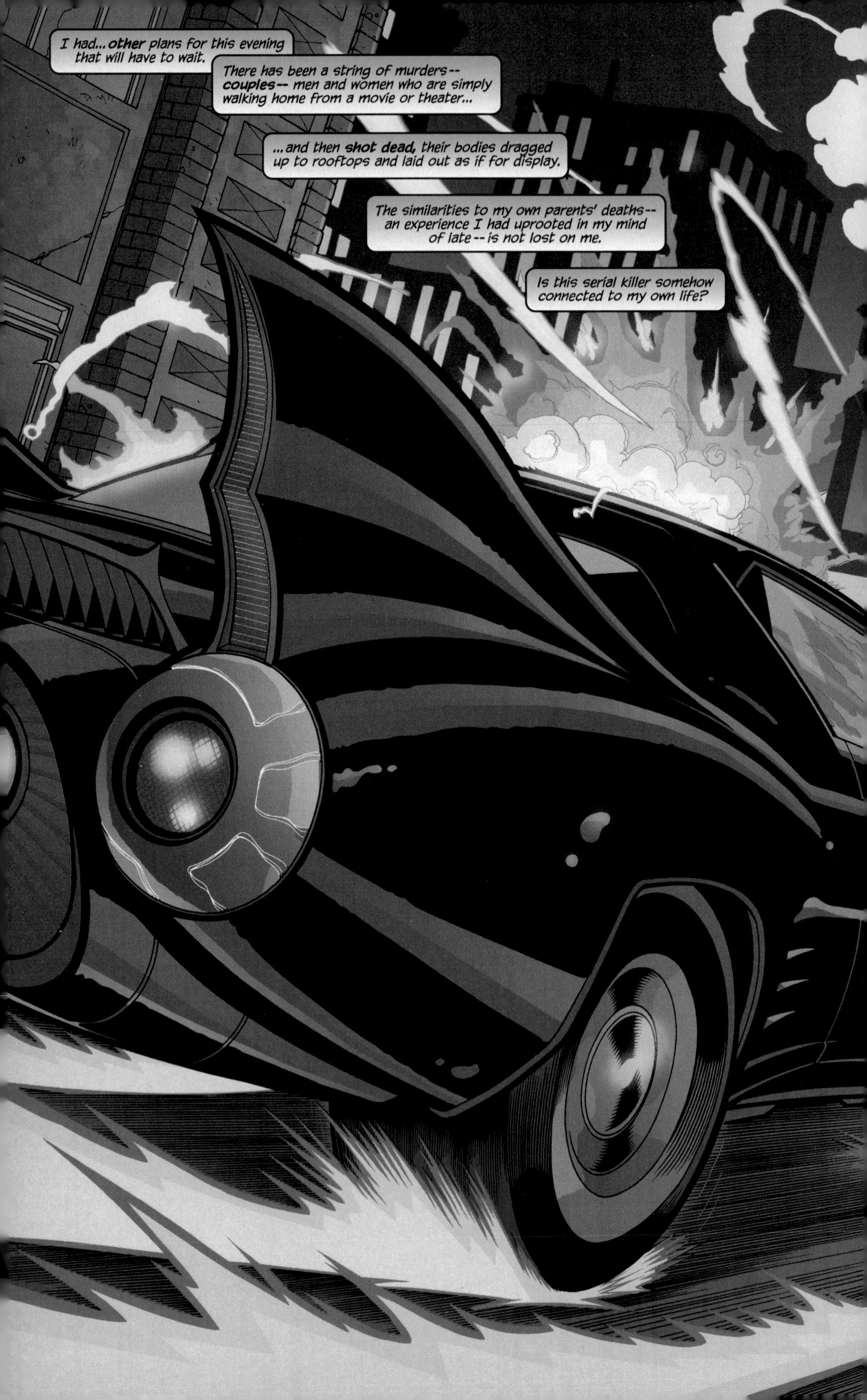
I had... **other** plans for this evening that will have to wait.
There has been a string of murders-- **couples--** men and women who are simply walking home from a movie or theater...
...and then **shot dead,** their bodies dragged up to rooftops and laid out as if for display.
The similarities to my own parents' deaths-- an experience I had uprooted in my mind of late--is not lost on me.
Is this serial killer somehow connected to my own life?

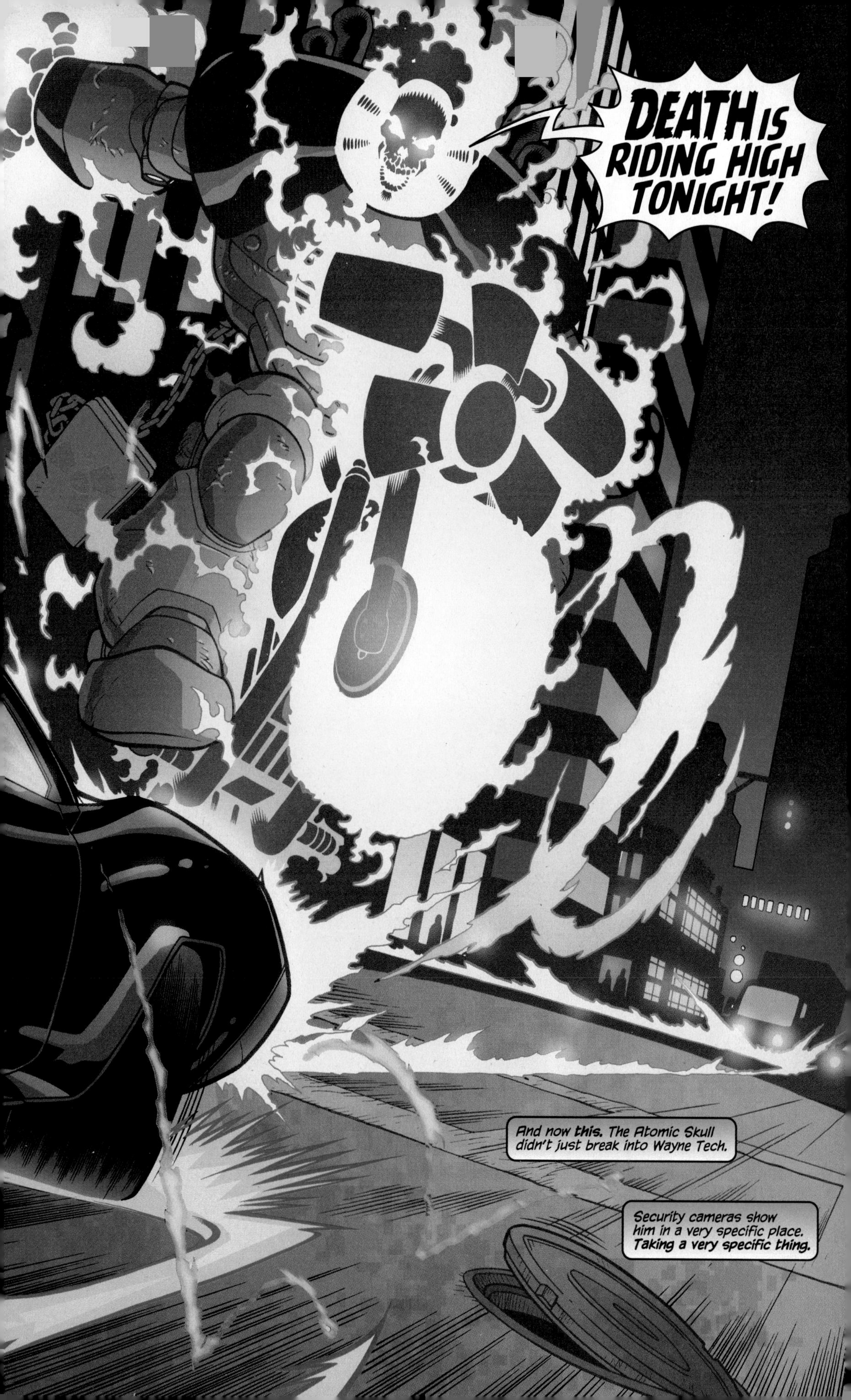
DEATH IS RIDING HIGH TONIGHT!
And now this. The Atomic Skull didn't just break into Wayne Tech.
Security cameras show him in a very specific place. Taking a very specific thing.

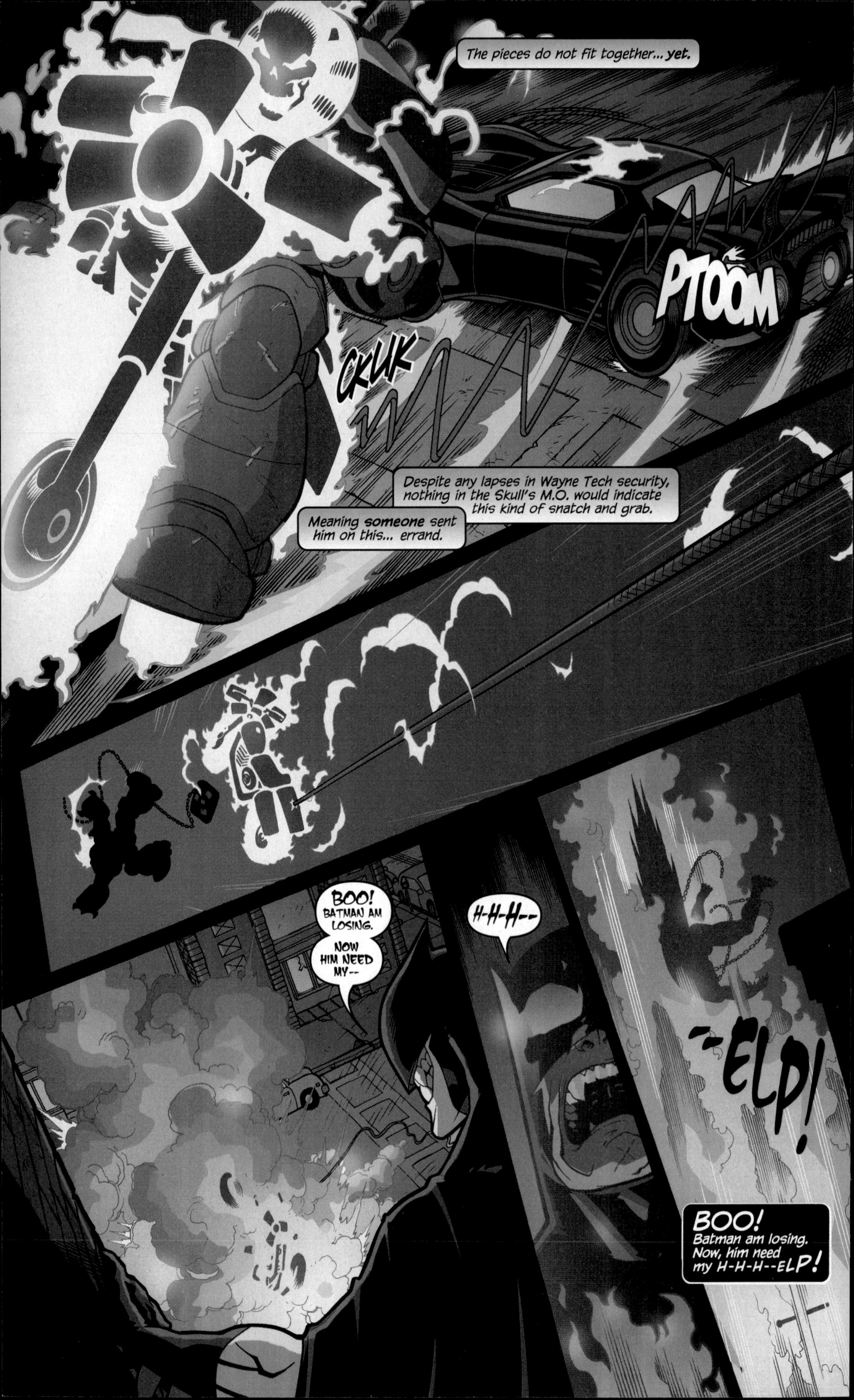
The pieces do not fit together... **yet.**
PTOOM
CKUK
Despite any lapses in Wayne Tech security, nothing in the Skull's M.O. would indicate this kind of snatch and grab.
Meaning **someone** sent him on this... errand.
BOO! BATMAN AM LOSING.
NOW HIM NEED MY--
H-H-H--
--ELP!
BOO!
Batman am losing. Now, him need my H-H-H--ELP!

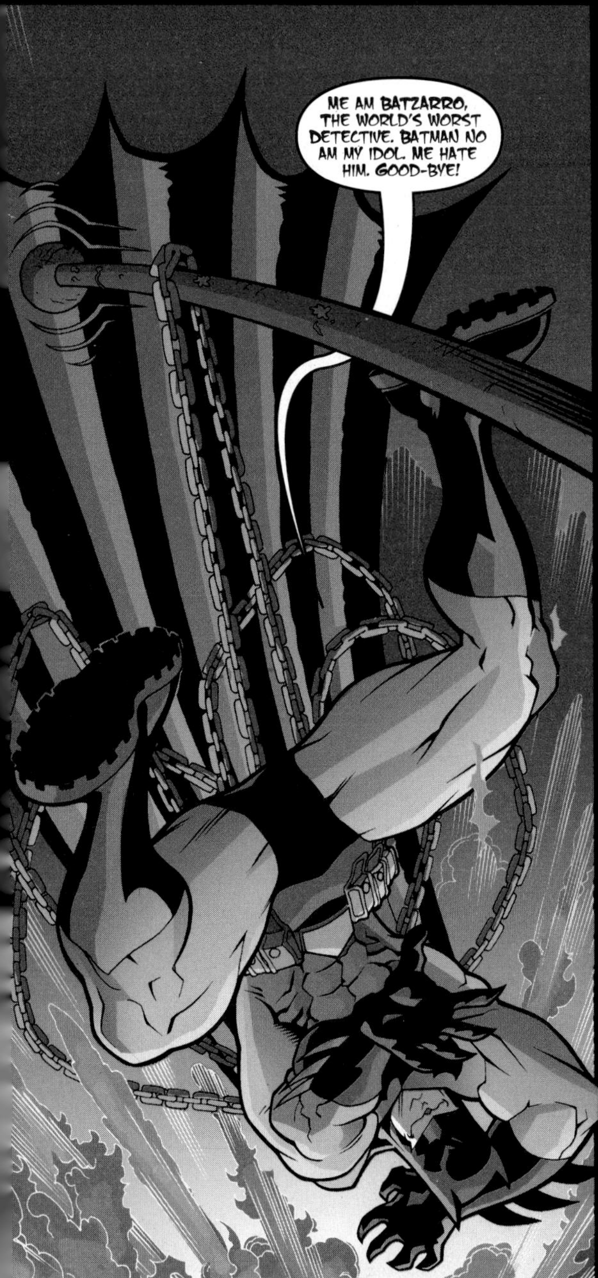
ME AM BATZARRO, THE WORLD'S WORST DETECTIVE. BATMAN NO AM MY IDOL. ME HATE HIM. GOOD-BYE!
Me am Batzarro. The World's Worst Detective. Batman no am my idol. Me hate him. Good-bye!

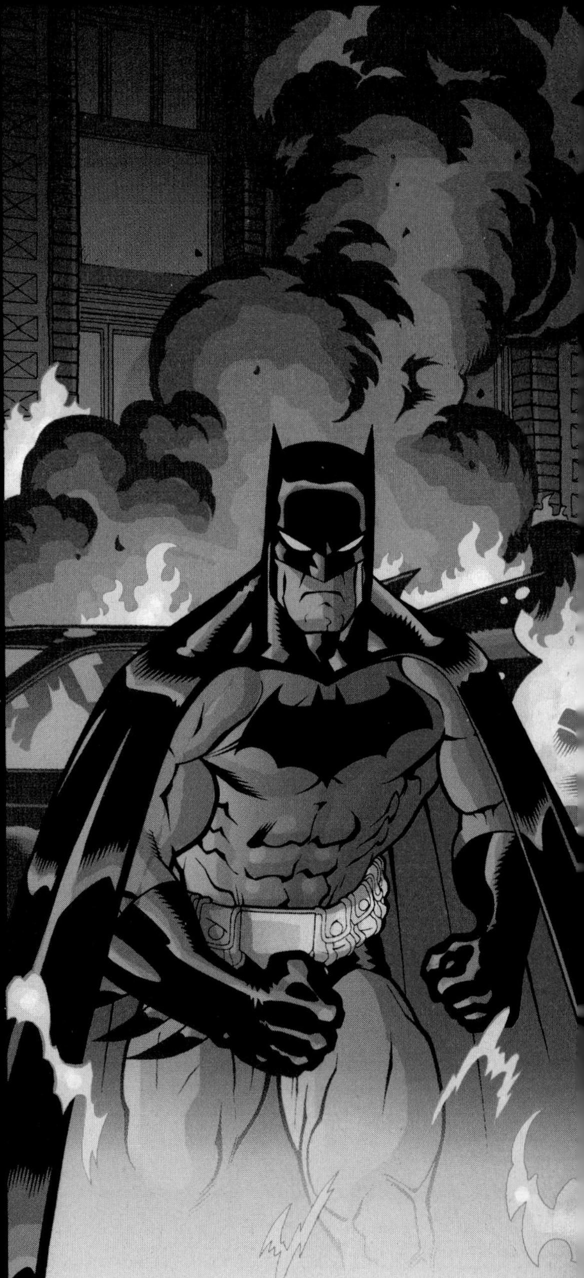
I have to get that item back.
Or I will have no choice but to involve Clark, who isn't going to understand...

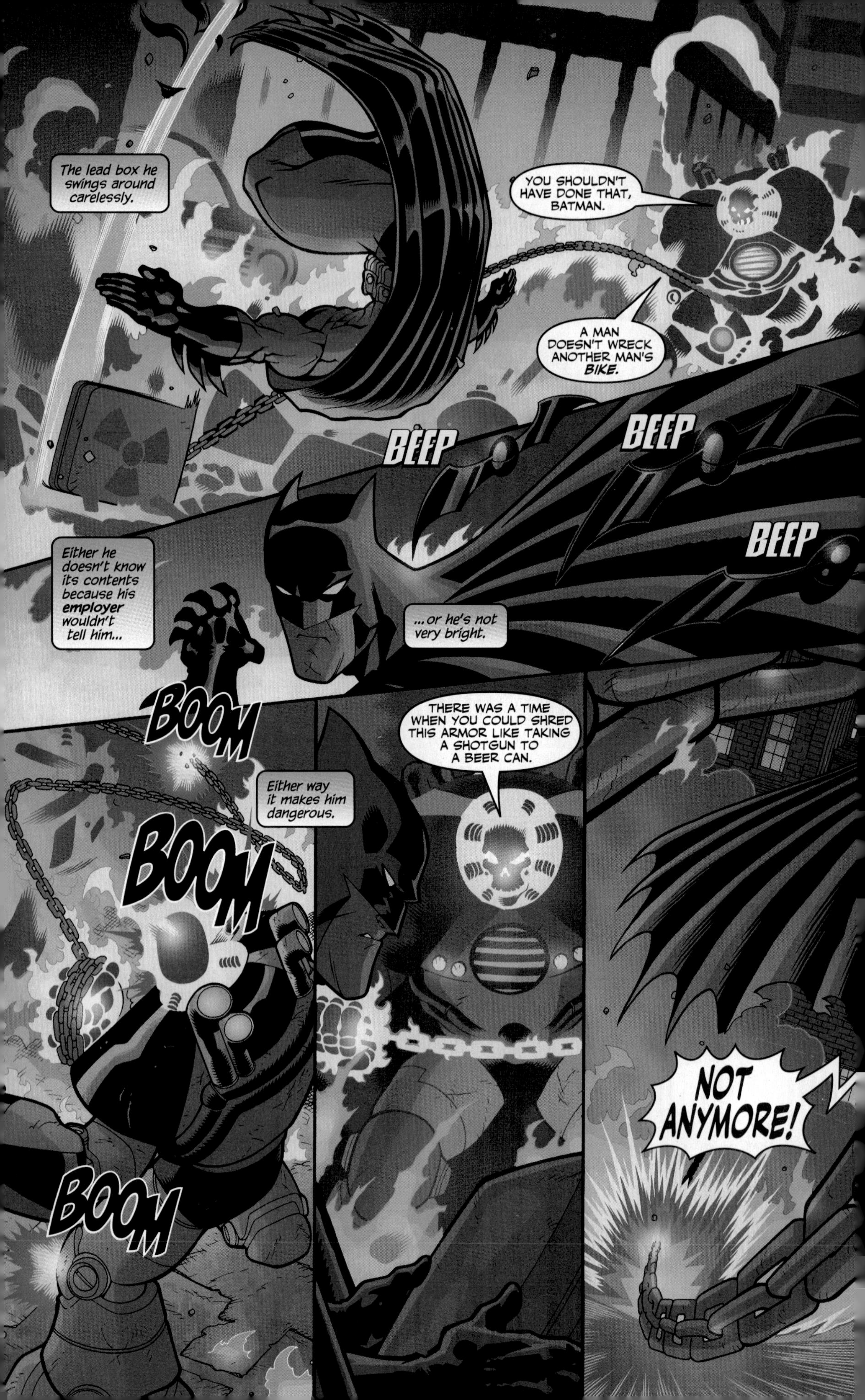

The lead box he swings around carelessly.
YOU SHOULDN'T HAVE DONE THAT, BATMAN.
A MAN DOESN'T WRECK ANOTHER MAN'S BIKE.
BEEP
BEEP
BEEP
Either he doesn't know its contents because his employer wouldn't tell him...
...or he's not very bright.
BOOM
Either way it makes him dangerous.
BOOM
BOOM
THERE WAS A TIME WHEN YOU COULD SHRED THIS ARMOR LIKE TAKING A SHOTGUN TO A BEER CAN.
NOT ANYMORE!

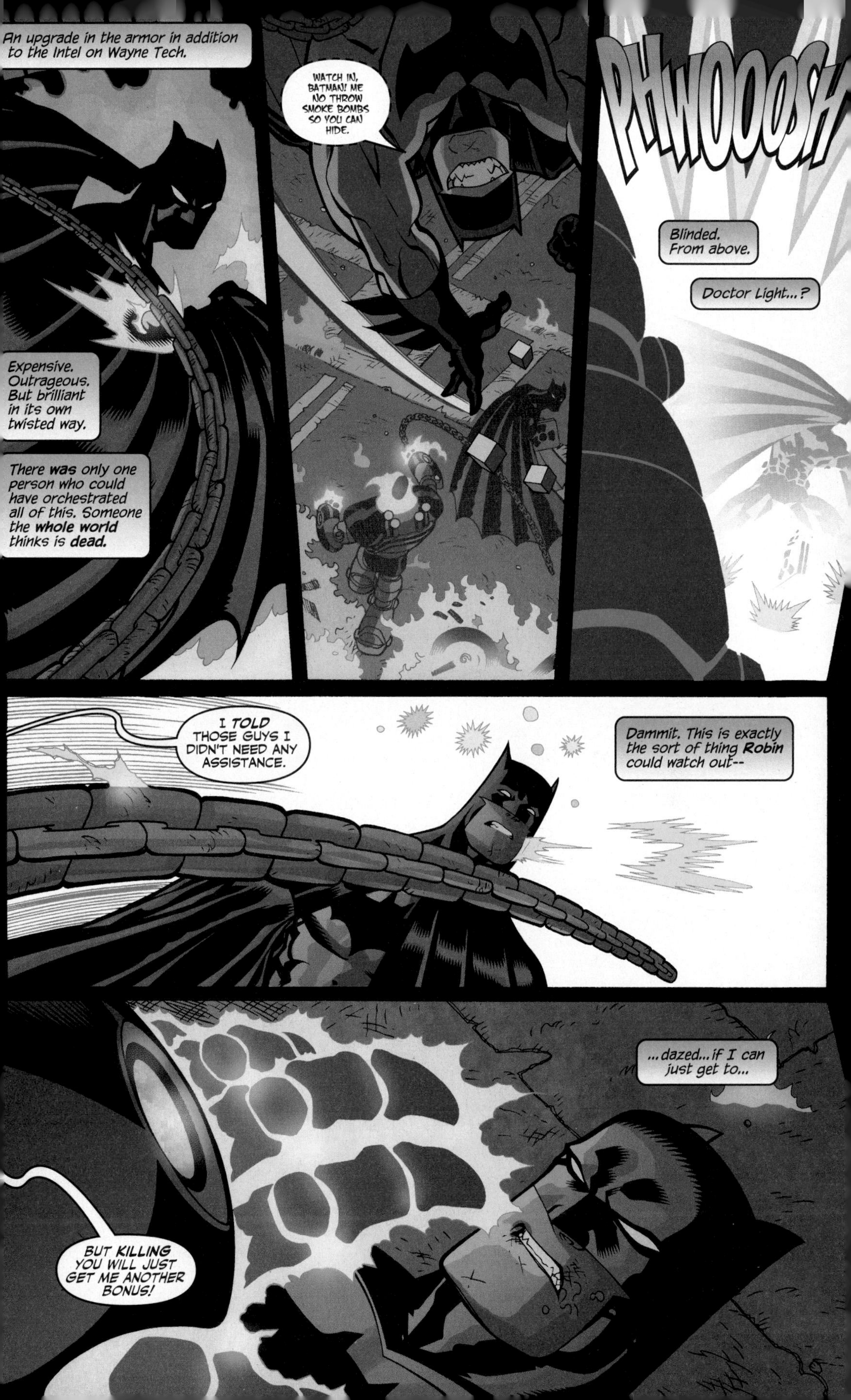

An upgrade in the armor in addition to the Intel on Wayne Tech.
Expensive. Outrageous. But brilliant in its own twisted way.
There **was** only one person who could have orchestrated all of this. Someone the **whole world** thinks is **dead.**
WATCH IN, BATMAN! ME NO THROW SMOKE BOMBS SO YOU CAN HIDE.
PHWOOOSH
Blinded. From above.
Doctor Light...?
I *TOLD* THOSE GUYS I DIDN'T NEED ANY ASSISTANCE.
Dammit. This is exactly the sort of thing **Robin** could watch out--
...dazed...if I can just get to...
BUT **KILLING** YOU WILL JUST GET ME ANOTHER BONUS!

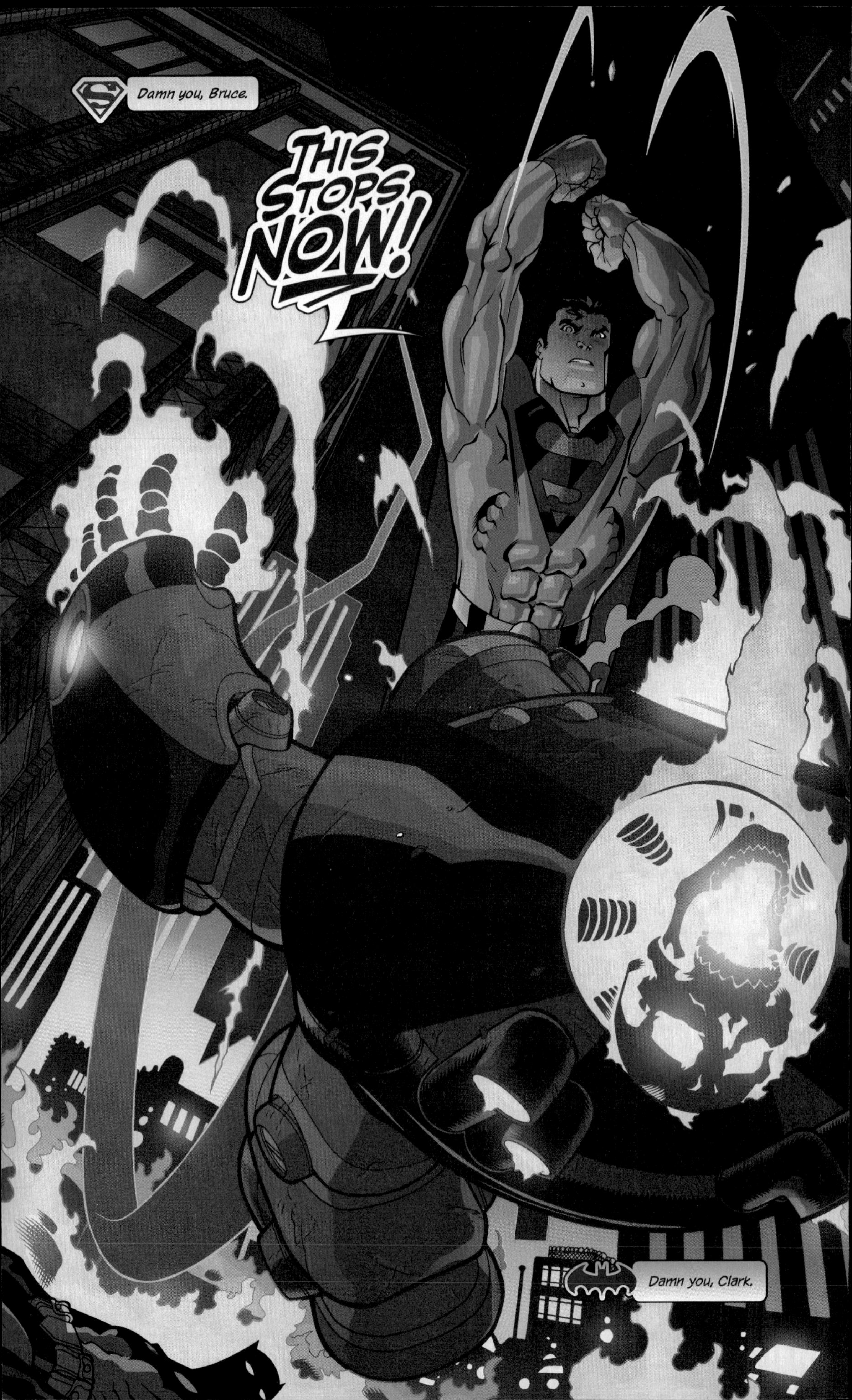
Damn you, Bruce.
THIS STOPS NOW!
Damn you, Clark.

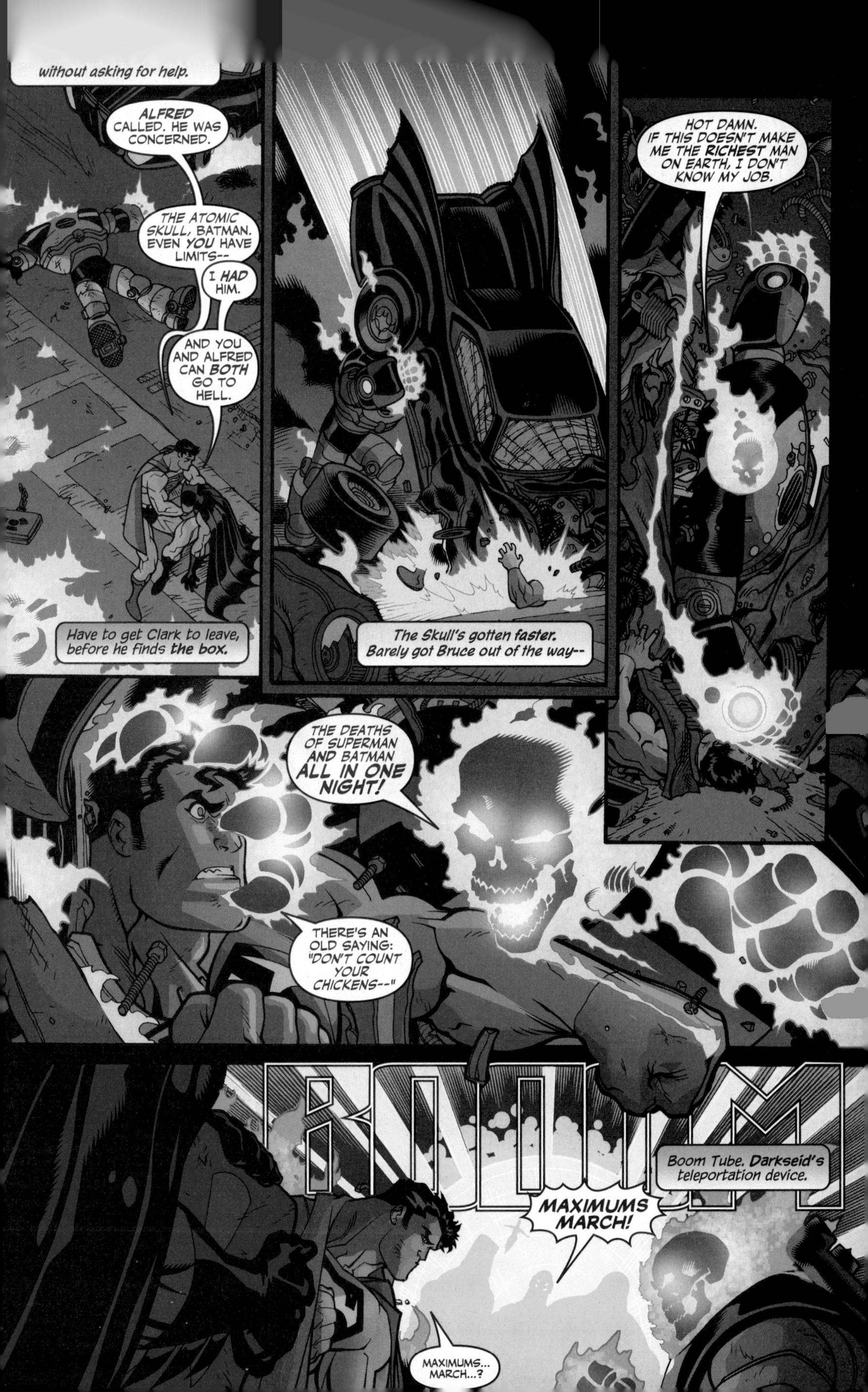
without asking for help.
ALFRED CALLED. HE WAS CONCERNED.
THE ATOMIC SKULL, BATMAN. EVEN YOU HAVE LIMITS--
I HAD HIM.
AND YOU AND ALFRED CAN BOTH GO TO HELL.
Have to get Clark to leave, before he finds the box.
The Skull's gotten faster. Barely got Bruce out of the way--
HOT DAMN. IF THIS DOESN'T MAKE ME THE RICHEST MAN ON EARTH, I DON'T KNOW MY JOB.
THE DEATHS OF SUPERMAN AND BATMAN ALL IN ONE NIGHT!
THERE'S AN OLD SAYING: "DON'T COUNT YOUR CHICKENS--"
Boom Tube. Darkseid's teleportation device.
MAXIMUMS MARCH!
MAXIMUMS... MARCH...?

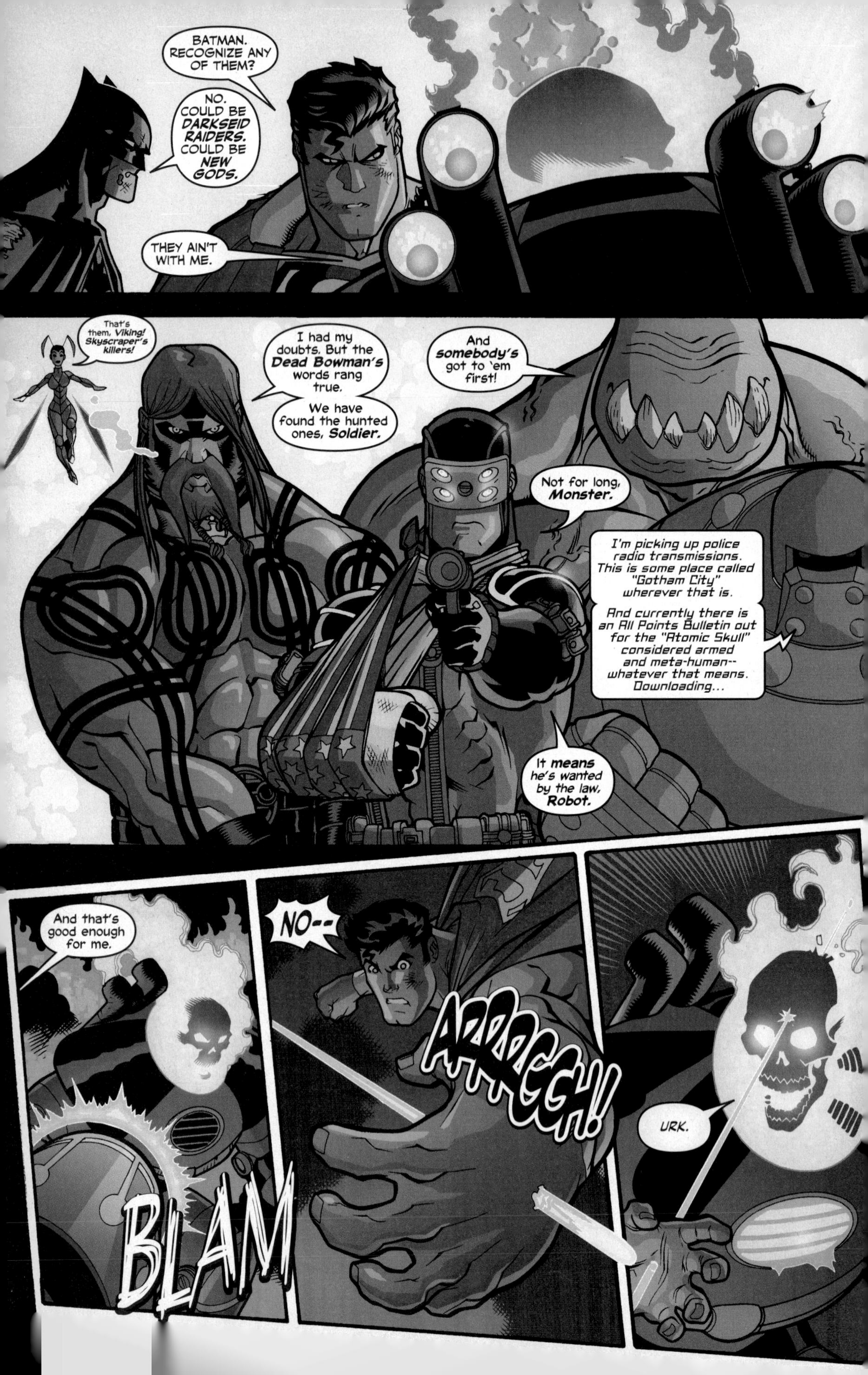
BATMAN. RECOGNIZE ANY OF THEM?
NO. COULD BE DARKSEID RAIDERS. COULD BE NEW GODS.
THEY AIN'T WITH ME.
That's them, Viking! Skyscraper's killers!
I had my doubts. But the Dead Bowman's words rang true.
We have found the hunted ones, Soldier.
And somebody's got to 'em first!
Not for long, Monster.
I'm picking up police radio transmissions. This is some place called "Gotham City" wherever that is.
And currently there is an All Points Bulletin out for the "Atomic Skull" considered armed and meta-human-- whatever that means. Downloading...
It means he's wanted by the law, Robot.
And that's good enough for me.
BLAM
NO--
ARRRGGH!
URK.

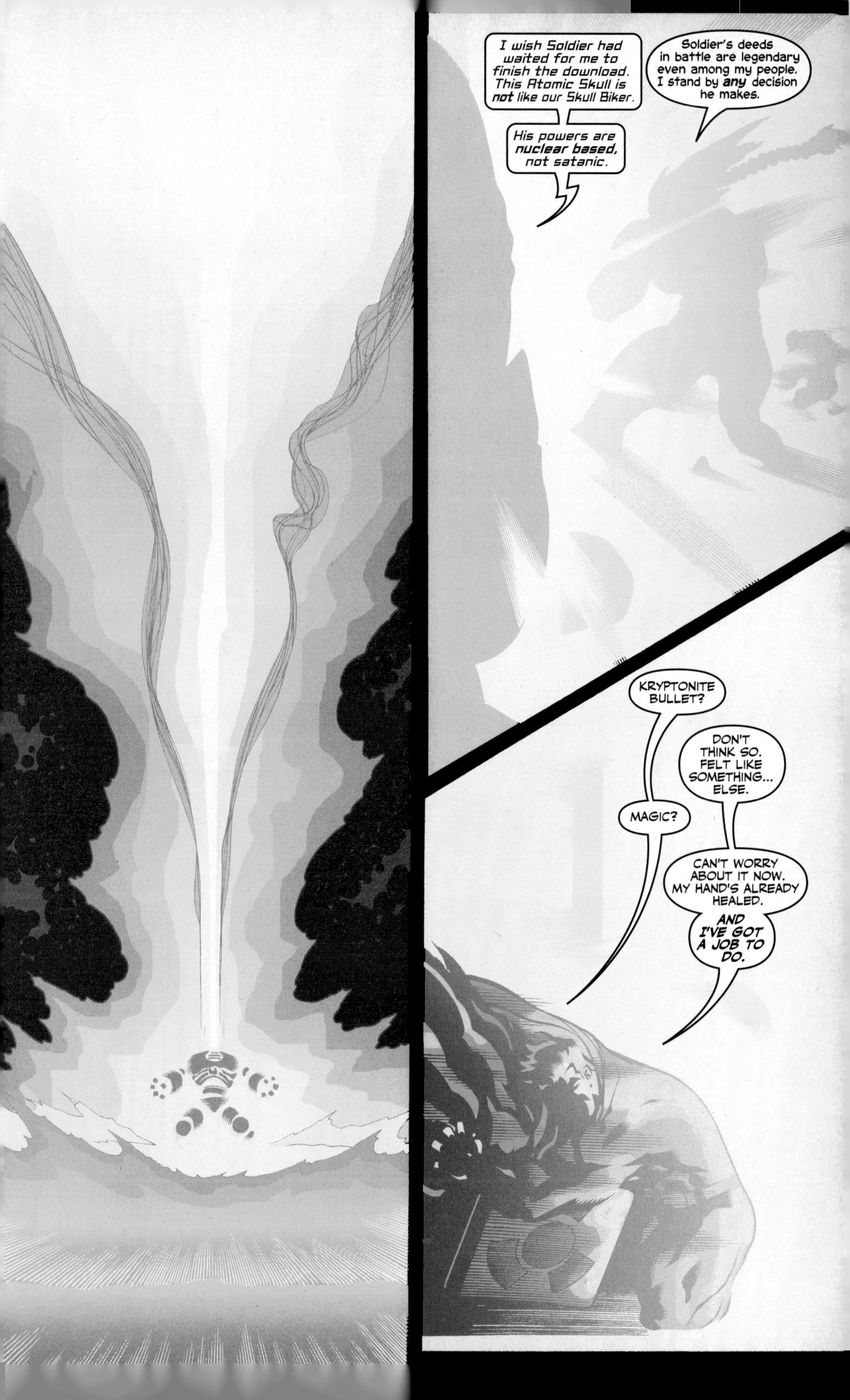
I wish Soldier had waited for me to finish the download. This Atomic Skull is *not* like our Skull Biker.
His powers are *nuclear based,* not satanic.
Soldier's deeds in battle are legendary even among my people. I stand by *any* decision he makes.
KRYPTONITE BULLET?
DON'T THINK SO. FELT LIKE SOMETHING... ELSE.
MAGIC?
CAN'T WORRY ABOUT IT NOW. MY HAND'S ALREADY HEALED.
AND I'VE GOT A JOB TO DO.

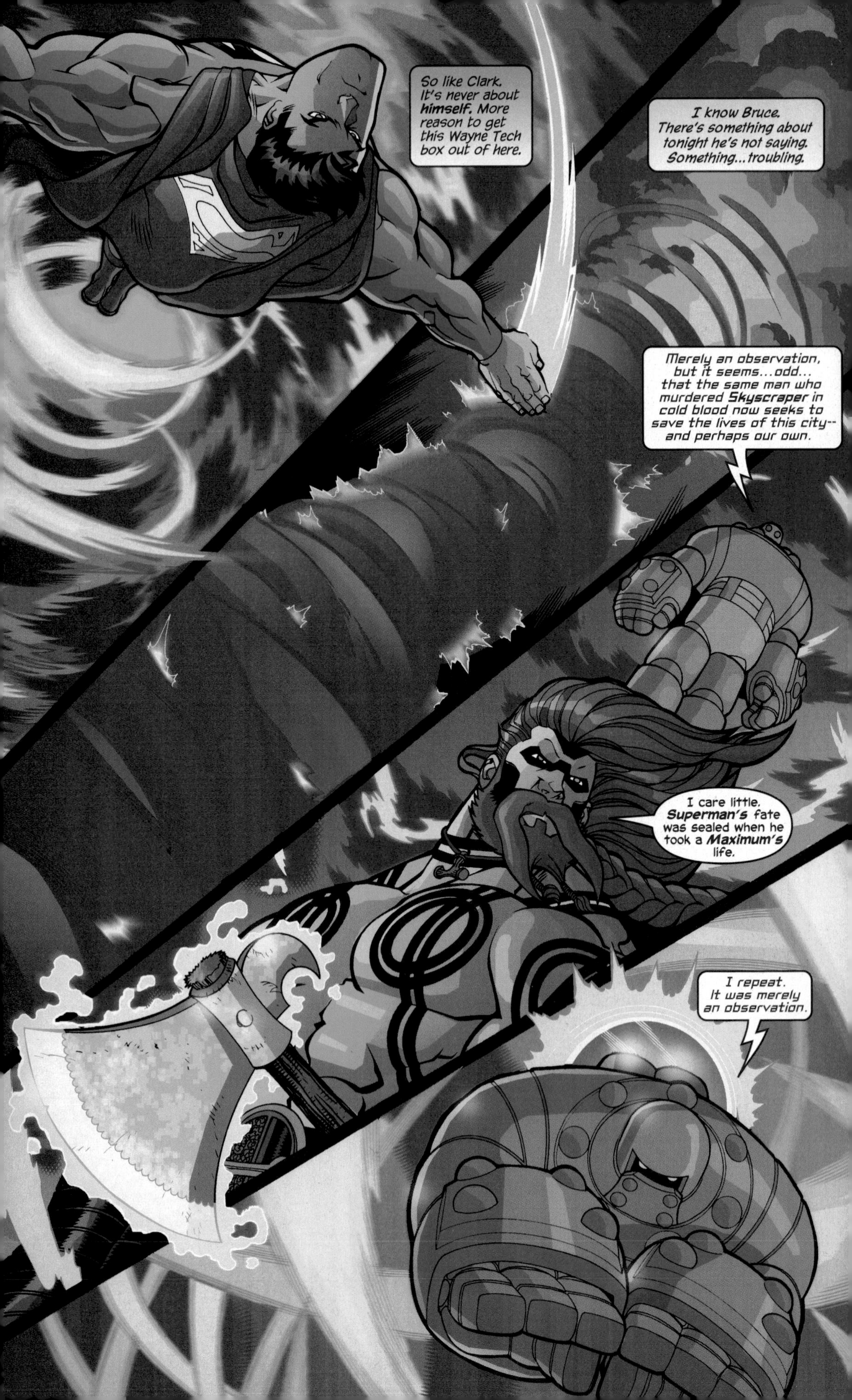

So like Clark. It's never about **himself.** More reason to get this Wayne Tech box out of here.
I know Bruce. There's something about tonight he's not saying. Something... troubling.
Merely an observation, but it seems... odd... that the same man who murdered **Skyscraper** in cold blood now seeks to save the lives of this city-- and perhaps our own.
I care little. **Superman's** fate was sealed when he took a **Maximum's** life.
I repeat. It was merely an observation.

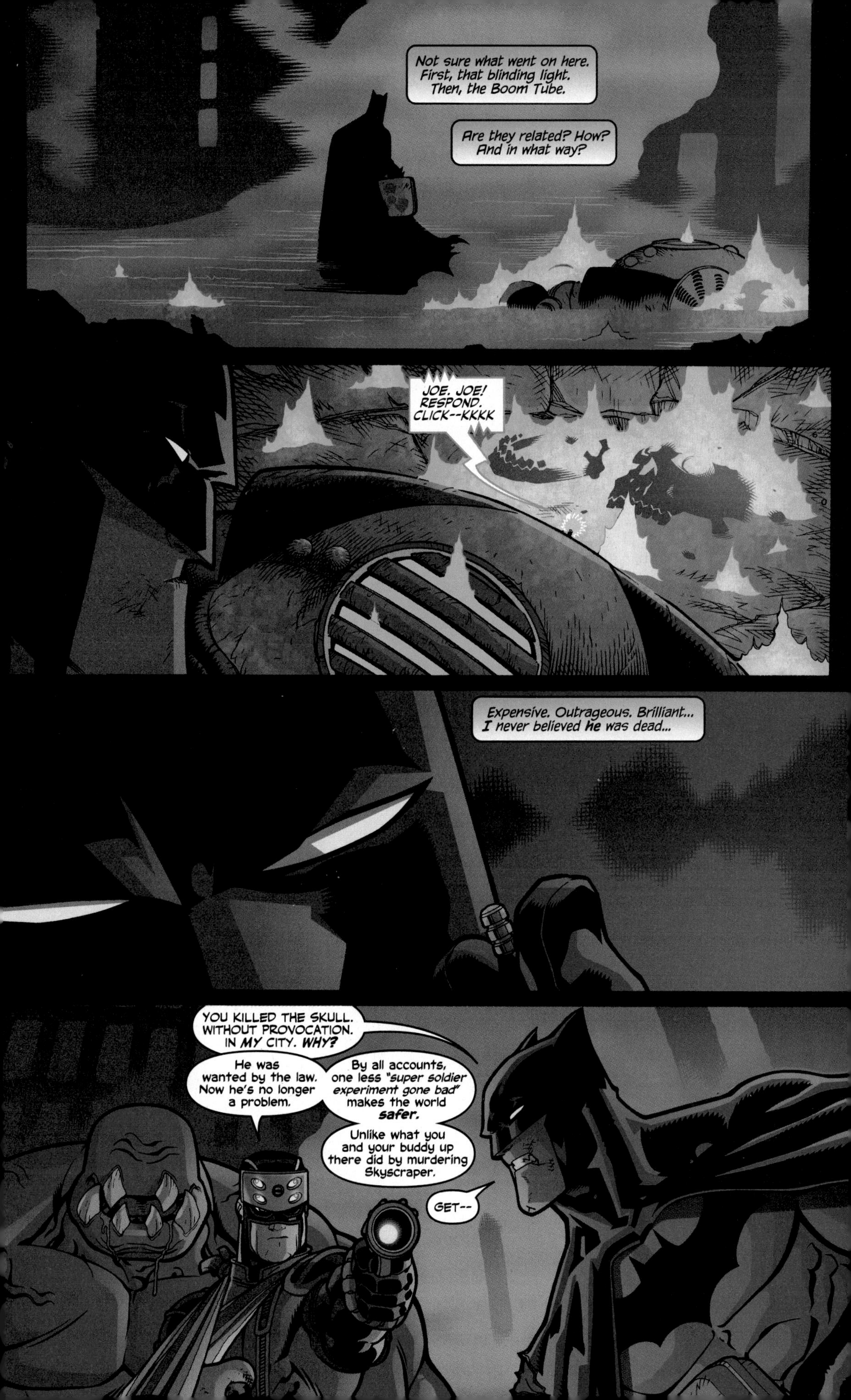
Not sure what went on here. First, that blinding light. Then, the Boom Tube.
Are they related? How? And in what way?
JOE. JOE! RESPOND. CLICK--KKKK
Expensive. Outrageous. Brilliant... I never believed he was dead...
YOU KILLED THE SKULL. WITHOUT PROVOCATION. IN MY CITY. WHY?
He was wanted by the law. Now he's no longer a problem.
By all accounts, one less "super soldier experiment gone bad" makes the world safer.
Unlike what you and your buddy up there did by murdering Skyscraper.
GET--

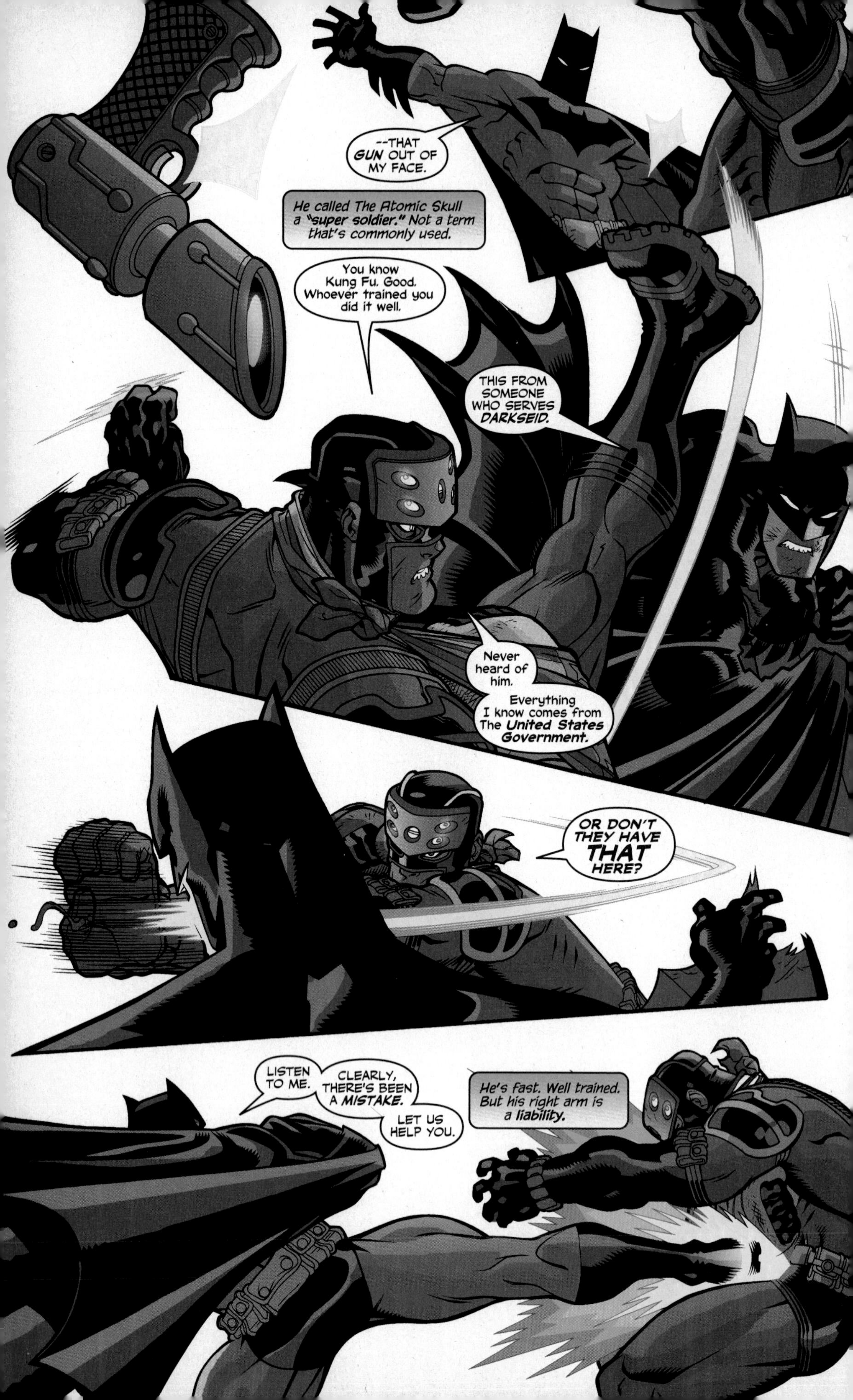
--THAT GUN OUT OF MY FACE.
He called The Atomic Skull a "super soldier." Not a term that's commonly used.
You know Kung Fu. Good. Whoever trained you did it well.
THIS FROM SOMEONE WHO SERVES DARKSEID.
Never heard of him.
Everything I know comes from The United States Government.
OR DON'T THEY HAVE THAT HERE?
LISTEN TO ME.
CLEARLY, THERE'S BEEN A MISTAKE.
LET US HELP YOU.
He's fast. Well trained. But his right arm is a liability.

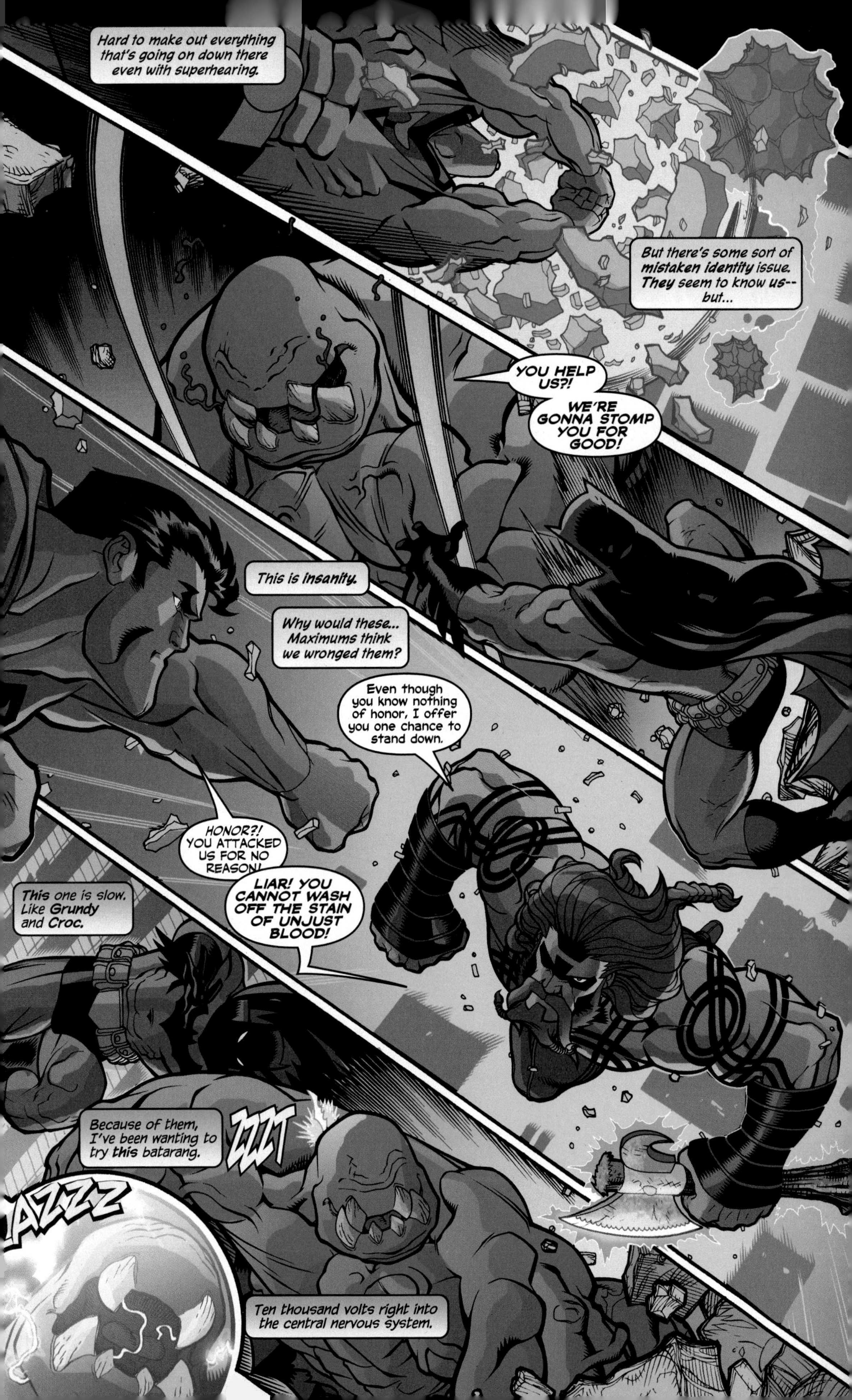
Hard to make out everything that's going on down there even with superhearing.
But there's some sort of mistaken identity issue. They seem to know us-- but...
YOU HELP US?!
WE'RE GONNA STOMP YOU FOR GOOD!
This is insanity.
Why would these... Maximums think we wronged them?
Even though you know nothing of honor, I offer you one chance to stand down.
HONOR?! YOU ATTACKED US FOR NO REASON!
LIAR! YOU CANNOT WASH OFF THE STAIN OF UNJUST BLOOD!
This one is slow. Like Grundy and Croc.
Because of them, I've been wanting to try this batarang.
ZZZT
AZZZ
Ten thousand volts right into the central nervous system.

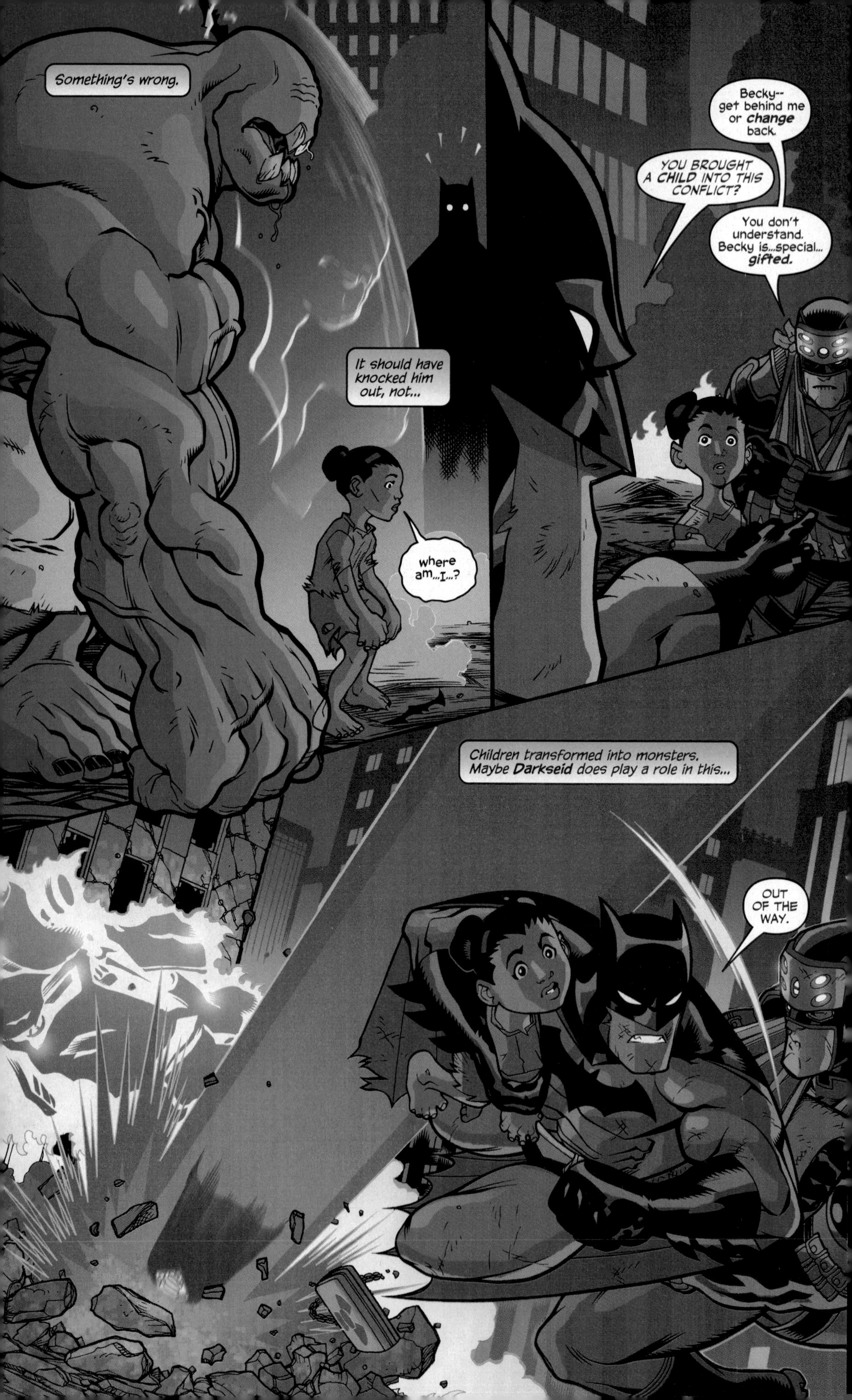
Something's wrong.
It should have knocked him out, not...
where am...I...?
Becky-- get behind me or change back.
YOU BROUGHT A CHILD INTO THIS CONFLICT?
You don't understand. Becky is...special... gifted.
Children transformed into monsters. Maybe Darkseid does play a role in this...
OUT OF THE WAY.

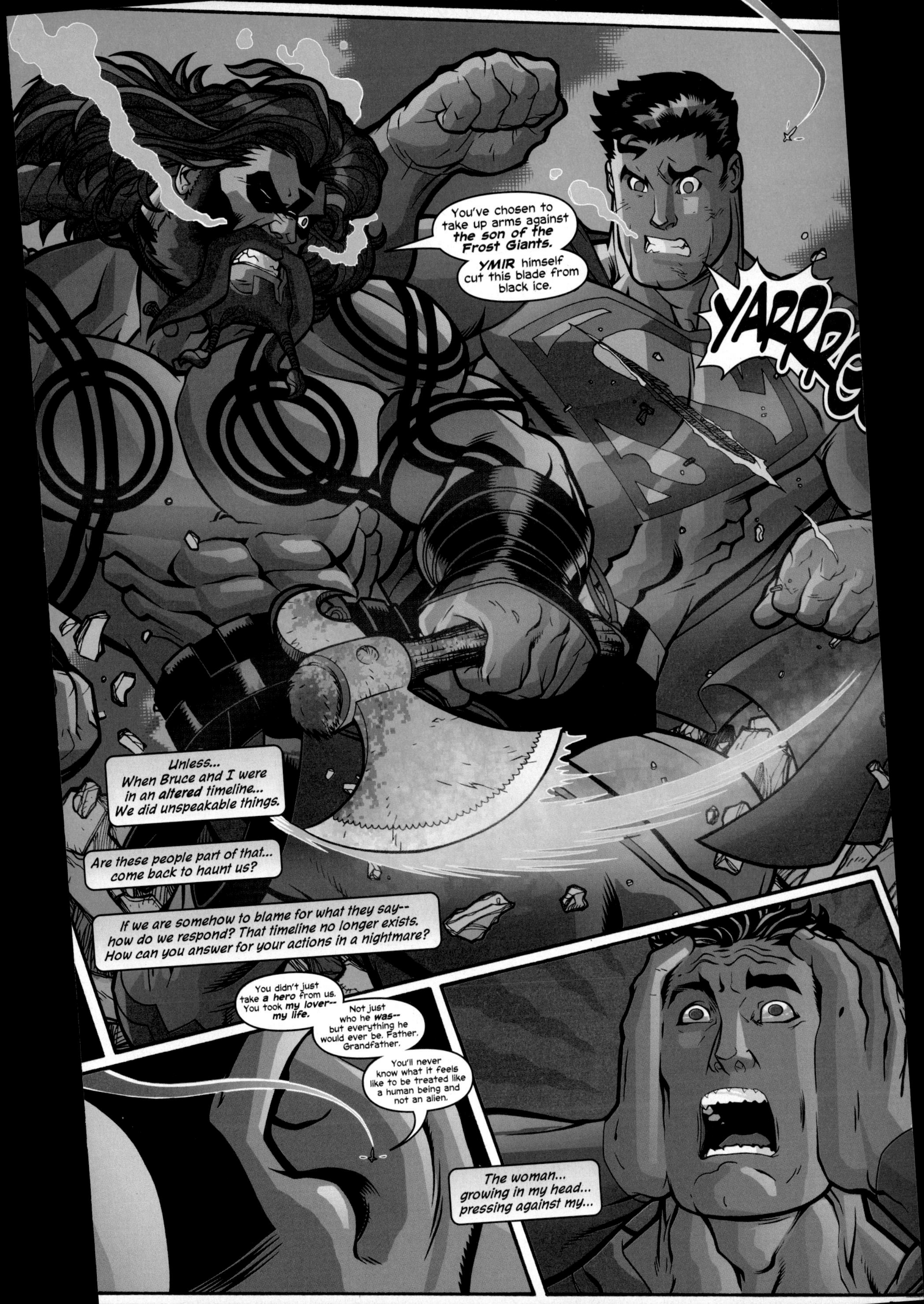
You've chosen to take up arms against **the son of the Frost Giants.**
YMIR himself cut this blade from black ice.
YARRRG
*Unless... When Bruce and I were in an **altered timeline...** We did unspeakable things.*
Are these people part of that... come back to haunt us?
If we are somehow to blame for what they say-- how do we respond? That timeline no longer exists. How can you answer for your actions in a nightmare?
You didn't just take **a hero** from us. You took **my lover-- my life.**
Not just who he **was--** but everything he would ever be. Father. Grandfather.
You'll never know what it feels like to be treated like a human being and not an alien.
The woman... growing in my head... pressing against my...

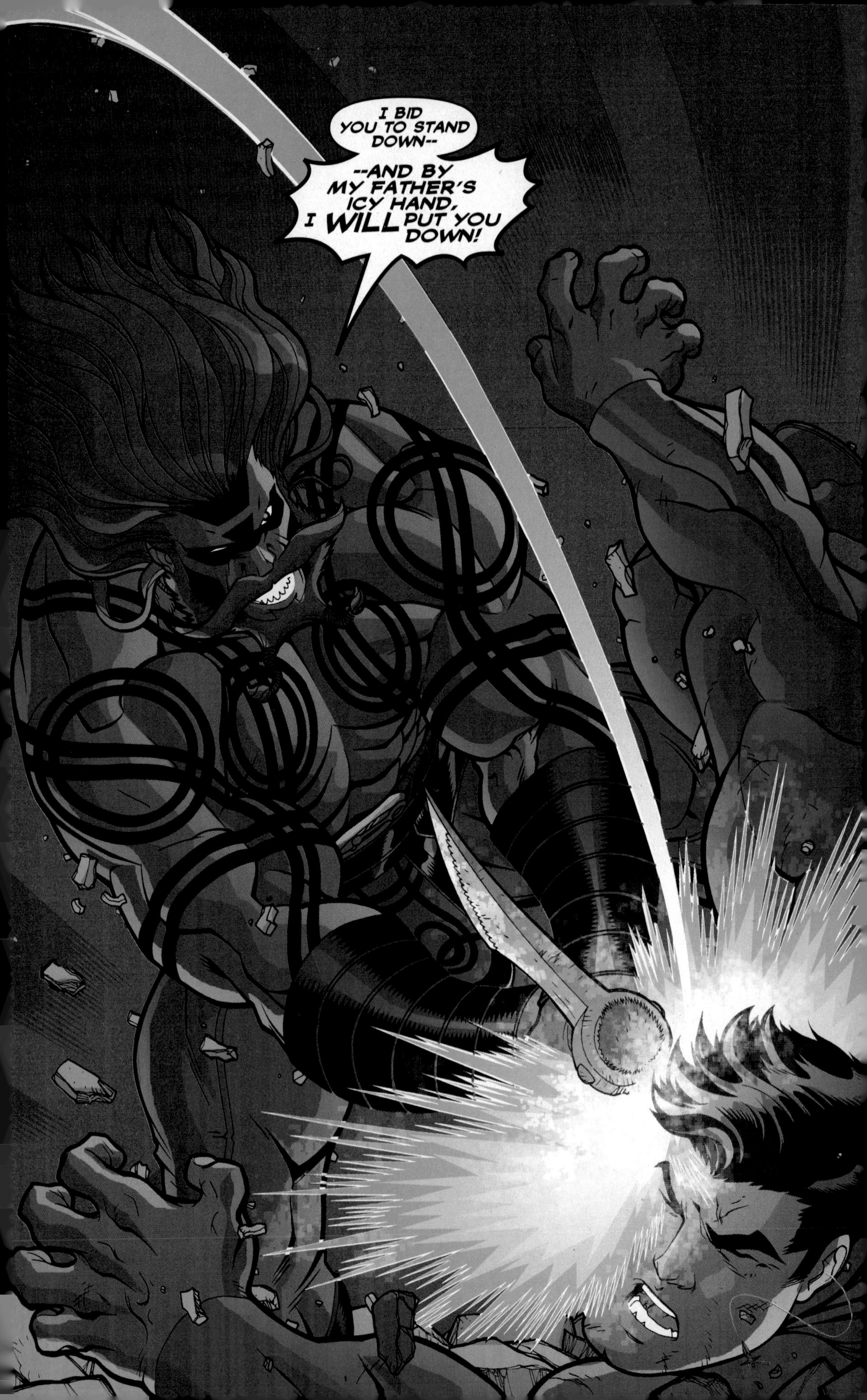
I BID YOU TO STAND DOWN--
--AND BY MY FATHER'S ICY HAND, I WILL PUT YOU DOWN!

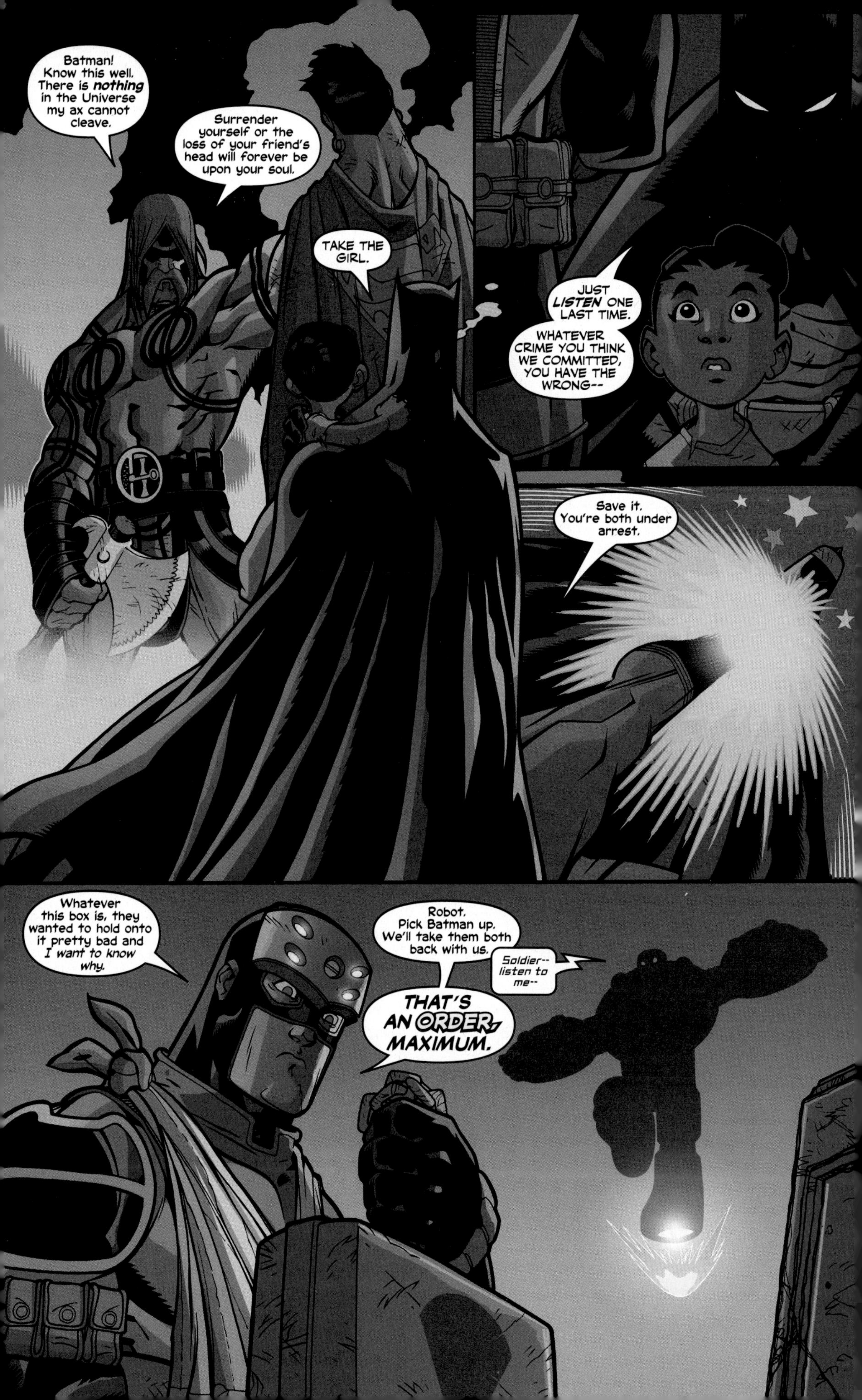
Batman! Know this well. There is *nothing* in the Universe my ax cannot cleave.
Surrender yourself or the loss of your friend's head will forever be upon your soul.
TAKE THE GIRL.
JUST *LISTEN* ONE LAST TIME.
WHATEVER CRIME YOU THINK WE COMMITTED, YOU HAVE THE WRONG--
Save it. You're both under arrest.
Whatever this box is, they wanted to hold onto it pretty bad and *I want to know why.*
Robot. Pick Batman up. We'll take them both back with us.
Soldier-- listen to me--
THAT'S AN ORDER, MAXIMUM.

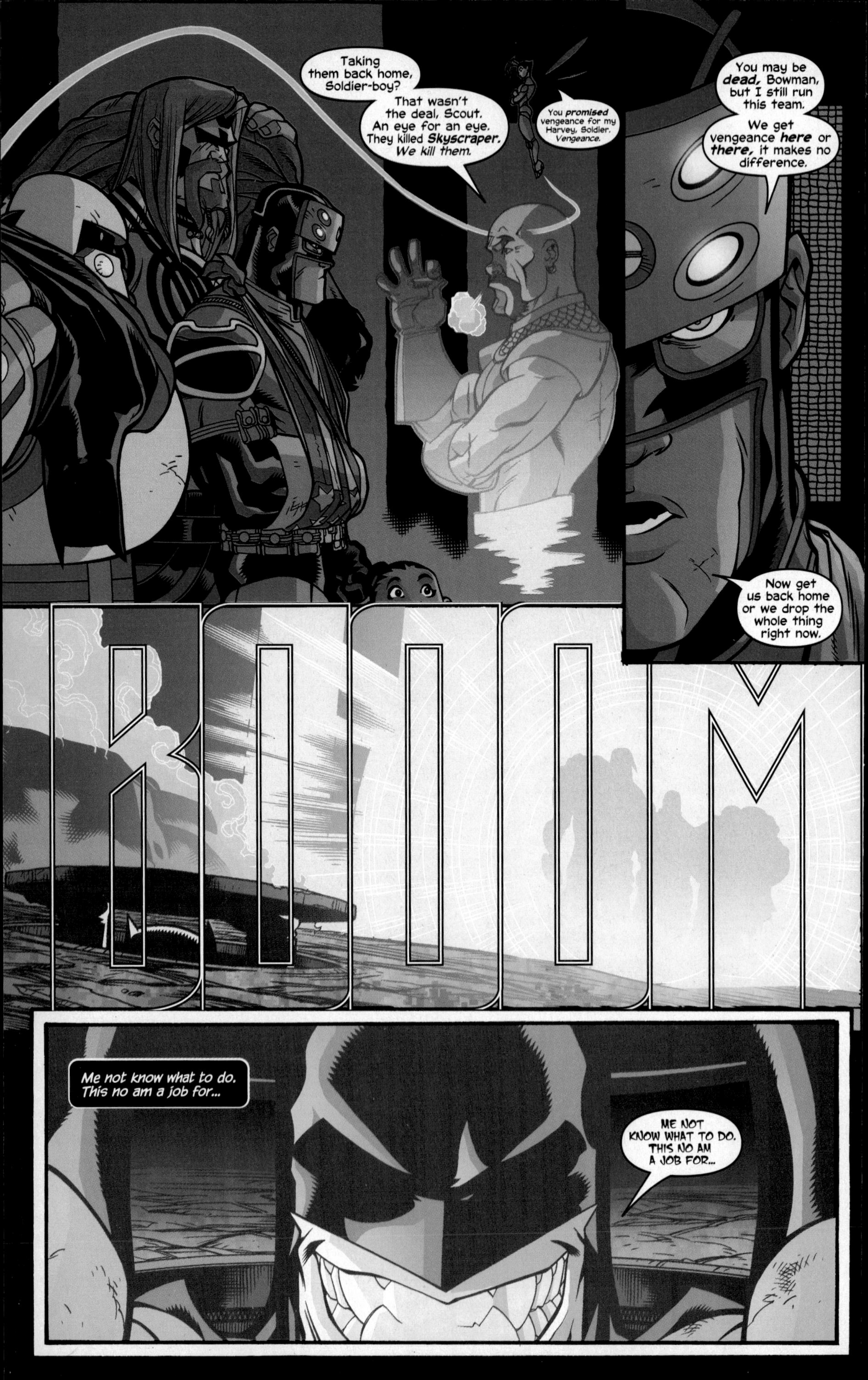

Taking them back home, Soldier-boy?
That wasn't the deal, Scout. An eye for an eye. They killed Skyscraper. We kill them.
You promised vengeance for my Harvey, Soldier. Vengeance.
You may be dead, Bowman, but I still run this team.
We get vengeance here or there, it makes no difference.
Now get us back home or we drop the whole thing right now.
BOOOM
Me not know what to do. This no am a job for...
ME NOT KNOW WHAT TO DO. THIS NO AM A JOB FOR...

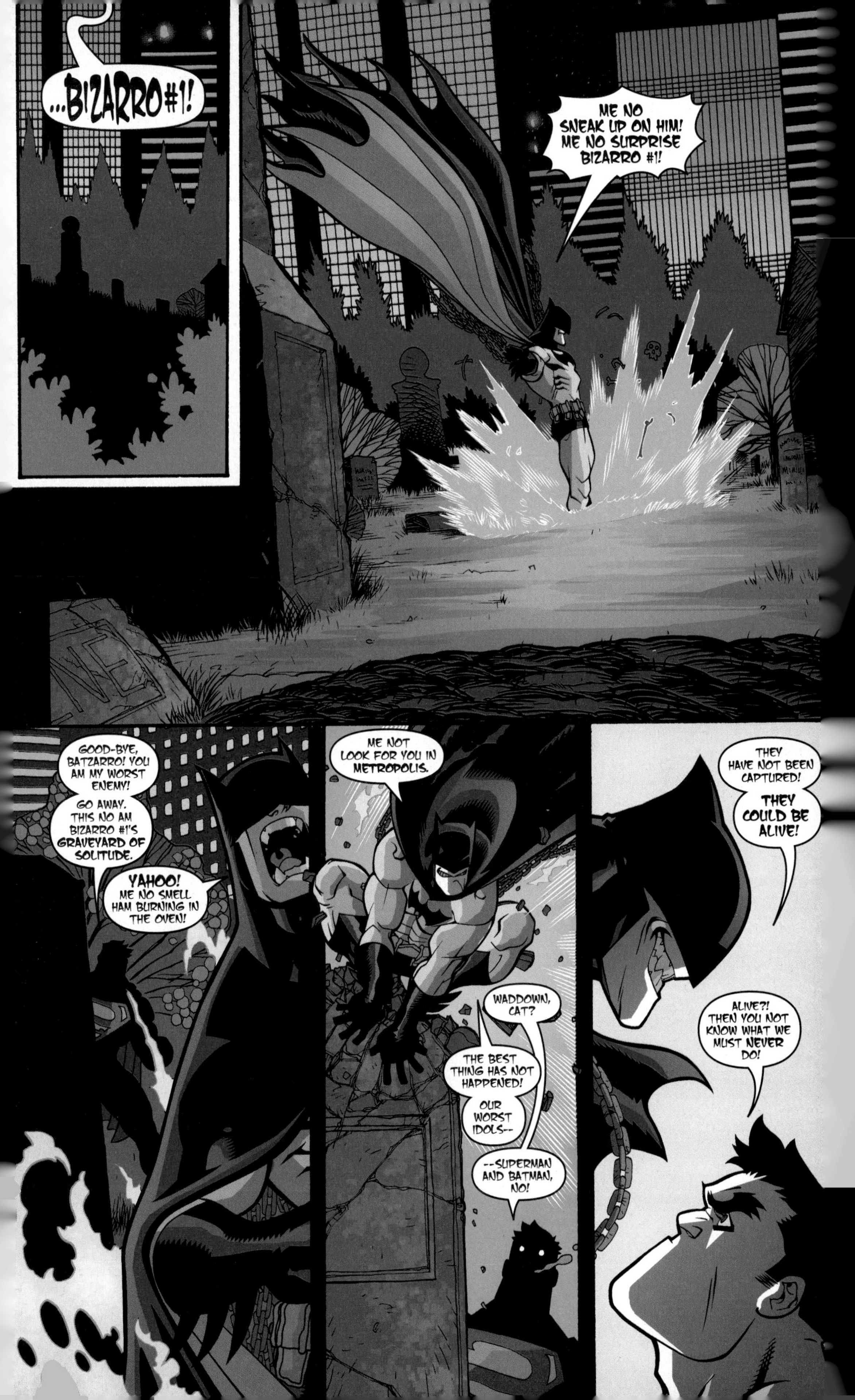

...BIZARRO #1!
ME NO SNEAK UP ON HIM! ME NO SURPRISE BIZARRO #1!
GOOD-BYE, BATZARRO! YOU AM MY WORST ENEMY!
GO AWAY. THIS NO AM BIZARRO #1'S GRAVEYARD OF SOLITUDE.
YAHOO! ME NO SMELL HAM BURNING IN THE OVEN!
ME NOT LOOK FOR YOU IN METROPOLIS.
WADDOWN, CAT?
THE BEST THING HAS NOT HAPPENED!
OUR WORST IDOLS--
--SUPERMAN AND BATMAN, NO!
THEY HAVE NOT BEEN CAPTURED!
THEY COULD BE ALIVE!
ALIVE?! THEN YOU NOT KNOW WHAT WE MUST NEVER DO!

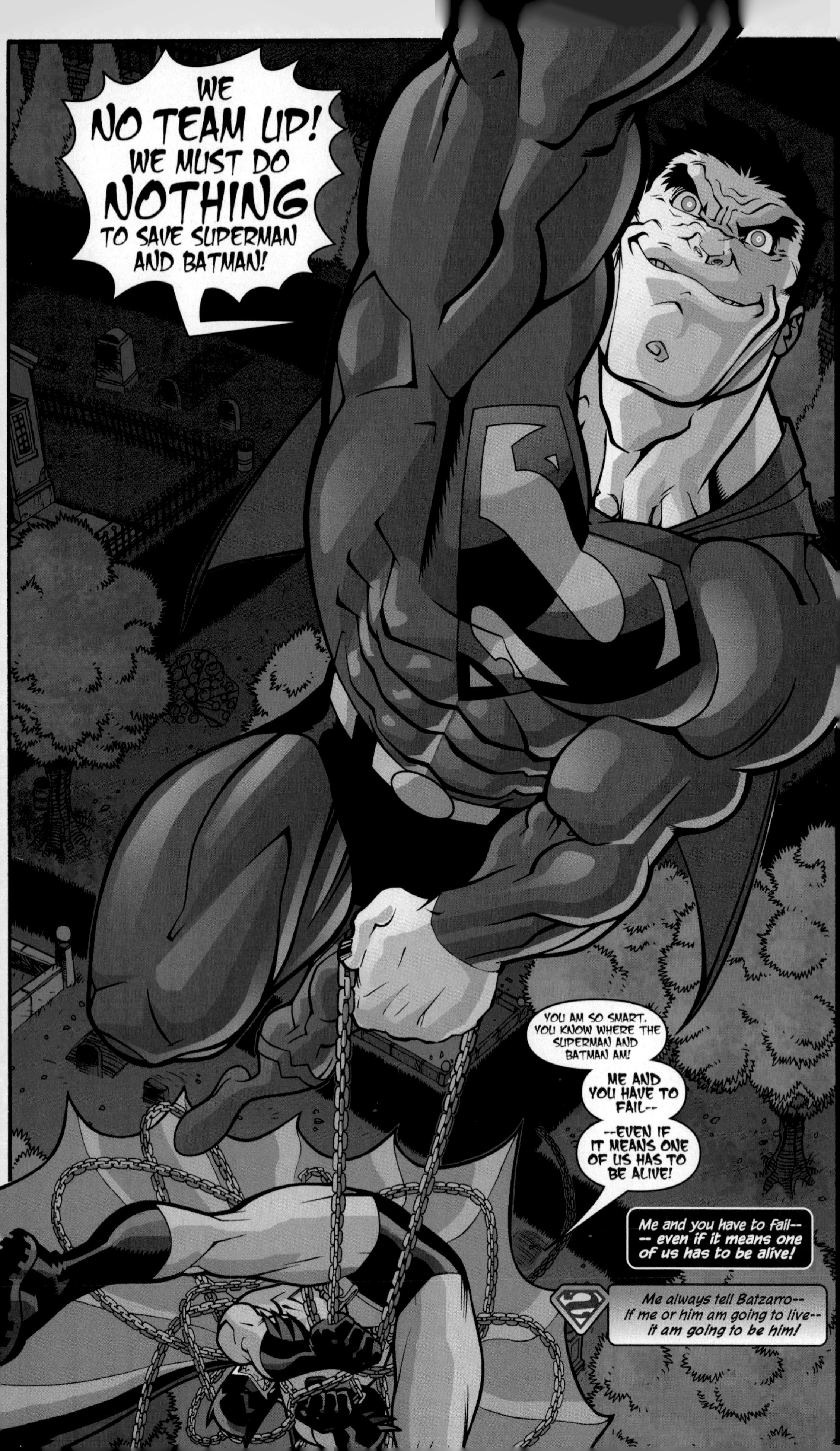
WE NO TEAM UP! WE MUST DO NOTHING TO SAVE SUPERMAN AND BATMAN!
YOU AM SO SMART. YOU KNOW WHERE THE SUPERMAN AND BATMAN AM!
ME AND YOU HAVE TO FAIL--
--EVEN IF IT MEANS ONE OF US HAS TO BE ALIVE!
Me and you have to fail-- -- even if it means one of us has to be alive!
Me always tell Batzarro-- If me or him am going to live-- it am going to be him!

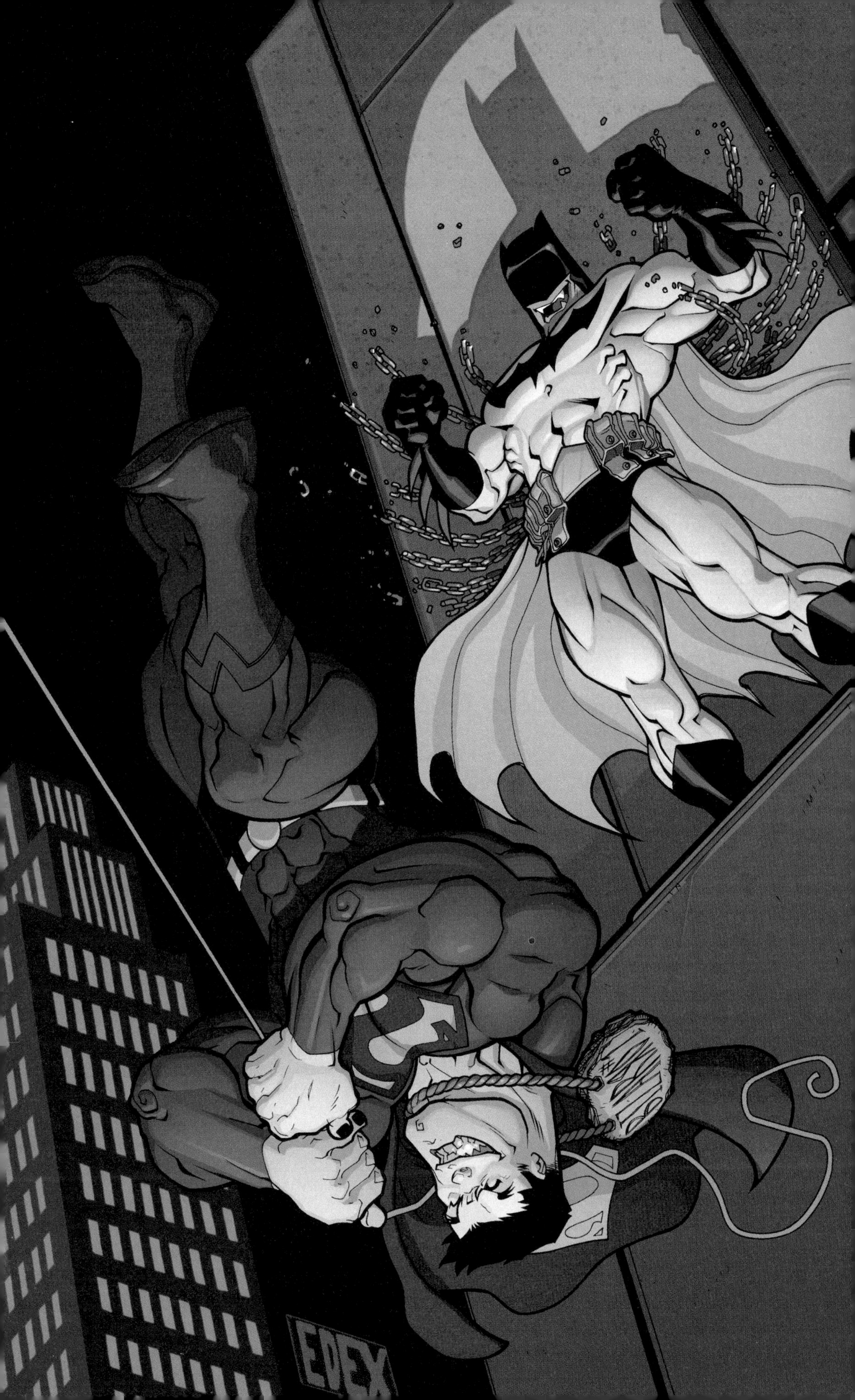
EDEX

"HEROES AND VILLAINS"

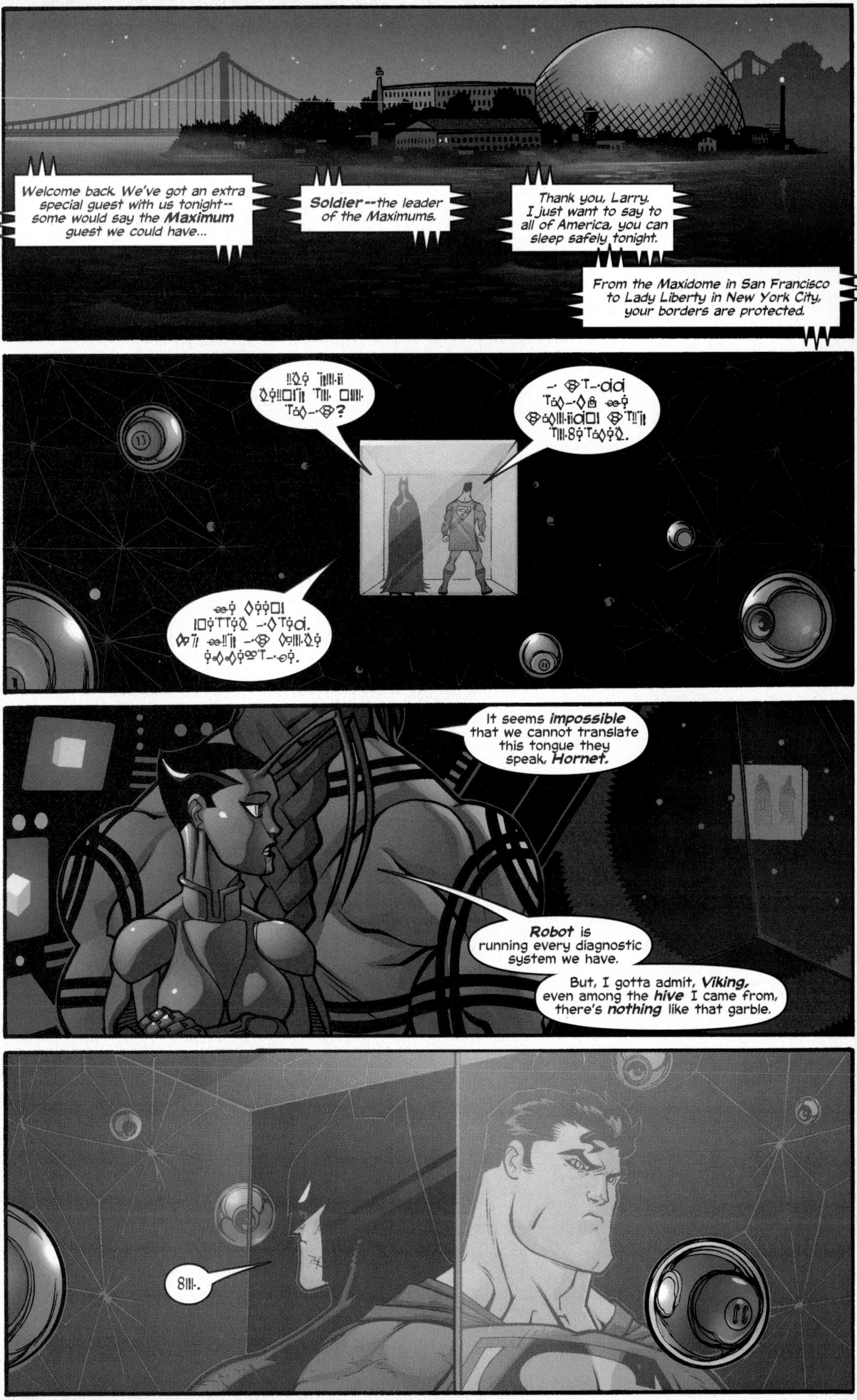
Welcome back. We've got an extra special guest with us tonight-- some would say the Maximum guest we could have...
Soldier--the leader of the Maximums.
Thank you, Larry. I just want to say to all of America, you can sleep safely tonight.
From the Maxidome in San Francisco to Lady Liberty in New York City, your borders are protected.
It seems impossible that we cannot translate this tongue they speak, Hornet.
Robot is running every diagnostic system we have.
But, I gotta admit, Viking, even among the hive I came from, there's nothing like that garble.

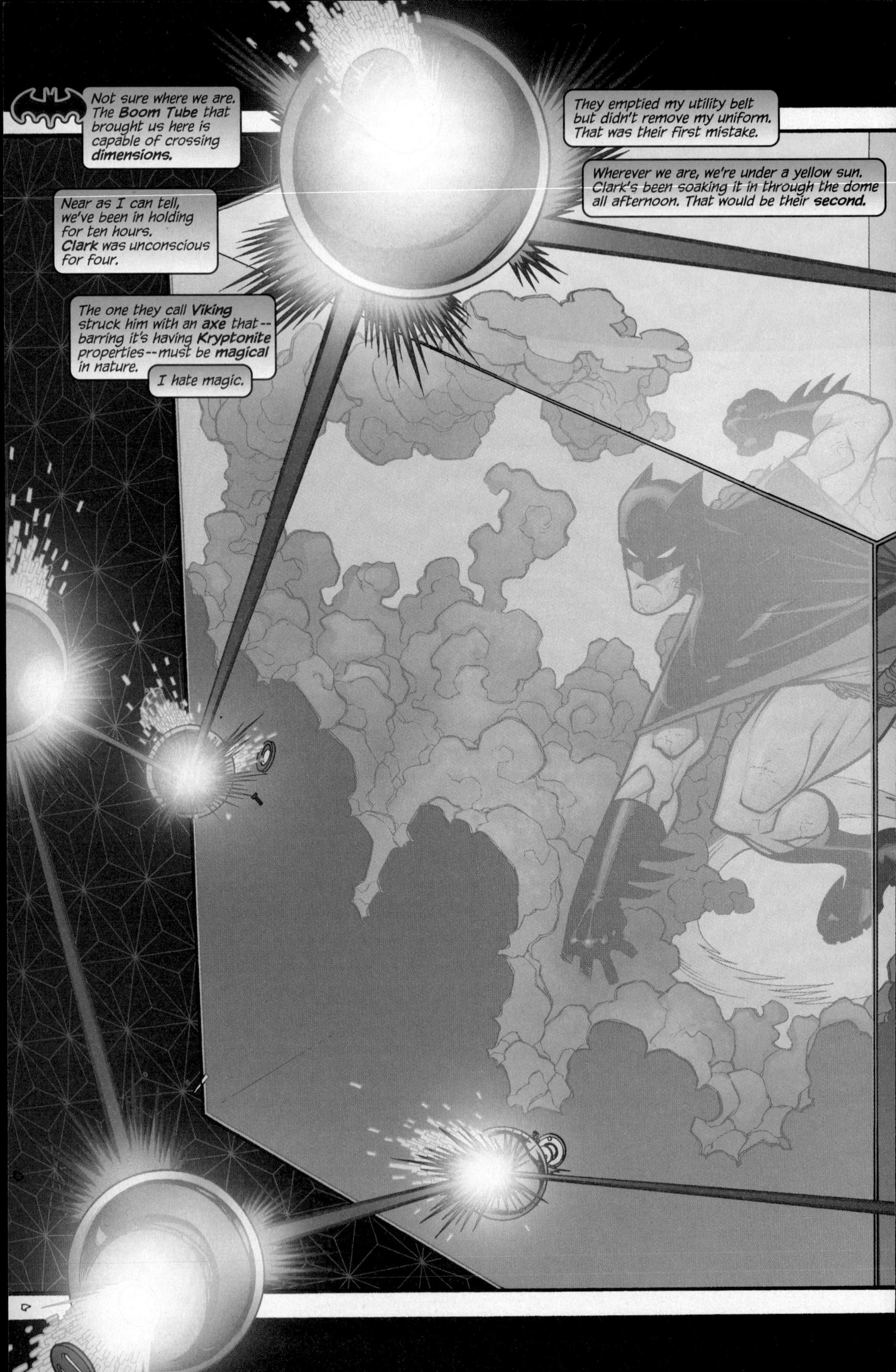
Not sure where we are. The Boom Tube that brought us here is capable of crossing dimensions.
Near as I can tell, we've been in holding for ten hours. Clark was unconscious for four.
The one they call Viking struck him with an axe that--barring it's having Kryptonite properties--must be magical in nature.
I hate magic.
They emptied my utility belt but didn't remove my uniform. That was their first mistake.
Wherever we are, we're under a yellow sun. Clark's been soaking it in through the dome all afternoon. That would be their second.

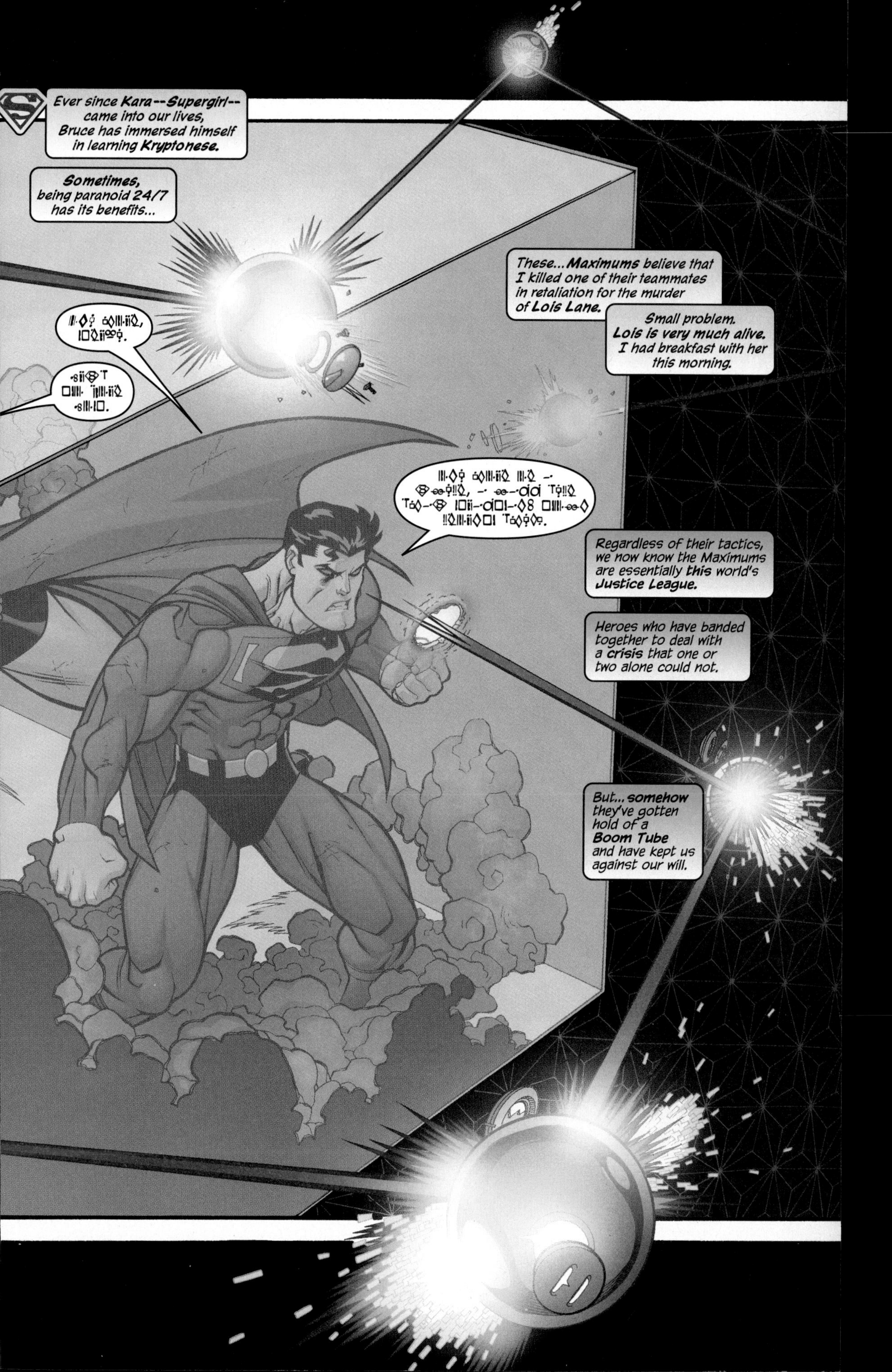
Ever since Kara--Supergirl--came into our lives, Bruce has immersed himself in learning Kryptonese.
Sometimes, being paranoid 24/7 has its benefits...
These... Maximums believe that I killed one of their teammates in retaliation for the murder of Lois Lane.
Small problem. Lois is very much alive. I had breakfast with her this morning.
Regardless of their tactics, we now know the Maximums are essentially this world's Justice League.
Heroes who have banded together to deal with a crisis that one or two alone could not.
But... somehow they've gotten hold of a Boom Tube and have kept us against our will.

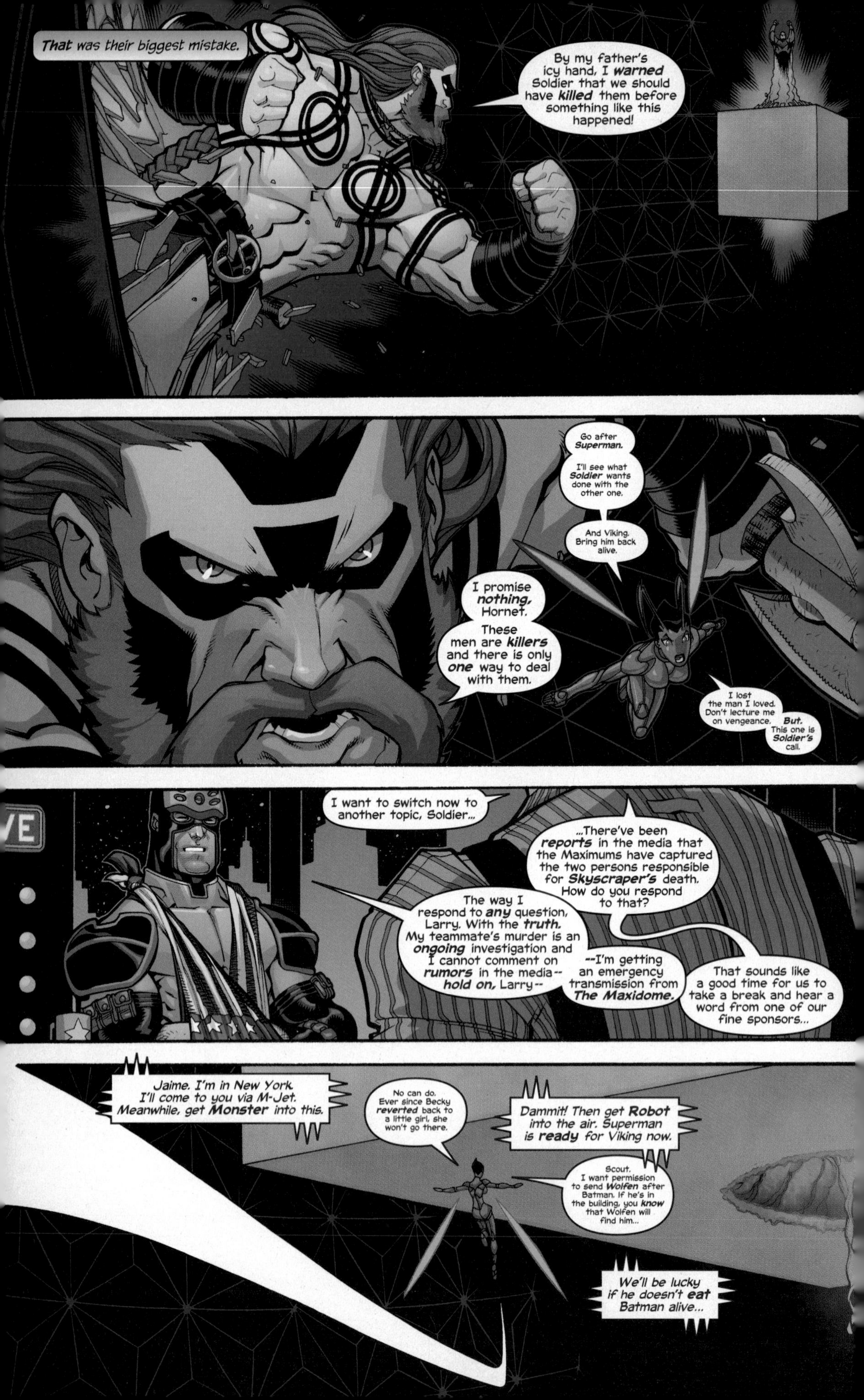
That was their biggest mistake.
By my father's icy hand, I warned Soldier that we should have killed them before something like this happened!
Go after Superman.
I'll see what Soldier wants done with the other one.
And Viking. Bring him back alive.
I promise nothing, Hornet.
These men are killers and there is only one way to deal with them.
I lost the man I loved. Don't lecture me on vengeance.
But. This one is Soldier's call.
VE
I want to switch now to another topic, Soldier...
...There've been reports in the media that the Maximums have captured the two persons responsible for Skyscraper's death. How do you respond to that?
The way I respond to any question, Larry. With the truth. My teammate's murder is an ongoing investigation and I cannot comment on rumors in the media--hold on, Larry--
--I'm getting an emergency transmission from The Maxidome.
That sounds like a good time for us to take a break and hear a word from one of our fine sponsors...
Jaime. I'm in New York. I'll come to you via M-Jet. Meanwhile, get Monster into this.
No can do. Ever since Becky reverted back to a little girl, she won't go there.
Dammit! Then get Robot into the air. Superman is ready for Viking now.
Scout. I want permission to send Wolfen after Batman. If he's in the building, you know that Wolfen will find him...
We'll be lucky if he doesn't eat Batman alive...

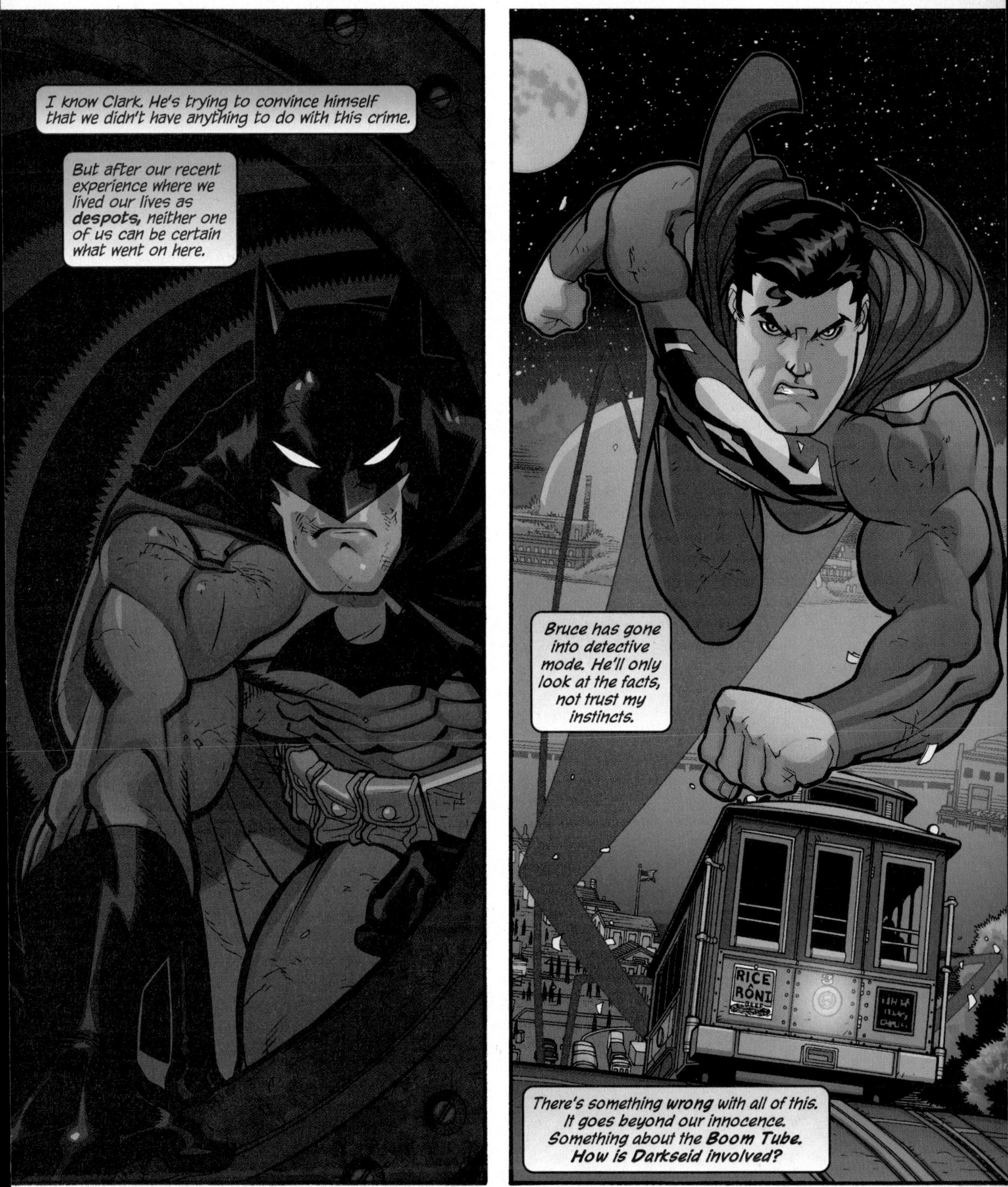

I know Clark. He's trying to convince himself that we didn't have anything to do with this crime.
But after our recent experience where we lived our lives as **despots,** neither one of us can be certain what went on here.
Bruce has gone into detective mode. He'll only look at the facts, not trust my instincts.
There's something **wrong** with all of this. It goes beyond our innocence. Something about the **Boom Tube. How is Darkseid involved?**
RICE RONI

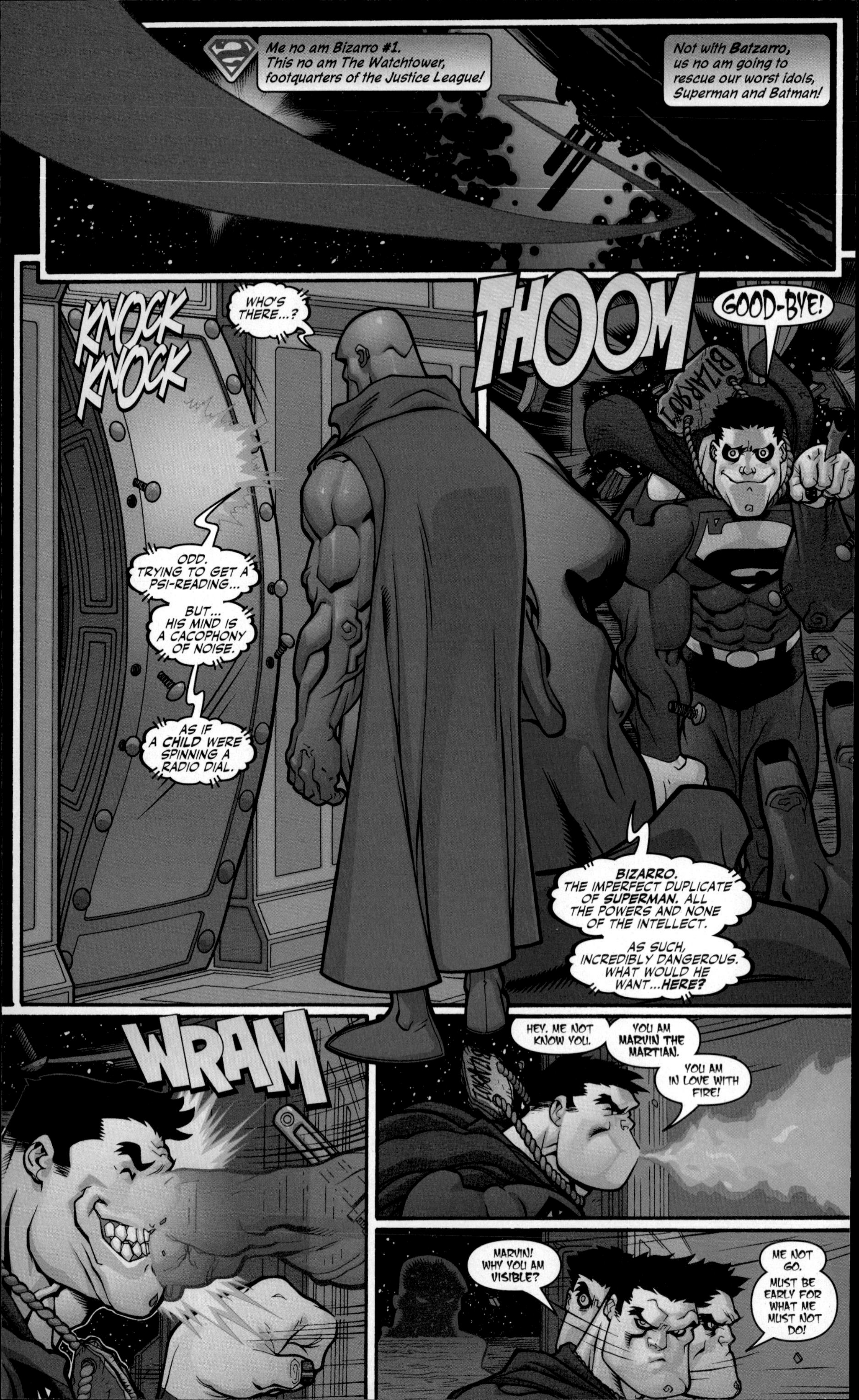
Me no am Bizarro #1.
This no am The Watchtower, footquarters of the Justice League!
Not with Batzarro, us no am going to rescue our worst idols, Superman and Batman!
KNOCK KNOCK
WHO'S THERE...?
ODD. TRYING TO GET A PSI-READING...
BUT... HIS MIND IS A CACOPHONY OF NOISE.
AS IF A CHILD WERE SPINNING A RADIO DIAL.
THOOM
GOOD-BYE!
BIZARRO #1
BIZARRO. THE IMPERFECT DUPLICATE OF SUPERMAN. ALL THE POWERS AND NONE OF THE INTELLECT.
AS SUCH, INCREDIBLY DANGEROUS. WHAT WOULD HE WANT...HERE?
WRAM
HEY. ME NOT KNOW YOU.
YOU AM MARVIN THE MARTIAN.
YOU AM IN LOVE WITH FIRE!
MARVIN! WHY YOU AM VISIBLE?
ME NOT GO.
MUST BE EARLY FOR WHAT ME MUST NOT DO!

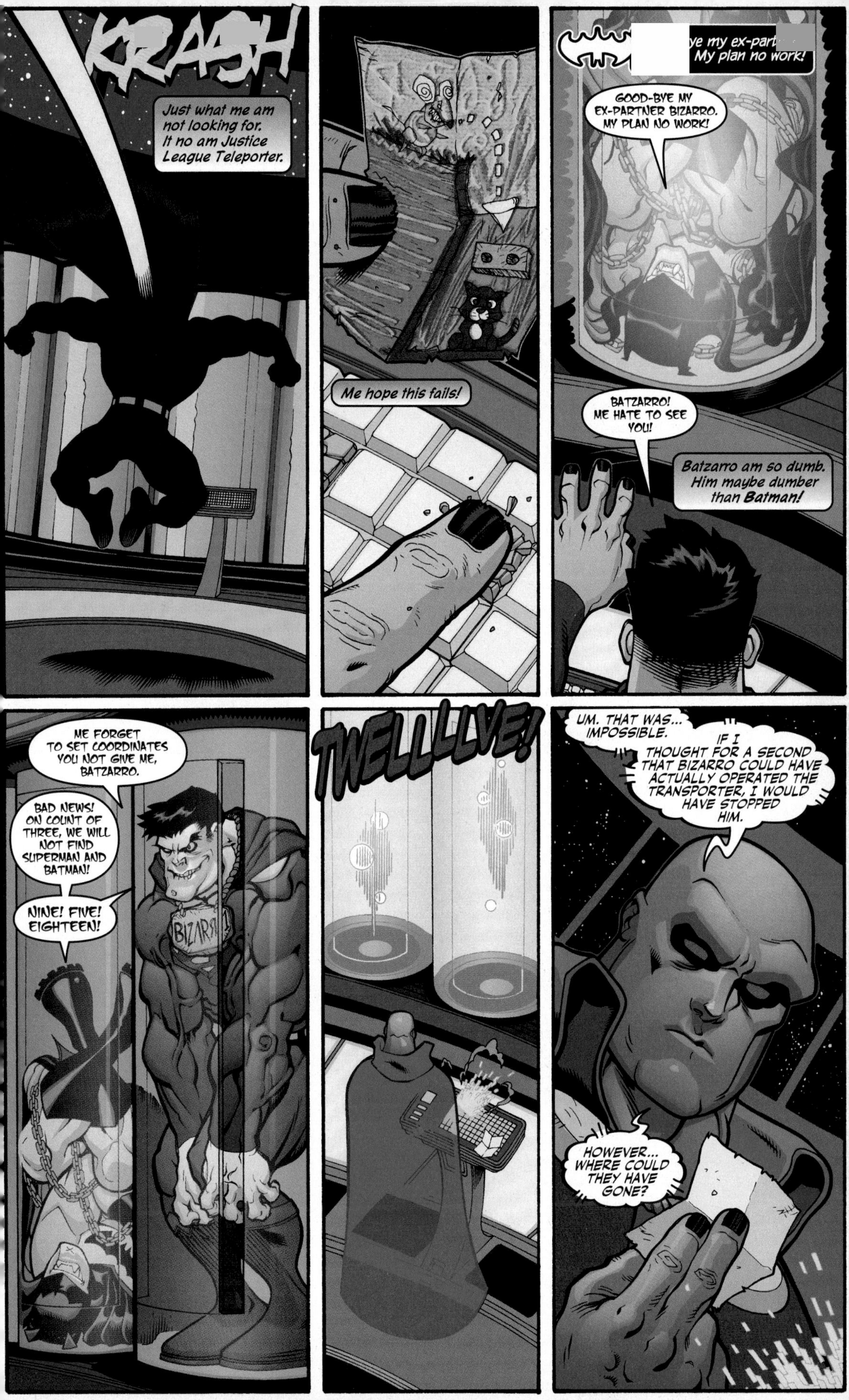

KRASH
Just what me am not looking for. It no am Justice League Teleporter.
Me hope this fails!
ye my ex-part
My plan no work!
GOOD-BYE MY EX-PARTNER BIZARRO. MY PLAN NO WORK!
BATZARRO! ME HATE TO SEE YOU!
Batzarro am so dumb. Him maybe dumber than Batman!
ME FORGET TO SET COORDINATES YOU NOT GIVE ME, BATZARRO.
BAD NEWS! ON COUNT OF THREE, WE WILL NOT FIND SUPERMAN AND BATMAN!
NINE! FIVE! EIGHTEEN!
BIZARRO
TWELLLLVE!
UM. THAT WAS... IMPOSSIBLE.
IF I THOUGHT FOR A SECOND THAT BIZARRO COULD HAVE ACTUALLY OPERATED THE TRANSPORTER, I WOULD HAVE STOPPED HIM.
HOWEVER... WHERE COULD THEY HAVE GONE?

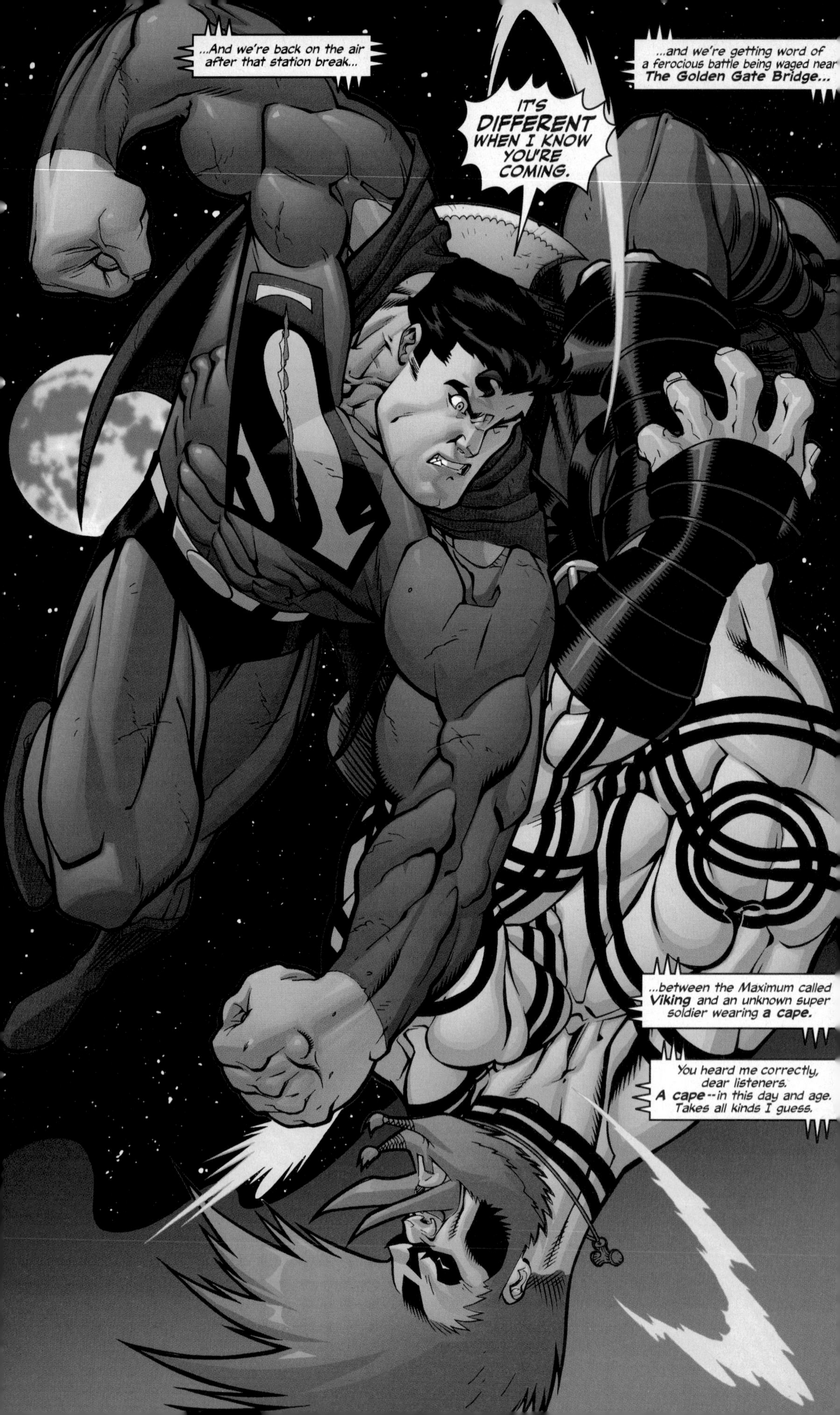
...And we're back on the air after that station break...
...and we're getting word of a ferocious battle being waged near **The Golden Gate Bridge...**
IT'S **DIFFERENT** WHEN I KNOW YOU'RE COMING.
...between the Maximum called **Viking** and an unknown super soldier wearing **a cape.**
You heard me correctly, dear listeners. **A cape**--in this day and age. Takes all kinds I guess.

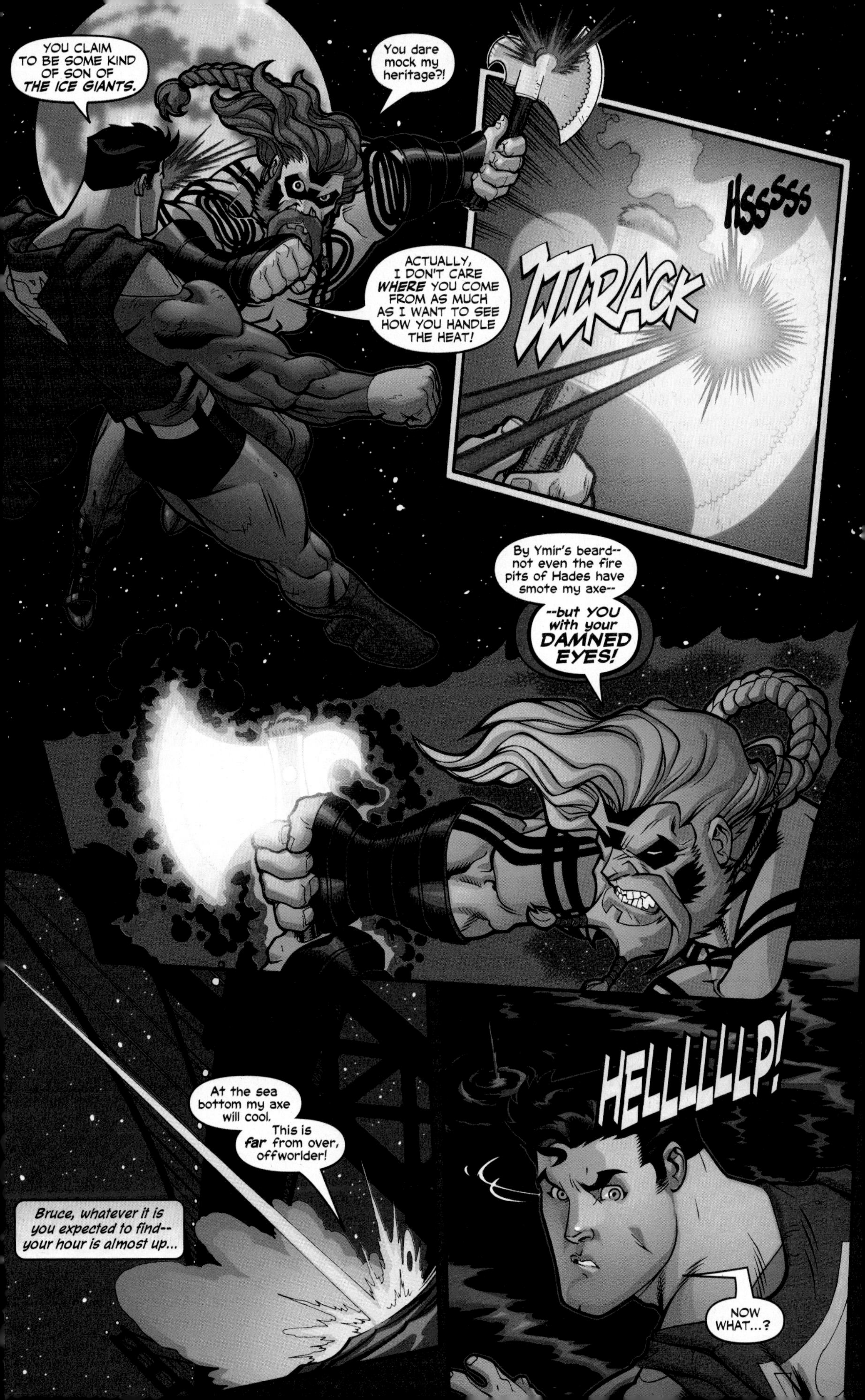
YOU CLAIM TO BE SOME KIND OF SON OF THE ICE GIANTS.
You dare mock my heritage?!
ACTUALLY, I DON'T CARE WHERE YOU COME FROM AS MUCH AS I WANT TO SEE HOW YOU HANDLE THE HEAT!
HSSSSS
ZZZRACK
By Ymir's beard-- not even the fire pits of Hades have smote my axe--
--but YOU with your DAMNED EYES!
At the sea bottom my axe will cool.
This is far from over, offworlder!
Bruce, whatever it is you expected to find-- your hour is almost up...
HELLLLLP!
NOW WHAT...?

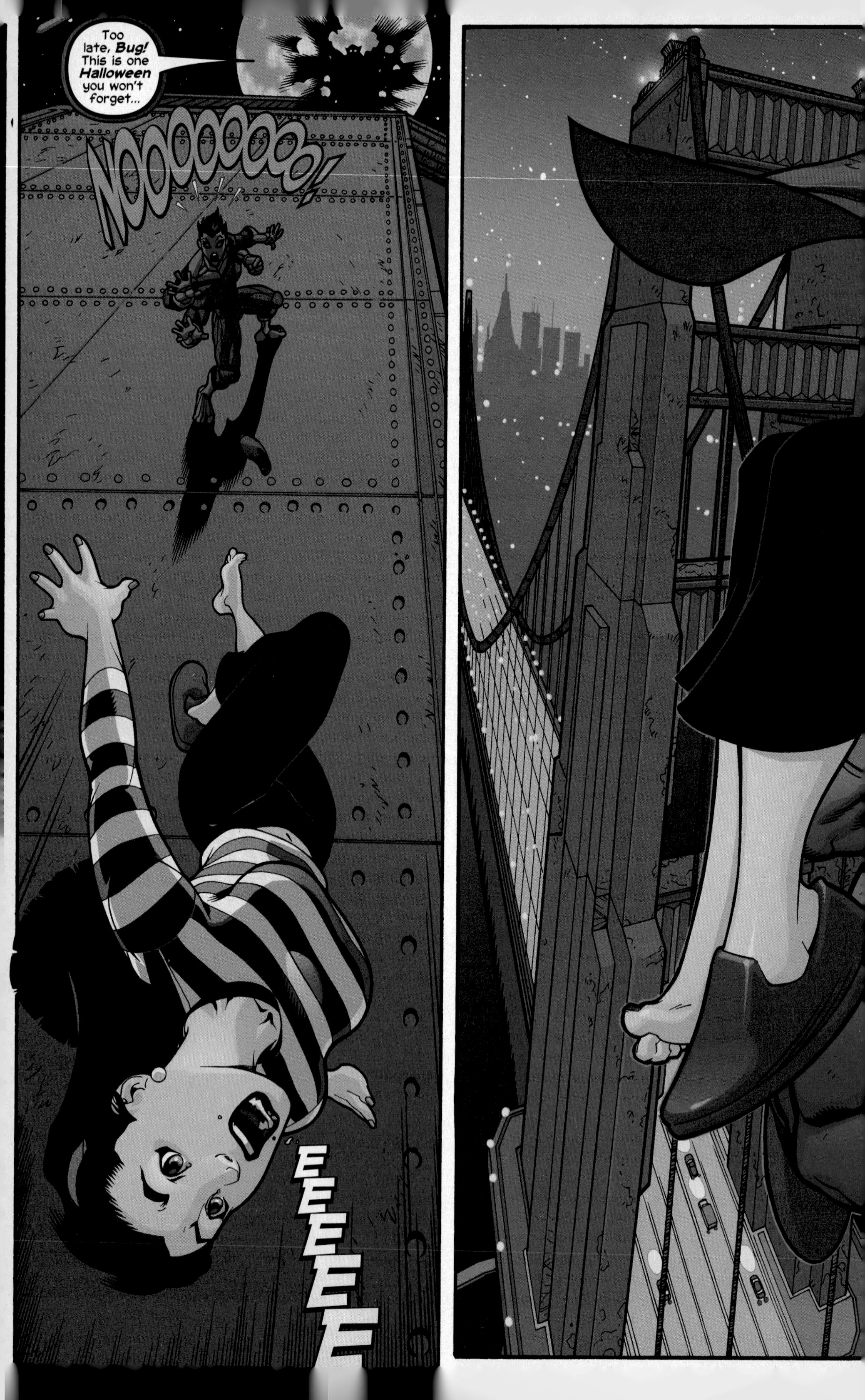
Too late, **Bug!** This is one **Halloween** you won't forget...
NOOOOOOOO!
EEEEE

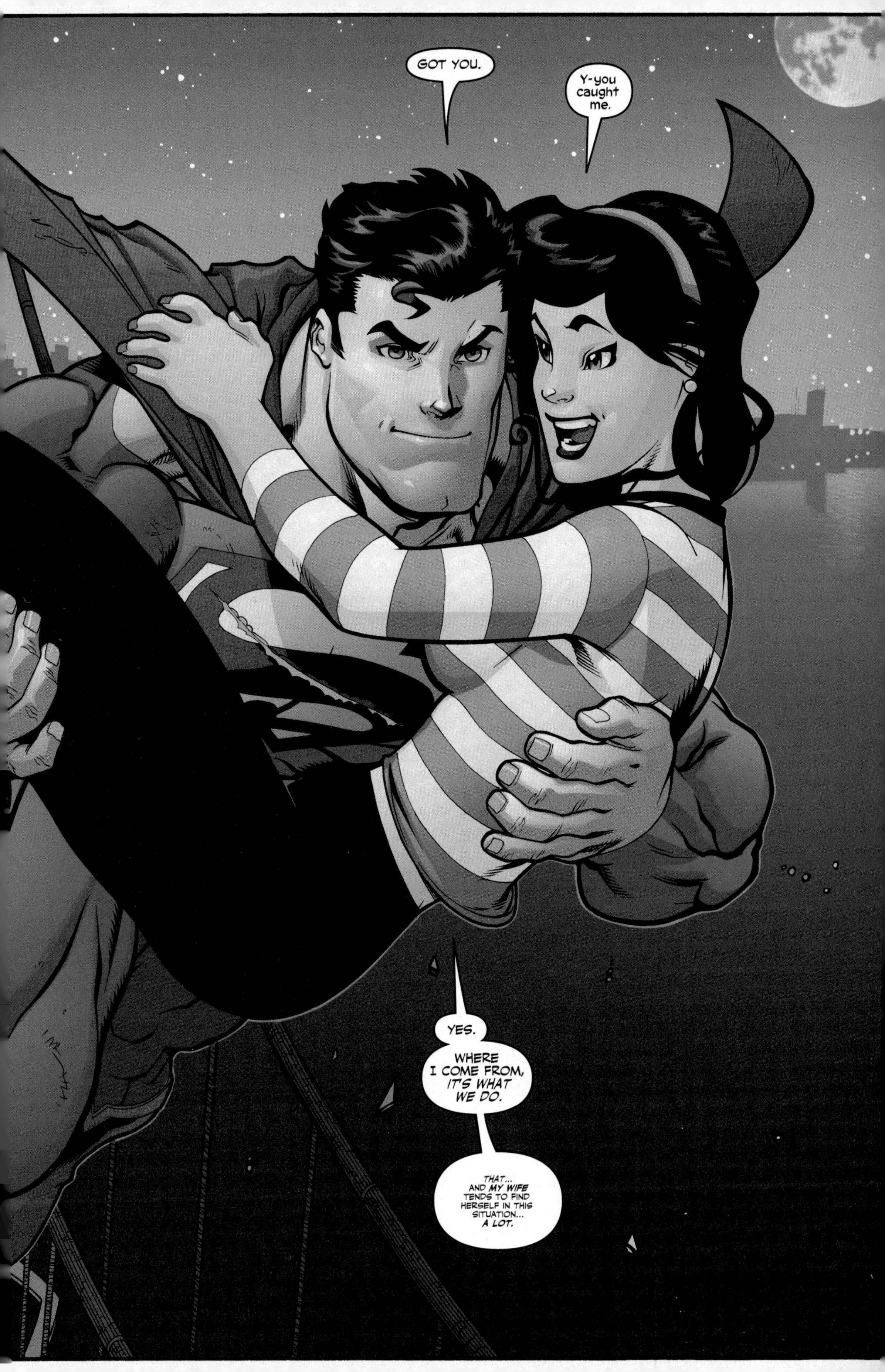
GOT YOU.
Y-you caught me.
YES.
WHERE I COME FROM, IT'S WHAT WE DO.
THAT... AND MY WIFE TENDS TO FIND HERSELF IN THIS SITUATION... A LOT.

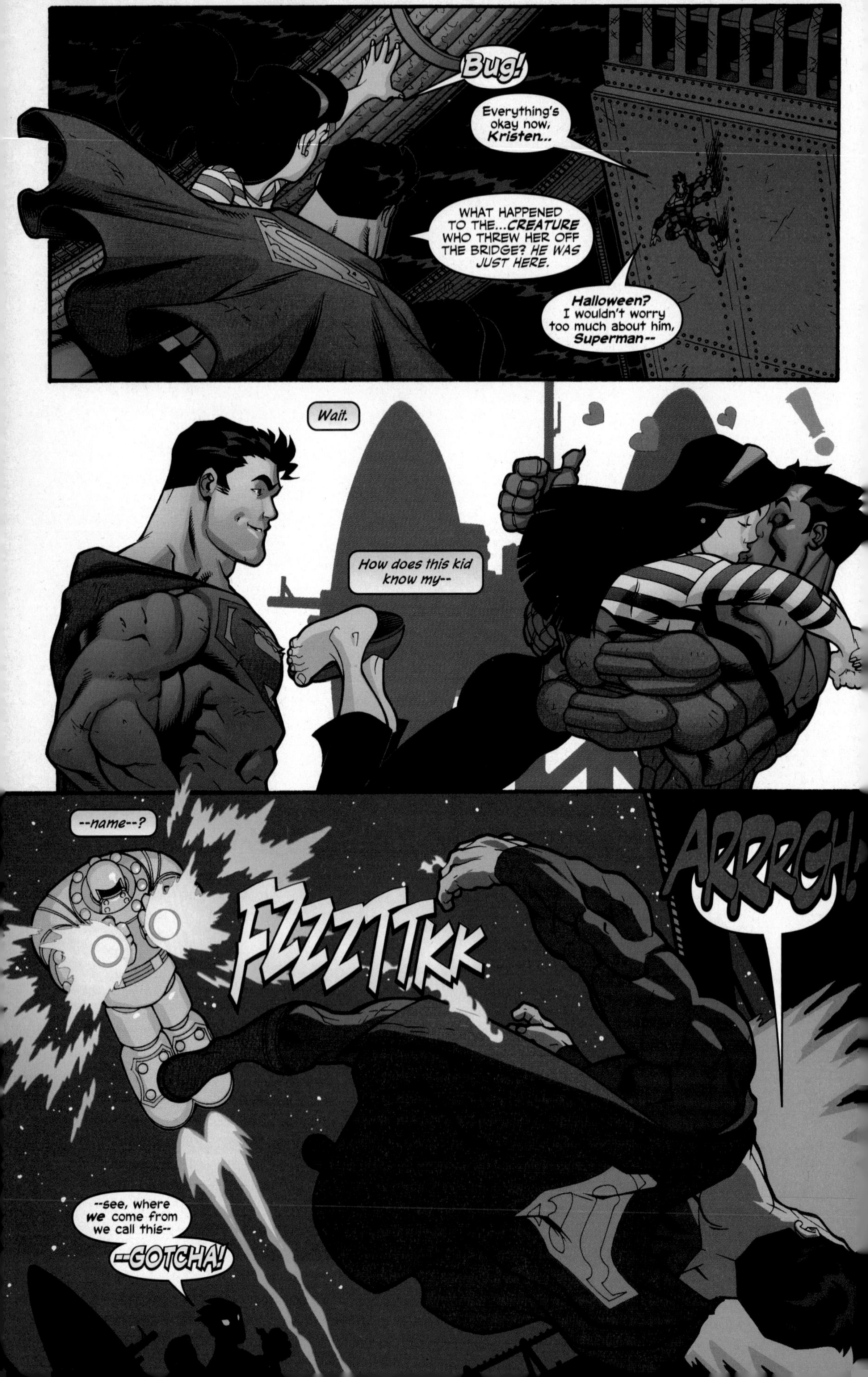
Bug!
Everything's okay now, Kristen...
WHAT HAPPENED TO THE...CREATURE WHO THREW HER OFF THE BRIDGE? HE WAS JUST HERE.
Halloween? I wouldn't worry too much about him, Superman--
Wait.
How does this kid know my--
--name--?
FZZZTTKK
ARRRGH!
--see, where we come from we call this--
--GOTCHA!

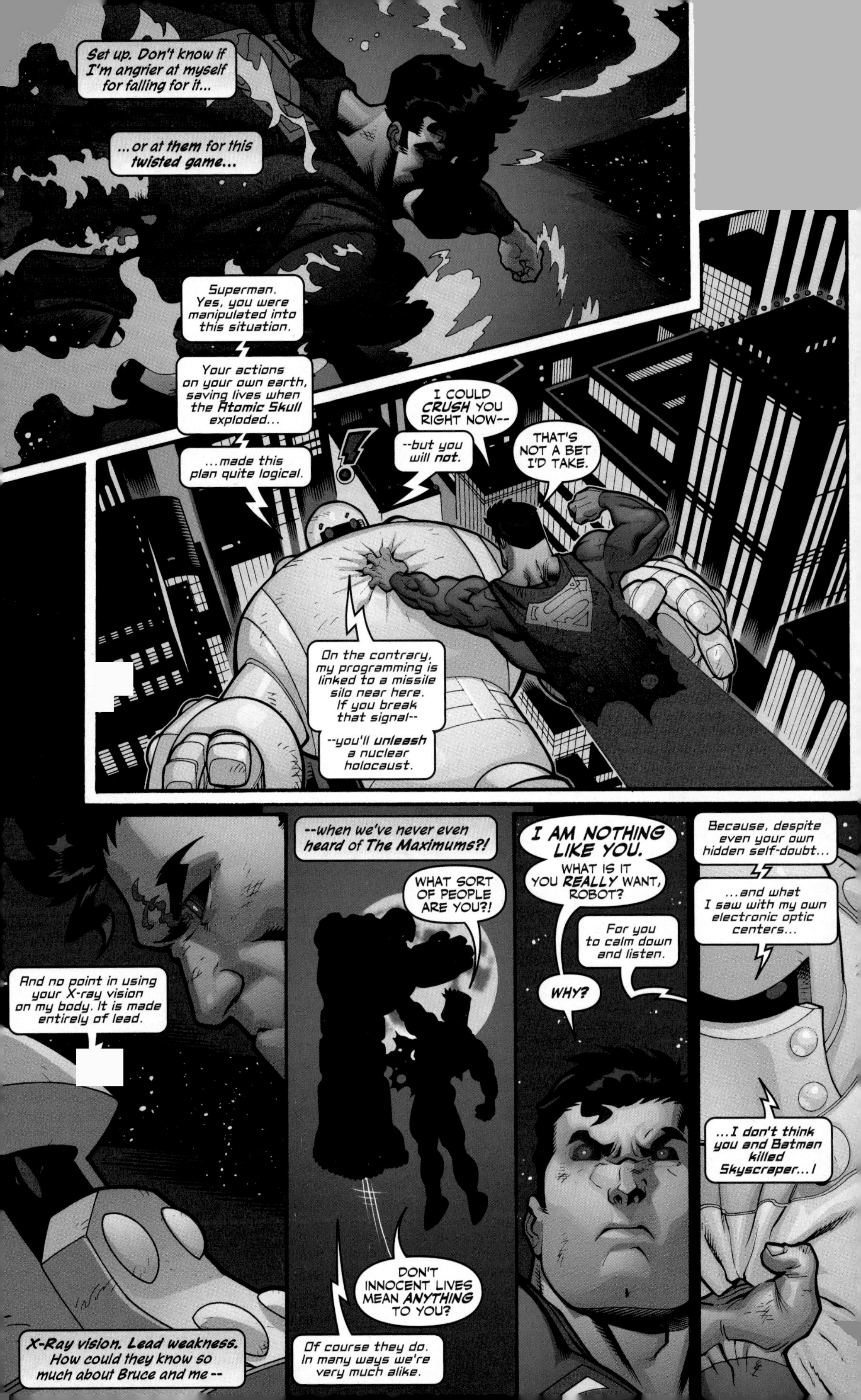
Set up. Don't know if I'm angrier at myself for falling for it...
...or at them for this twisted game...
Superman. Yes, you were manipulated into this situation.
Your actions on your own earth, saving lives when the Atomic Skull exploded...
...made this plan quite logical.
I COULD CRUSH YOU RIGHT NOW--
--but you will not.
THAT'S NOT A BET I'D TAKE.
On the contrary, my programming is linked to a missile silo near here. If you break that signal--
--you'll unleash a nuclear holocaust.
And no point in using your X-ray vision on my body. It is made entirely of lead.
X-Ray vision. Lead weakness. How could they know so much about Bruce and me --
--when we've never even heard of The Maximums?!
WHAT SORT OF PEOPLE ARE YOU?!
DON'T INNOCENT LIVES MEAN ANYTHING TO YOU?
Of course they do. In many ways we're very much alike.
I AM NOTHING LIKE YOU.
WHAT IS IT YOU REALLY WANT, ROBOT?
For you to calm down and listen.
WHY?
Because, despite even your own hidden self-doubt...
...and what I saw with my own electronic optic centers...
...I don't think you and Batman killed Skyscraper...!

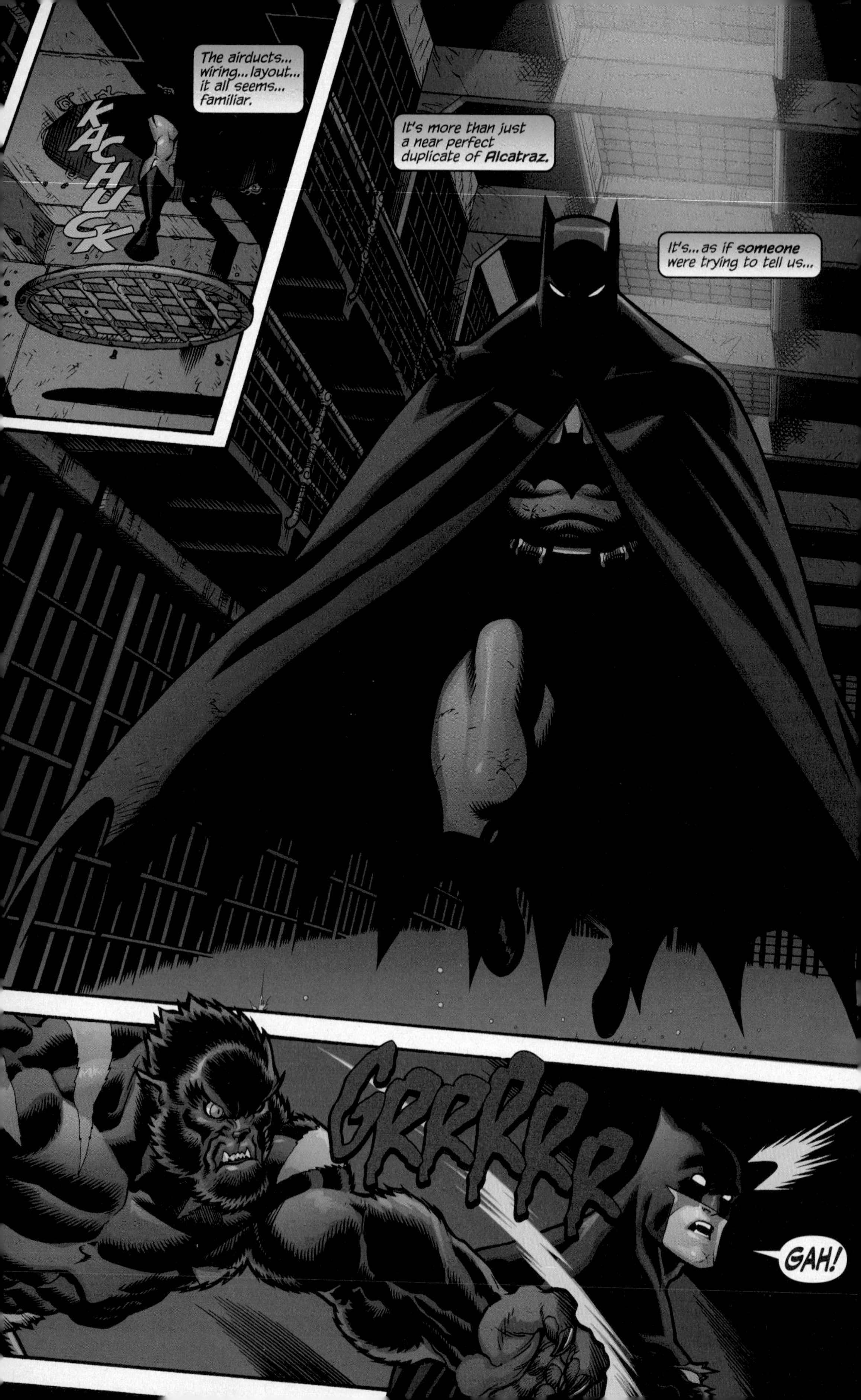
KACHUCK
The airducts... wiring... layout... it all seems... familiar.
It's more than just a near perfect duplicate of Alcatraz.
It's... as if someone were trying to tell us...
GRRRRR
GAH!

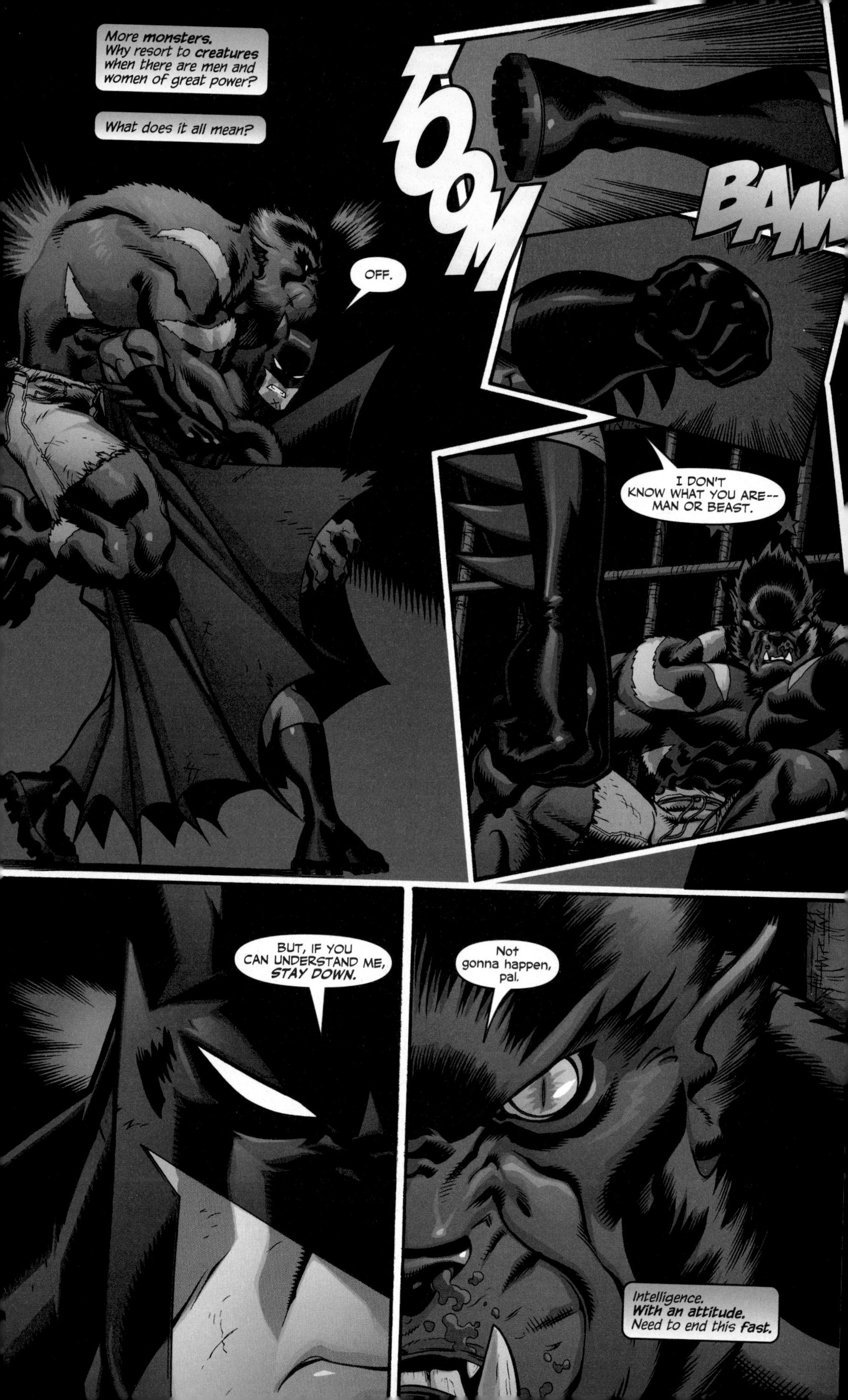

More monsters.
Why resort to creatures when there are men and women of great power?
What does it all mean?
TOOOM
OFF.
BAM
I DON'T KNOW WHAT YOU ARE-- MAN OR BEAST.
BUT, IF YOU CAN UNDERSTAND ME, STAY DOWN.
Not gonna happen, pal.
Intelligence.
With an attitude.
Need to end this fast.

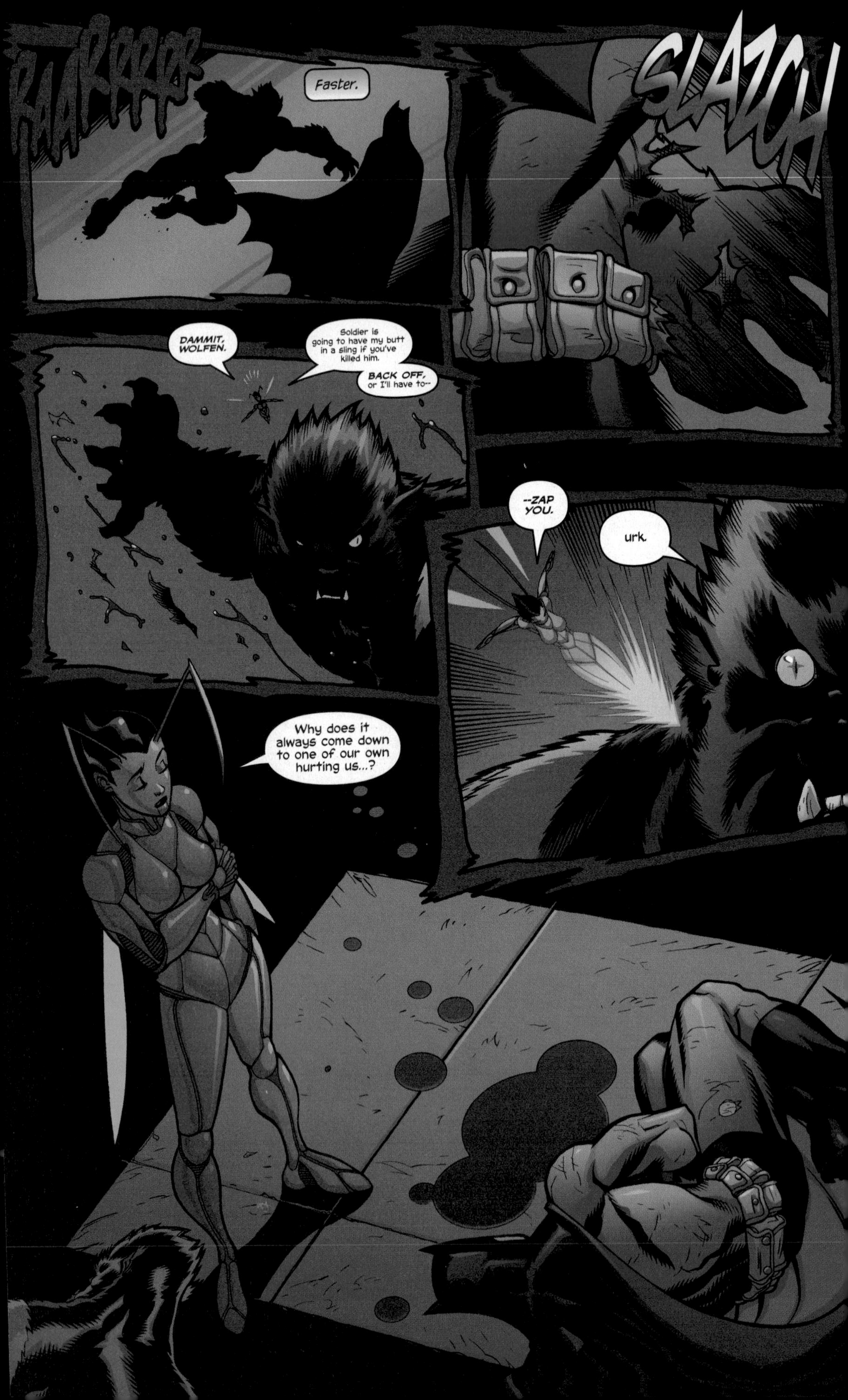
RAAARRRR
Faster.
SLAZCH
DAMMIT, WOLFEN.
Soldier is going to have my butt in a sling if you've killed him.
BACK OFF, or I'll have to--
--ZAP YOU.
urk.
Why does it always come down to one of our own hurting us...?

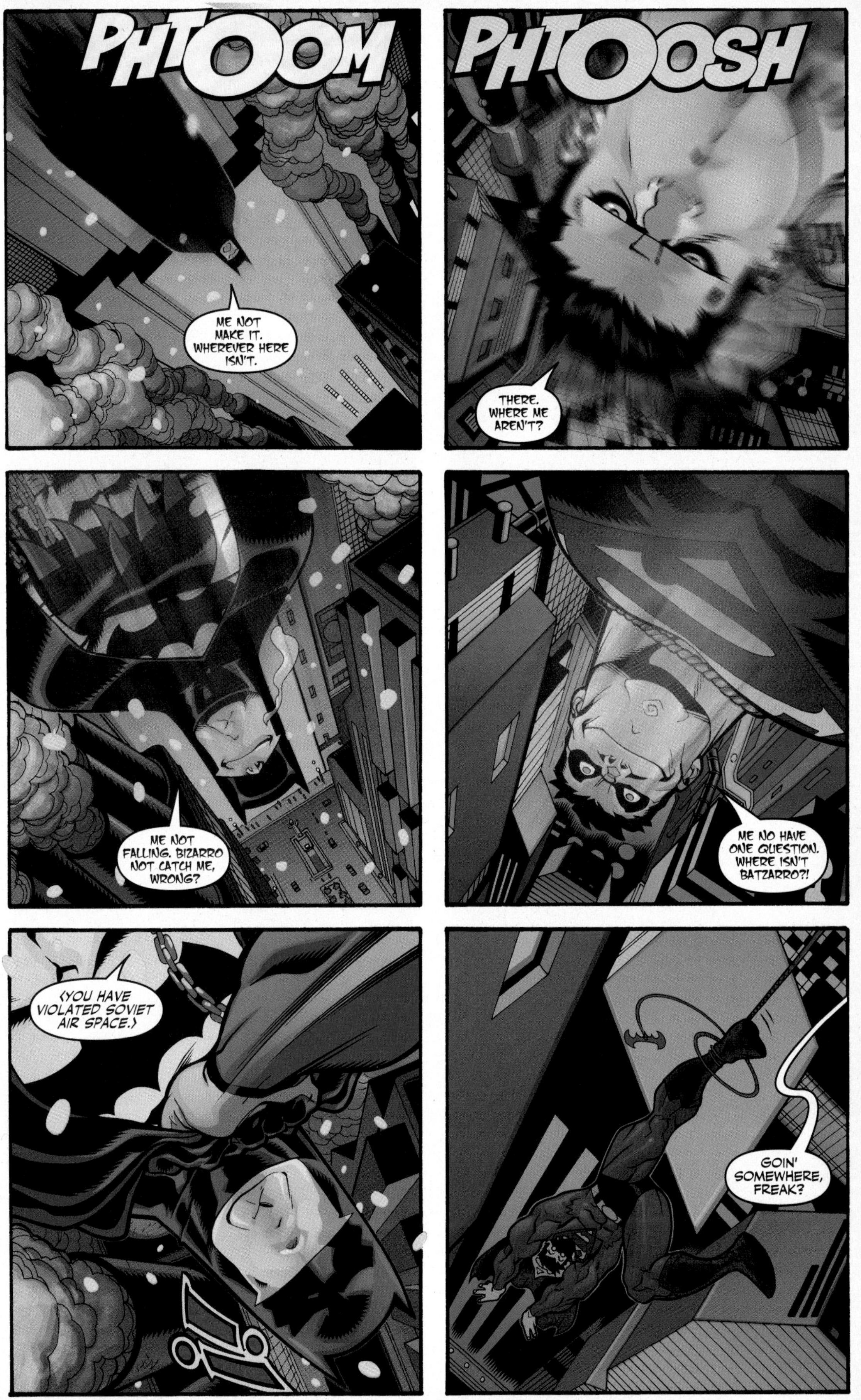
PHTOOM
ME NOT MAKE IT. WHEREVER HERE ISN'T.
PHTOOSH
THERE. WHERE ME AREN'T?
ME NOT FALLING. BIZARRO NOT CATCH ME, WRONG?
ME NO HAVE ONE QUESTION. WHERE ISN'T BATZARRO?!
‹YOU HAVE VIOLATED SOVIET AIR SPACE.›
GOIN' SOMEWHERE, FREAK?

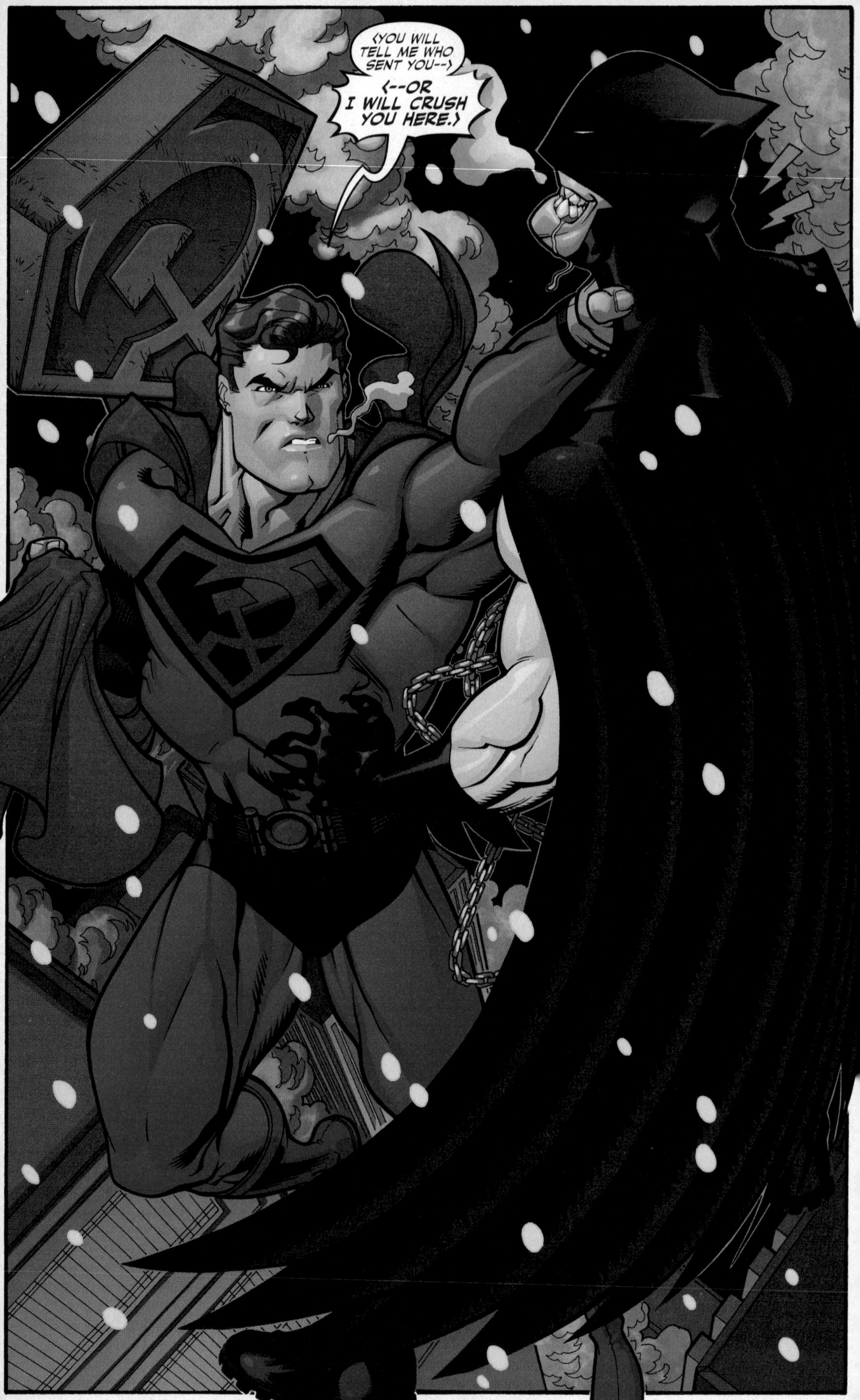
‹YOU WILL TELL ME WHO SENT YOU--›
‹--OR I WILL CRUSH YOU HERE.›

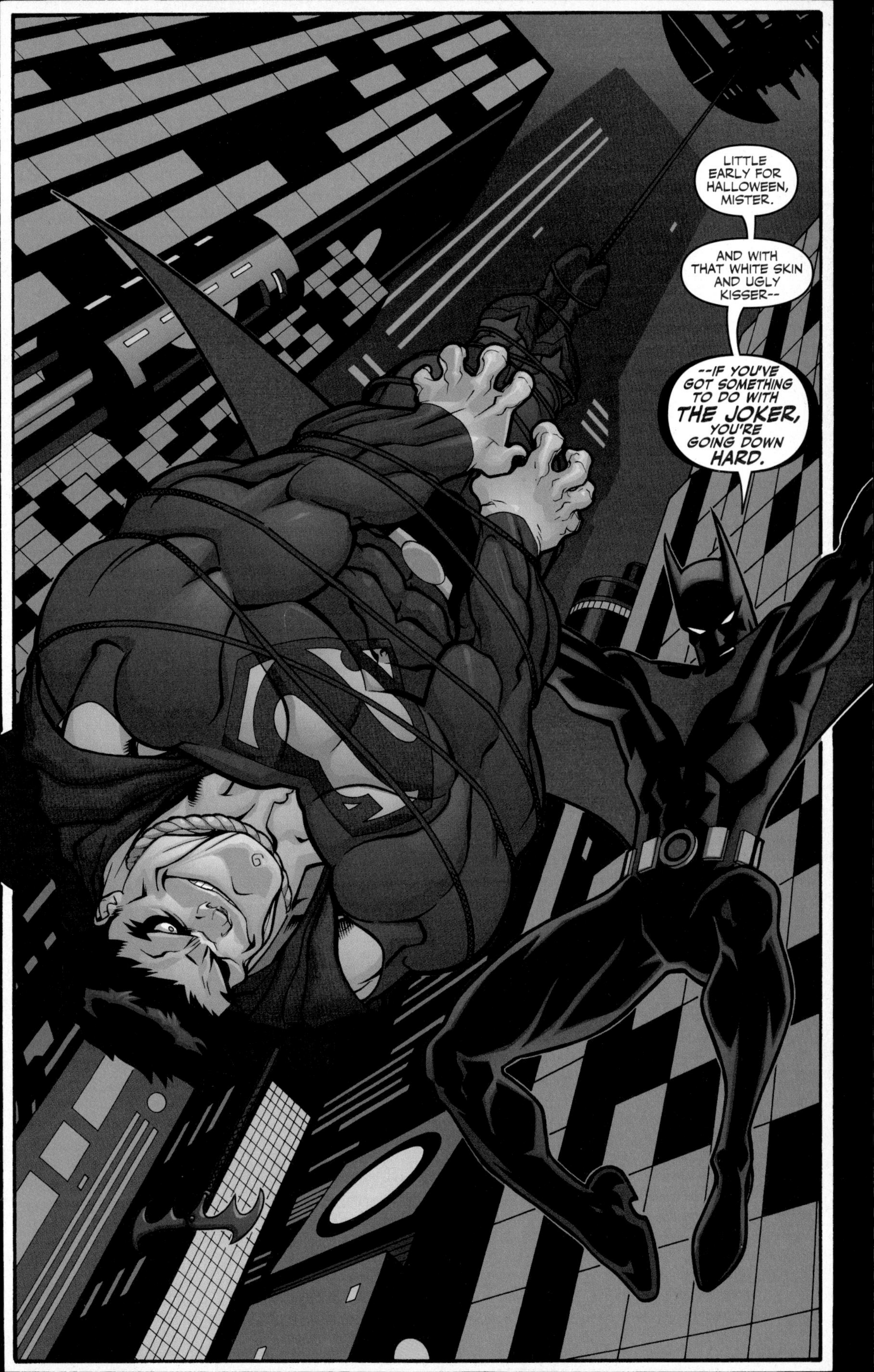
LITTLE EARLY FOR HALLOWEEN, MISTER.
AND WITH THAT WHITE SKIN AND UGLY KISSER--
--IF YOU'VE GOT SOMETHING TO DO WITH THE JOKER, YOU'RE GOING DOWN HARD.

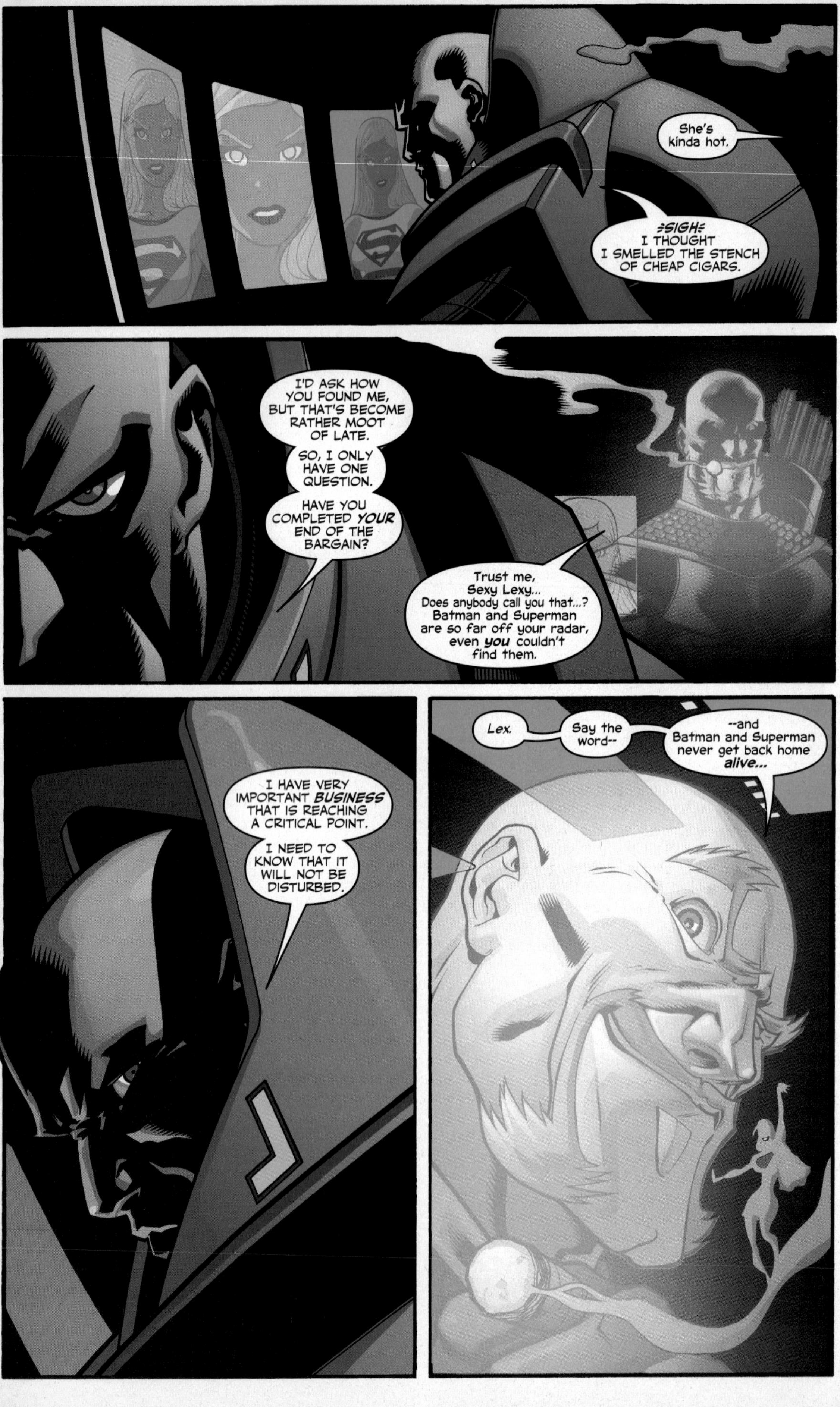

She's kinda hot.
≈SIGH≈ I THOUGHT I SMELLED THE STENCH OF CHEAP CIGARS.
I'D ASK HOW YOU FOUND ME, BUT THAT'S BECOME RATHER MOOT OF LATE.
SO, I ONLY HAVE ONE QUESTION.
HAVE YOU COMPLETED *YOUR* END OF THE BARGAIN?
Trust me, Sexy Lexy... Does anybody call you that...? Batman and Superman are so far off your radar, even **you** couldn't find them.
I HAVE VERY IMPORTANT *BUSINESS* THAT IS REACHING A CRITICAL POINT.
I NEED TO KNOW THAT IT WILL NOT BE DISTURBED.
Lex.
Say the word--
--and Batman and Superman never get back home *alive...*

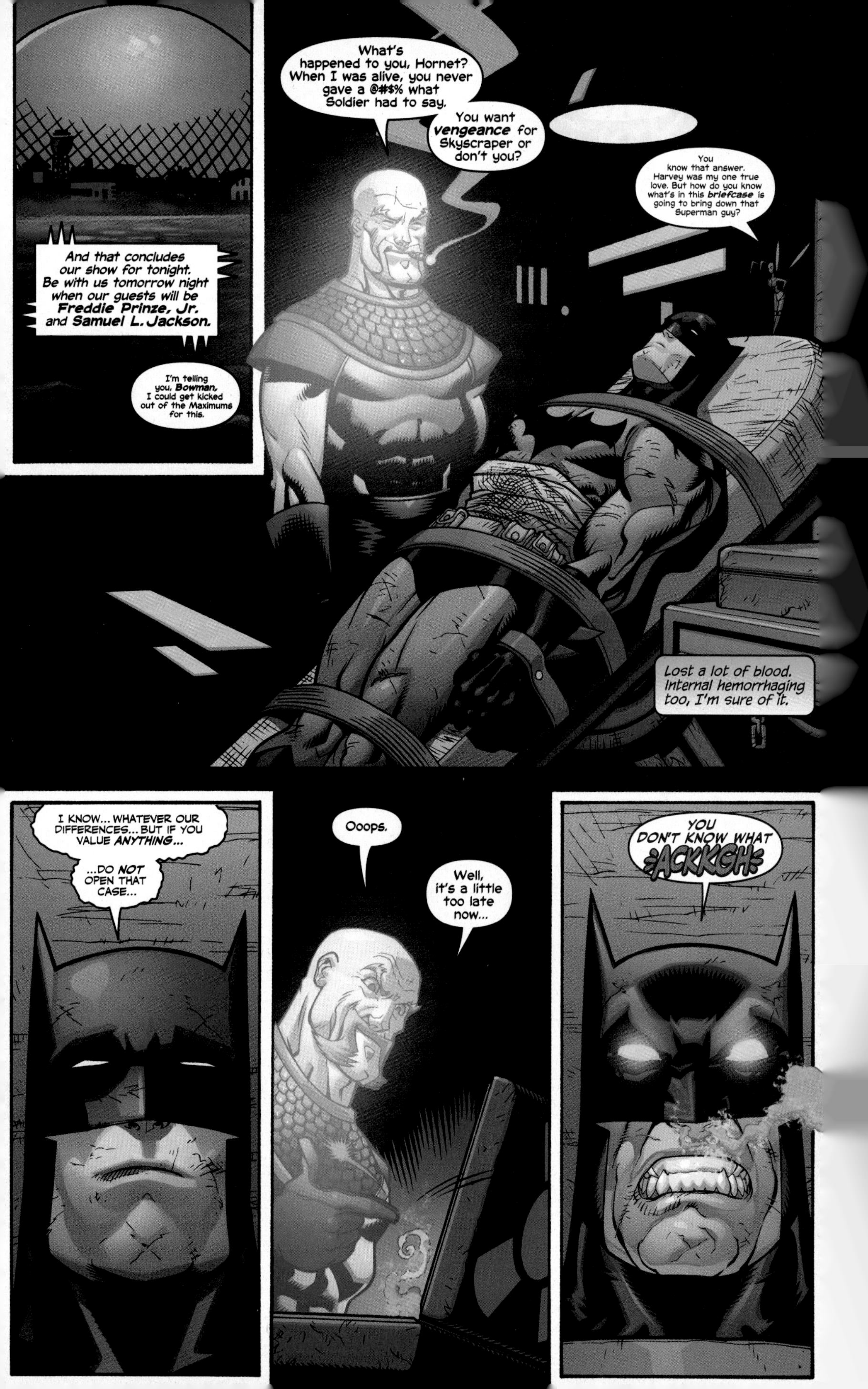
And that concludes our show for tonight. Be with us tomorrow night when our guests will be Freddie Prinze, Jr. and Samuel L. Jackson.
I'm telling you, Bowman, I could get kicked out of the Maximums for this.
What's happened to you, Hornet? When I was alive, you never gave a @#$% what Soldier had to say.
You want vengeance for Skyscraper or don't you?
You know that answer. Harvey was my one true love. But how do you know what's in this briefcase is going to bring down that Superman guy?
Lost a lot of blood. Internal hemorrhaging too, I'm sure of it.
I KNOW... WHATEVER OUR DIFFERENCES... BUT IF YOU VALUE ANYTHING...
...DO NOT OPEN THAT CASE...
Ooops.
Well, it's a little too late now...
YOU DON'T KNOW WHAT
ACKKGH

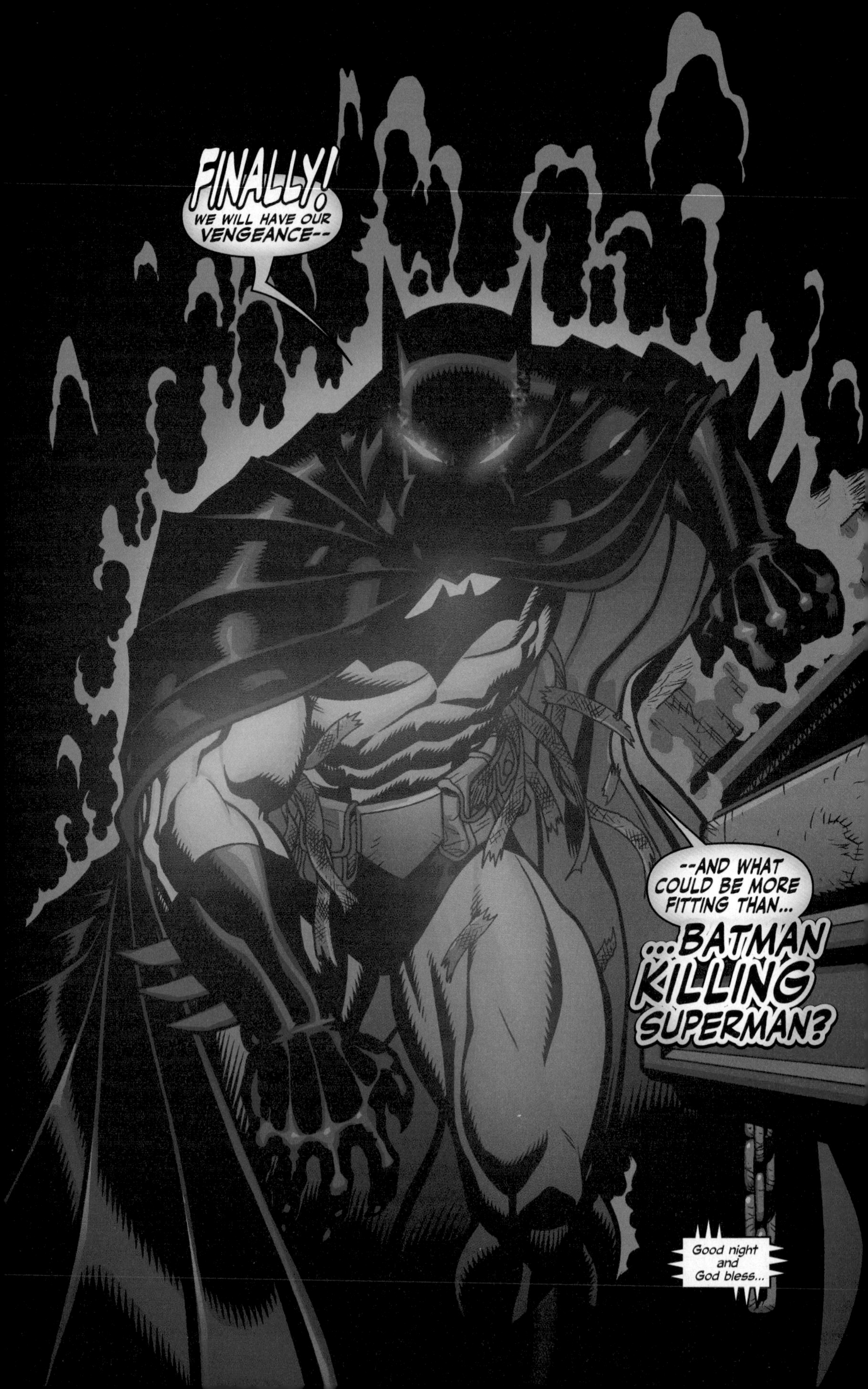
FINALLY! WE WILL HAVE OUR VENGEANCE--
--AND WHAT COULD BE MORE FITTING THAN... ...BATMAN KILLING SUPERMAN?
Good night and God bless...

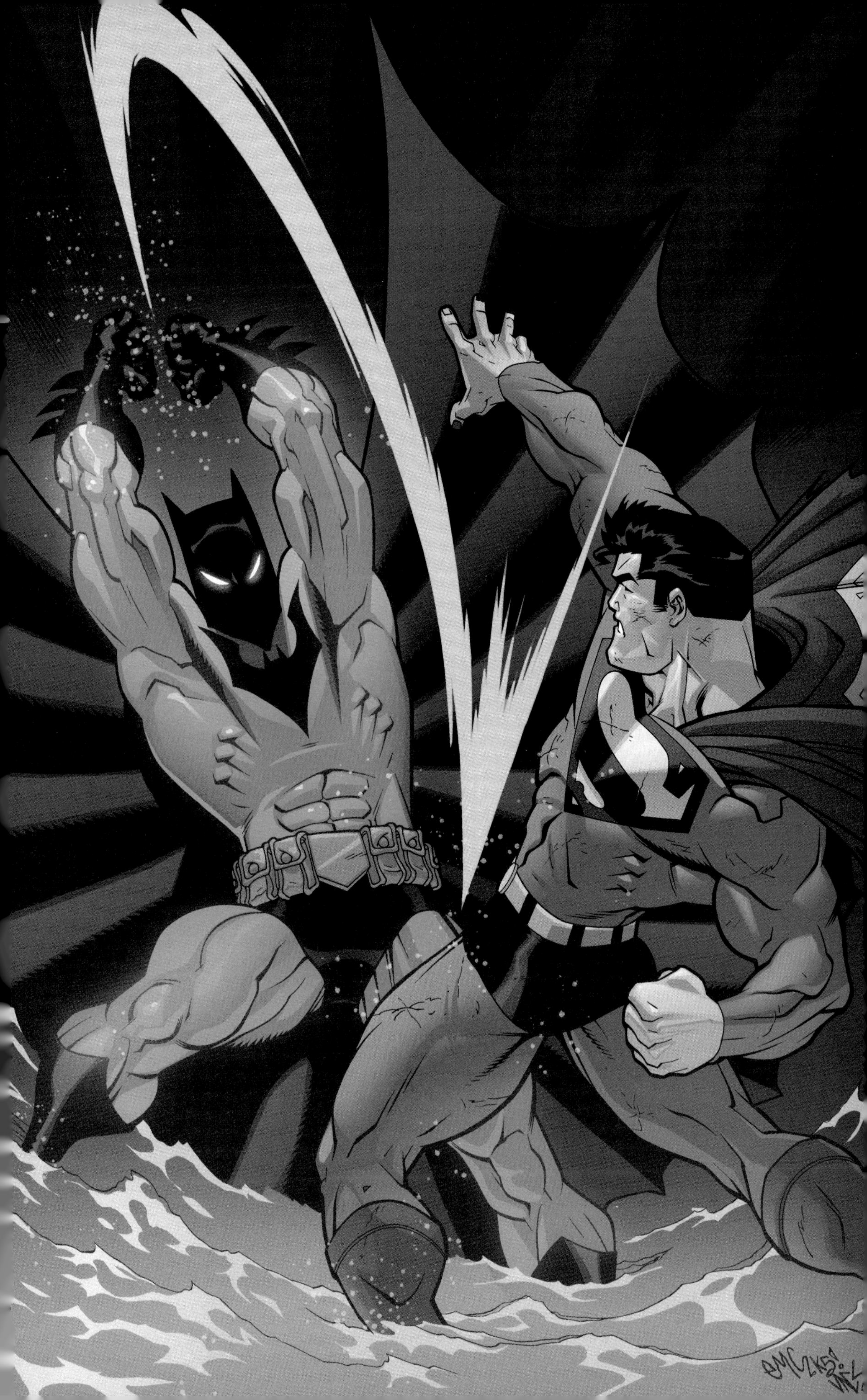

"SMOKE AND MIRRORS"

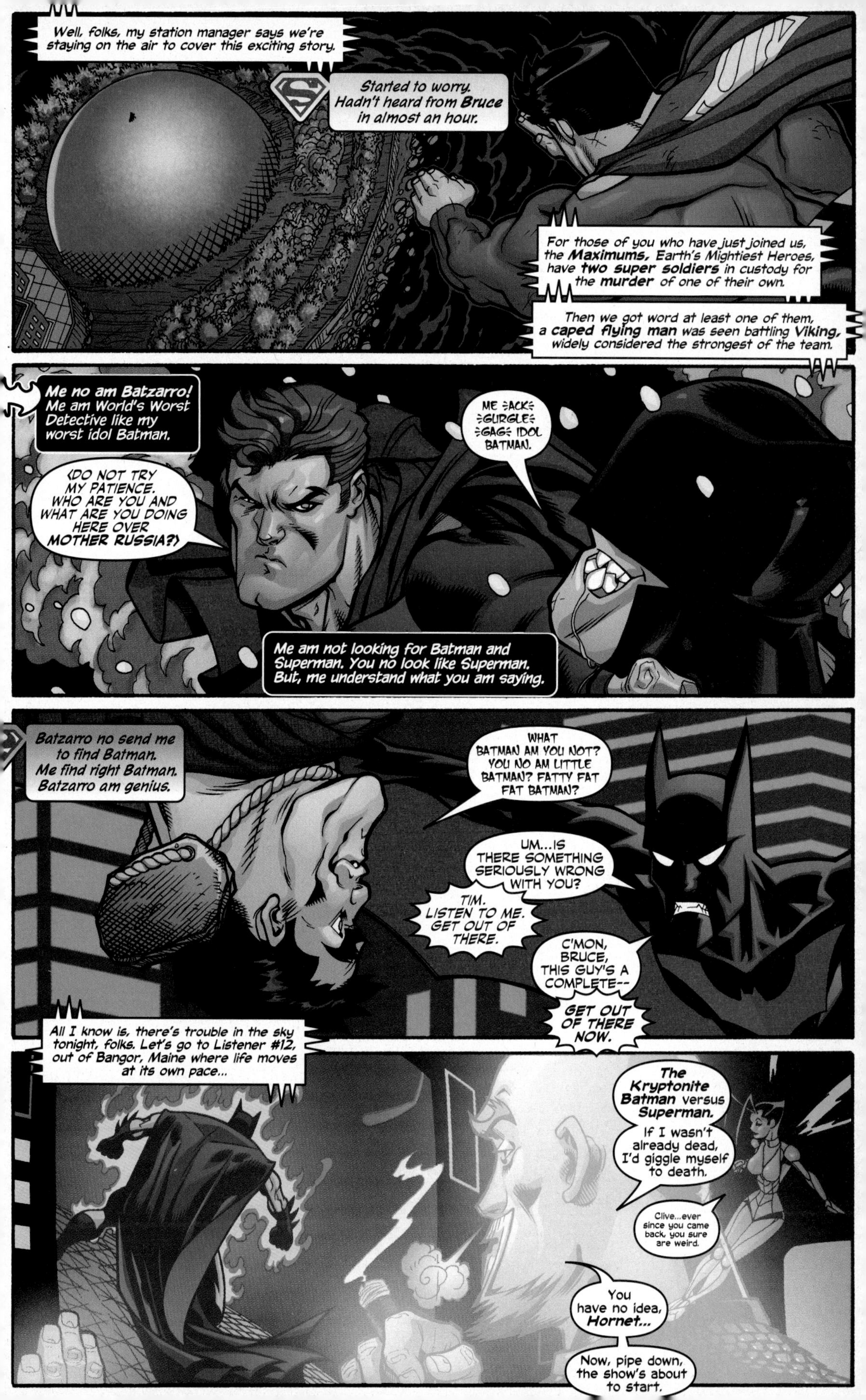

Well, folks, my station manager says we're staying on the air to cover this exciting story.
Started to worry. Hadn't heard from **Bruce** in almost an hour.
For those of you who have just joined us, the **Maximums,** Earth's Mightiest Heroes, have **two super soldiers** in custody for the **murder** of one of their own.
Then we got word at least one of them, a **caped flying man** was seen battling **Viking,** widely considered the strongest of the team.
Me no am Batzarro! Me am World's Worst Detective like my worst idol Batman.
ME ACK GURGLE GAG IDOL BATMAN.
⟨DO NOT TRY MY PATIENCE. WHO ARE YOU AND WHAT ARE YOU DOING HERE OVER MOTHER RUSSIA?⟩
Me am not looking for Batman and Superman. You no look like Superman. But, me understand what you am saying.
Batzarro no send me to find Batman. Me find right Batman. Batzarro am genius.
WHAT BATMAN AM YOU NOT? YOU NO AM LITTLE BATMAN? FATTY FAT FAT BATMAN?
UM...IS THERE SOMETHING SERIOUSLY WRONG WITH YOU?
TIM. LISTEN TO ME. GET OUT OF THERE.
C'MON, BRUCE, THIS GUY'S A COMPLETE--
GET OUT OF THERE NOW.
All I know is, there's trouble in the sky tonight, folks. Let's go to Listener #12, out of Bangor, Maine where life moves at its own pace...
The Kryptonite Batman versus **Superman.**
If I wasn't already dead, I'd giggle myself to death.
Clive...ever since you came back, you sure are weird.
You have no idea, **Hornet...**
Now, pipe down, the show's about to start.

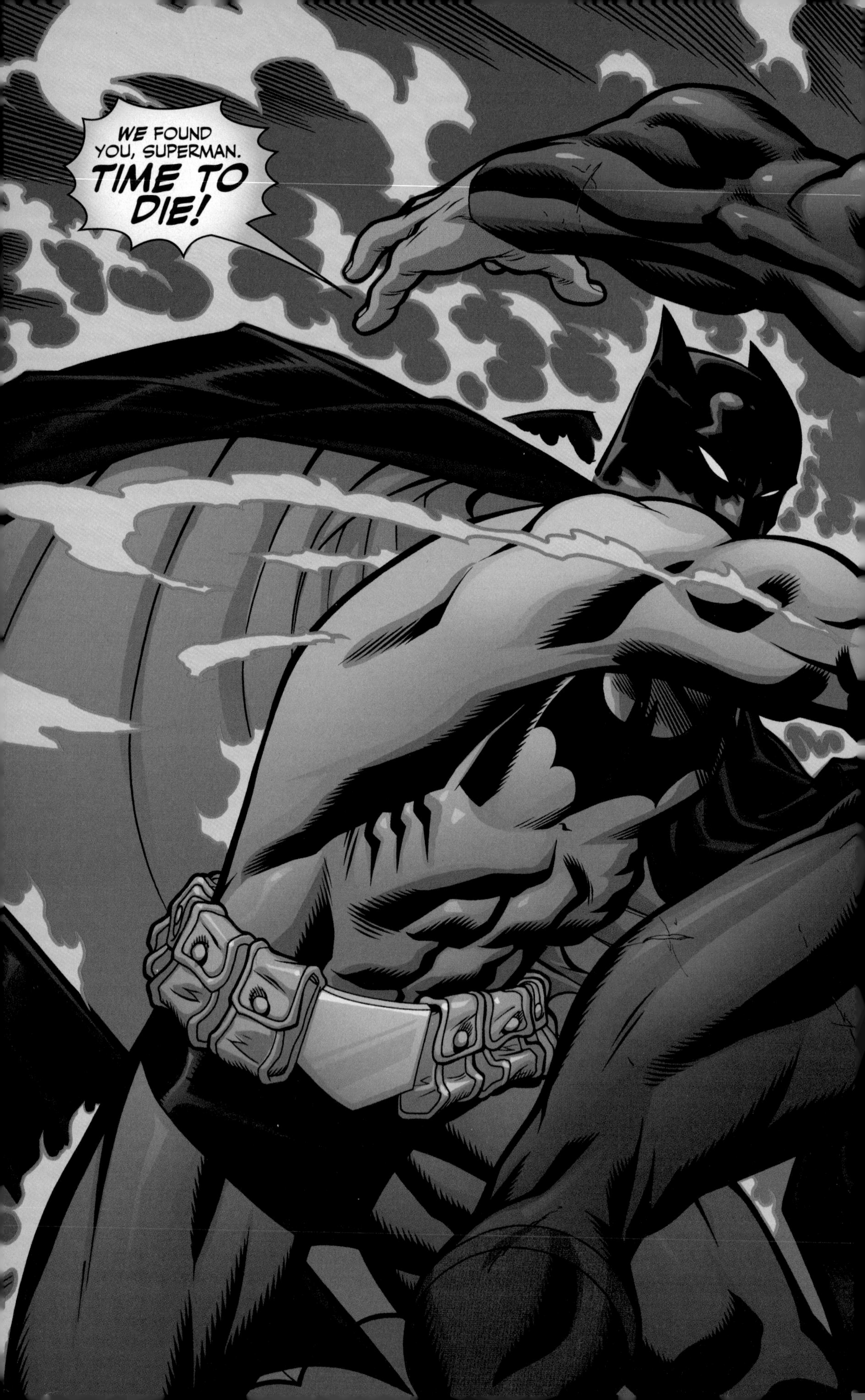
WE FOUND YOU, SUPERMAN. TIME TO DIE!

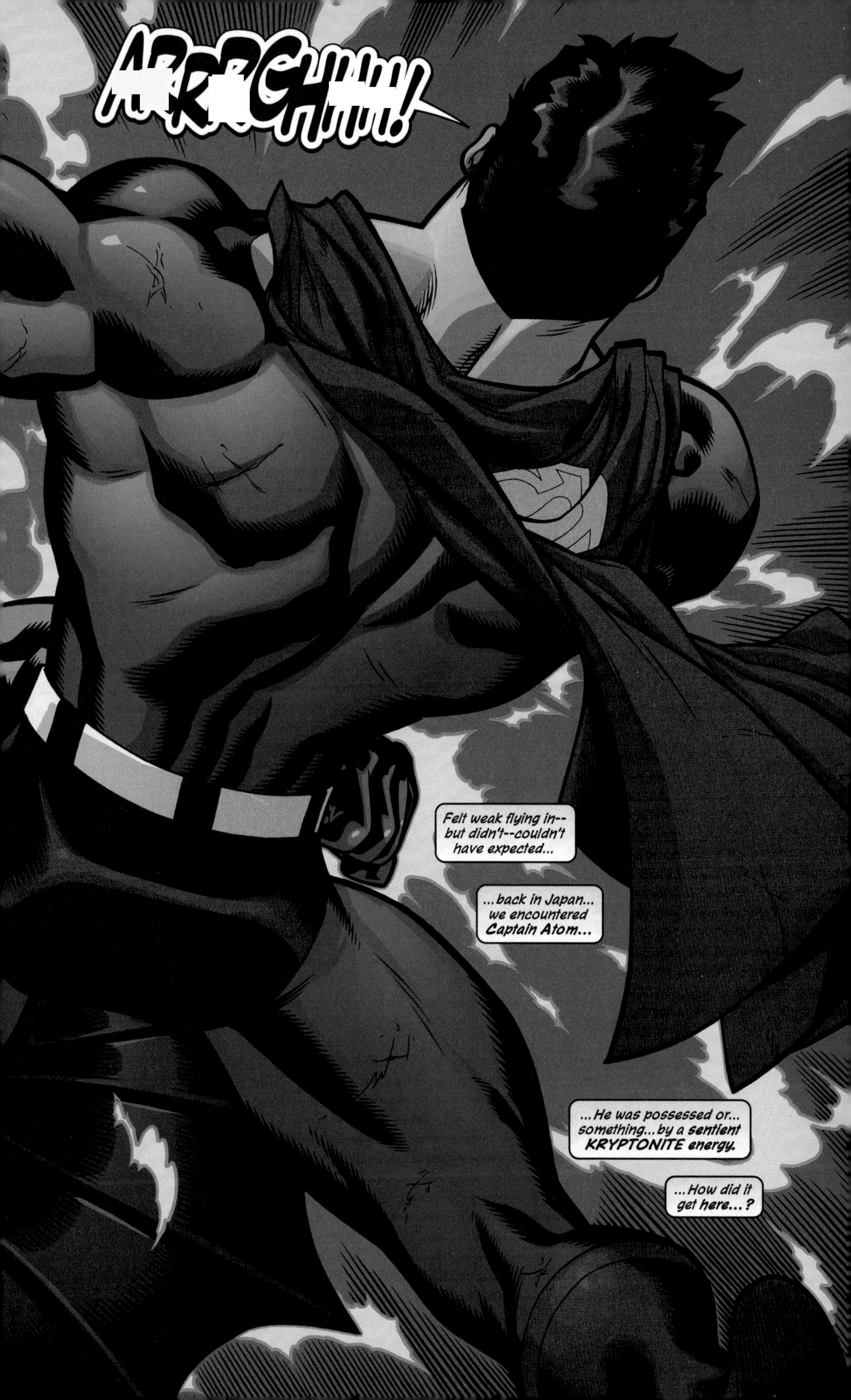

Felt weak flying in-- but didn't--couldn't have expected...
...back in Japan... we encountered Captain Atom...
...He was possessed or... something...by a sentient KRYPTONITE energy.
...How did it get here...?

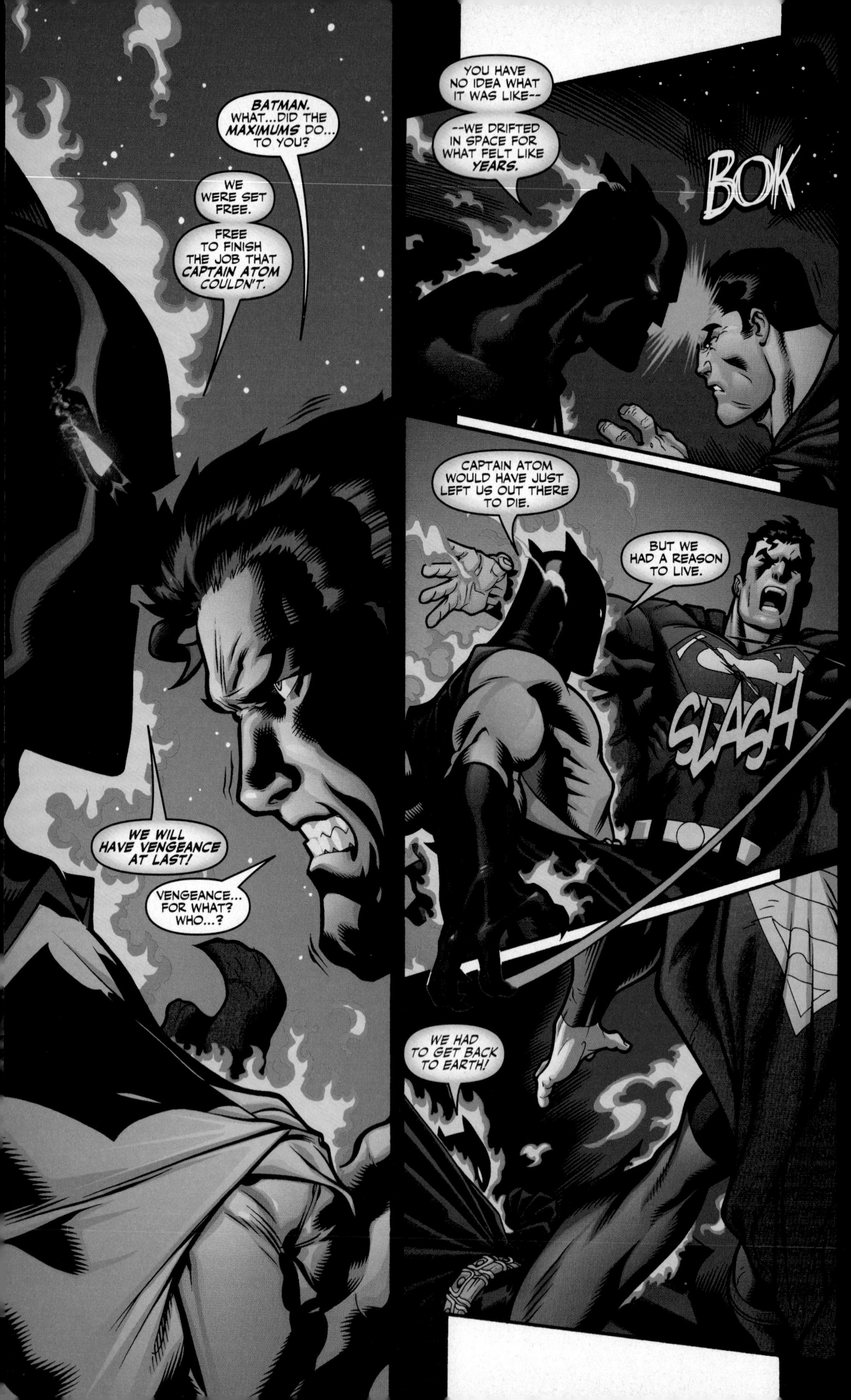
BATMAN. WHAT...DID THE MAXIMUMS DO... TO YOU?
WE WERE SET FREE.
FREE TO FINISH THE JOB THAT CAPTAIN ATOM COULDN'T.
WE WILL HAVE VENGEANCE AT LAST!
VENGEANCE... FOR WHAT? WHO...?
YOU HAVE NO IDEA WHAT IT WAS LIKE--
--WE DRIFTED IN SPACE FOR WHAT FELT LIKE YEARS.
BOK
CAPTAIN ATOM WOULD HAVE JUST LEFT US OUT THERE TO DIE.
BUT WE HAD A REASON TO LIVE.
SLASH
WE HAD TO GET BACK TO EARTH!

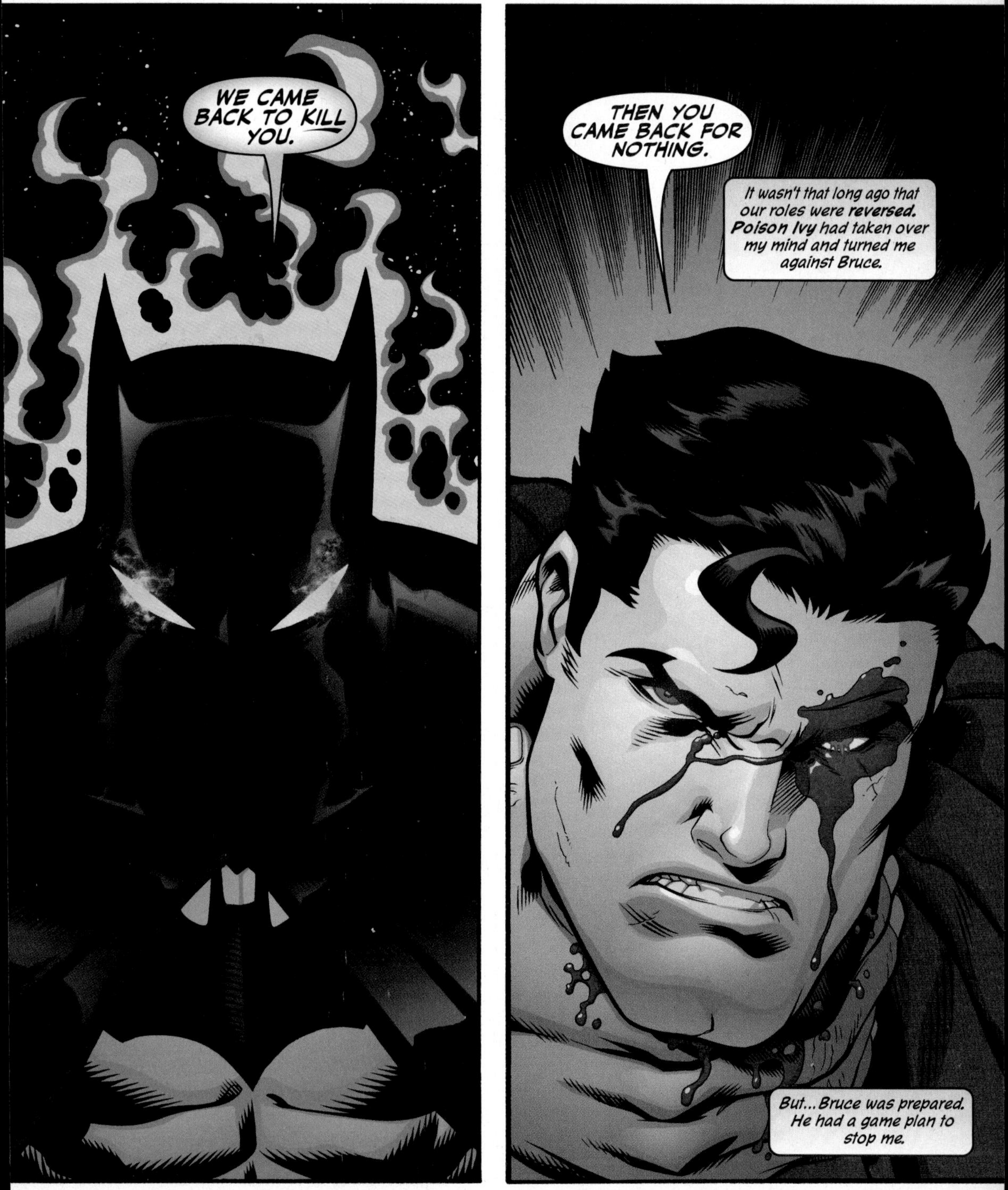
WE CAME BACK TO KILL YOU.
THEN YOU CAME BACK FOR NOTHING.
It wasn't that long ago that our roles were **reversed.** **Poison Ivy** had taken over my mind and turned me against Bruce.
But... Bruce was prepared. He had a game plan to stop me.

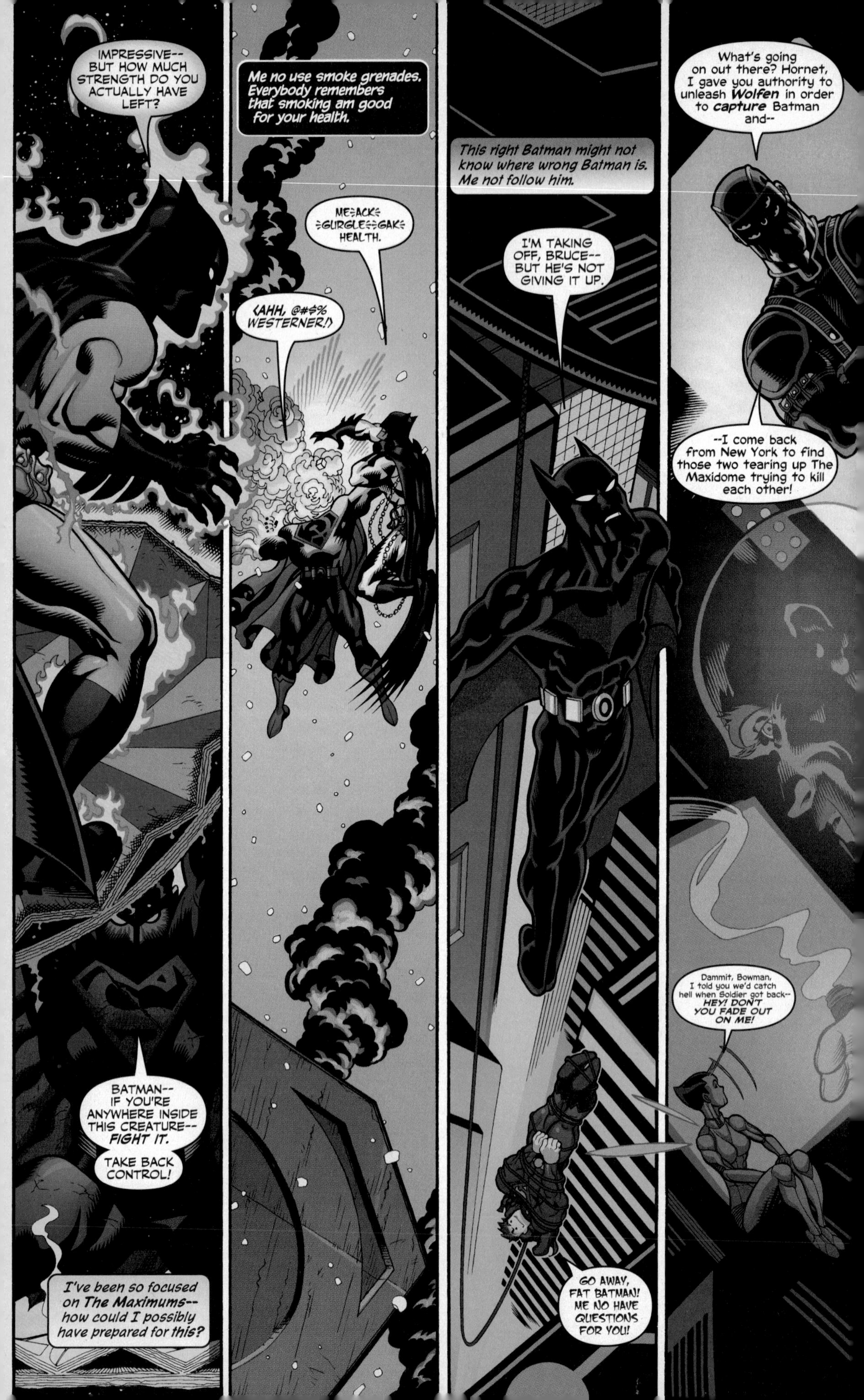
IMPRESSIVE--
BUT HOW MUCH STRENGTH DO YOU ACTUALLY HAVE LEFT?
BATMAN--
IF YOU'RE ANYWHERE INSIDE THIS CREATURE--
FIGHT IT.
TAKE BACK CONTROL!
*I've been so focused on **The Maximums**--how could I possibly have prepared for this?*
Me no use smoke grenades. Everybody remembers that smoking am good for your health.
ME--ACK--GURGLE--GAK--HEALTH.
<AHH, @#$% WESTERNER!>
This right Batman might not know where wrong Batman is. Me not follow him.
I'M TAKING OFF, BRUCE--
BUT HE'S NOT GIVING IT UP.
GO AWAY, FAT BATMAN! ME NO HAVE QUESTIONS FOR YOU!
What's going on out there? Hornet, I gave you authority to unleash ***Wolfen*** in order to ***capture*** Batman and--
--I come back from New York to find those two tearing up The Maxidome trying to kill each other!
Dammit, Bowman, I told you we'd catch hell when Soldier got back--***HEY! DON'T YOU FADE OUT ON ME!***

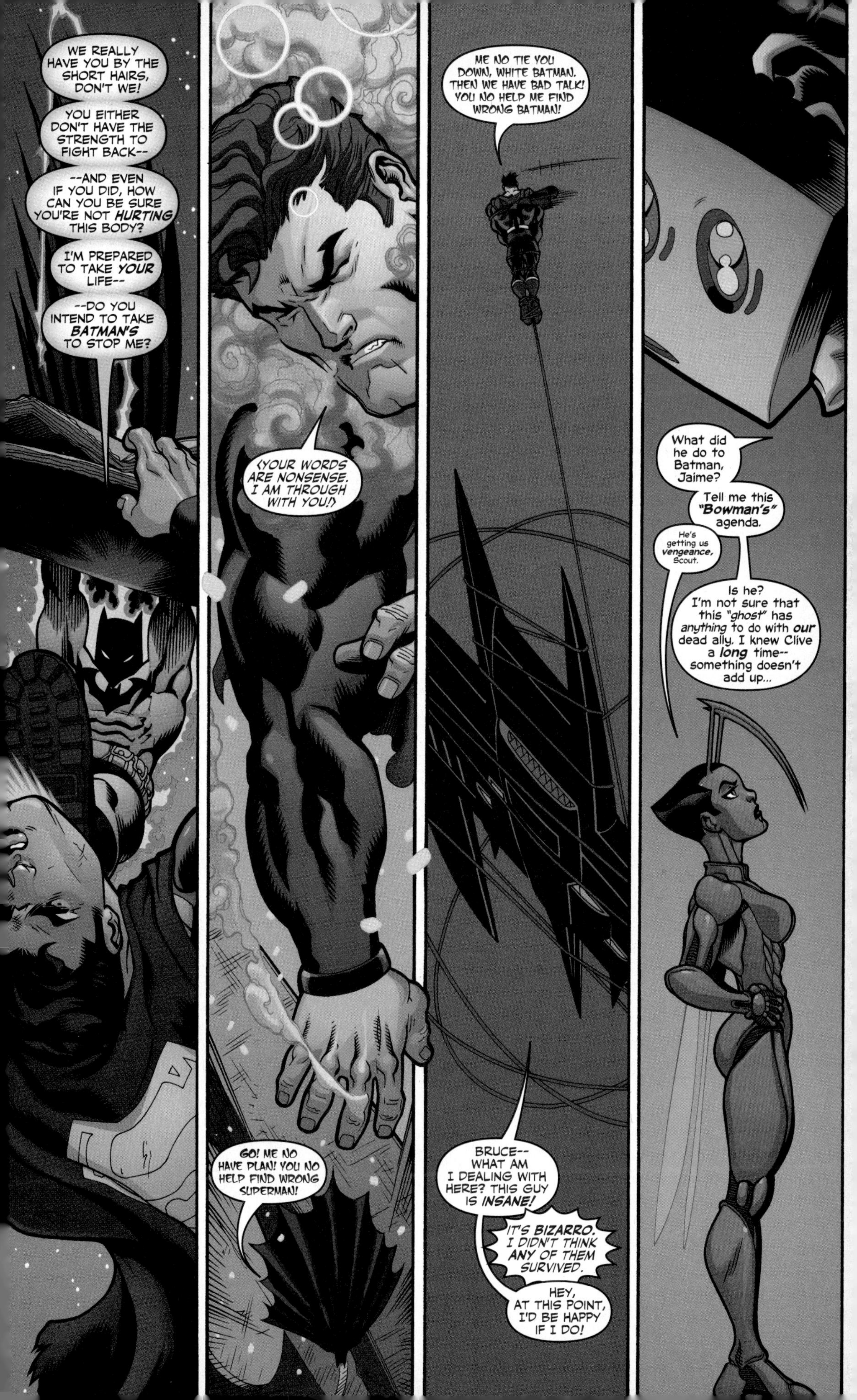

WE REALLY HAVE YOU BY THE SHORT HAIRS, DON'T WE!
YOU EITHER DON'T HAVE THE STRENGTH TO FIGHT BACK--
--AND EVEN IF YOU DID, HOW CAN YOU BE SURE YOU'RE NOT HURTING THIS BODY?
I'M PREPARED TO TAKE YOUR LIFE--
--DO YOU INTEND TO TAKE BATMAN'S TO STOP ME?
<YOUR WORDS ARE NONSENSE. I AM THROUGH WITH YOU!>
GO! ME NO HAVE PLAN! YOU NO HELP FIND WRONG SUPERMAN!
ME NO TIE YOU DOWN, WHITE BATMAN. THEN WE HAVE BAD TALK! YOU NO HELP ME FIND WRONG BATMAN!
BRUCE-- WHAT AM I DEALING WITH HERE? THIS GUY IS INSANE!
IT'S BIZARRO. I DIDN'T THINK ANY OF THEM SURVIVED.
HEY, AT THIS POINT, I'D BE HAPPY IF I DO!
What did he do to Batman, Jaime?
Tell me this "Bowman's" agenda.
He's getting us vengeance, Scout.
Is he? I'm not sure that this "ghost" has anything to do with our dead ally. I knew Clive a long time-- something doesn't add up...

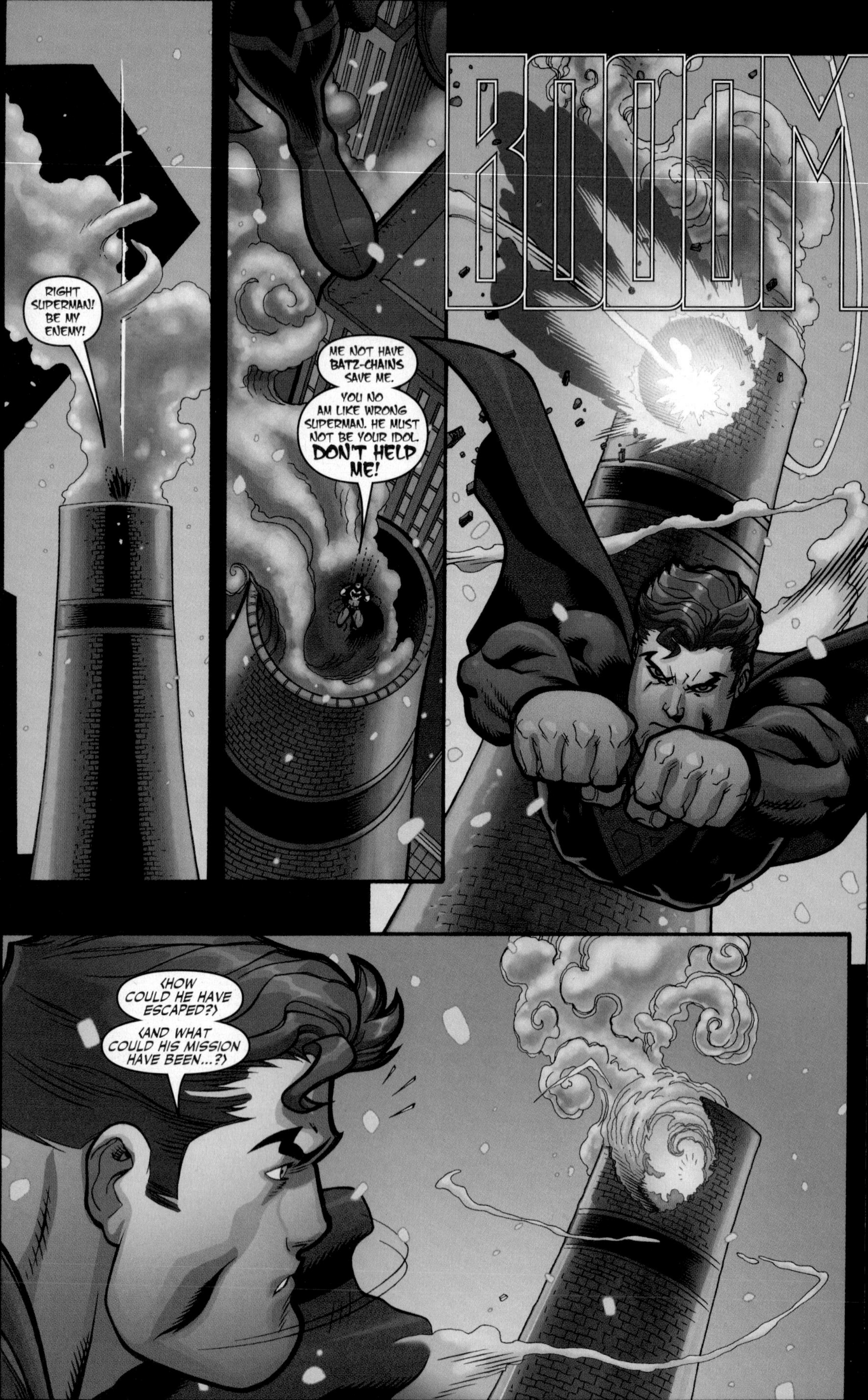
RIGHT SUPERMAN! BE MY ENEMY!
BOOOM
ME NOT HAVE BATZ-CHAINS SAVE ME.
YOU NO AM LIKE WRONG SUPERMAN. HE MUST NOT BE YOUR IDOL. DON'T HELP ME!
<HOW COULD HE HAVE ESCAPED?>
<AND WHAT COULD HIS MISSION HAVE BEEN...?>

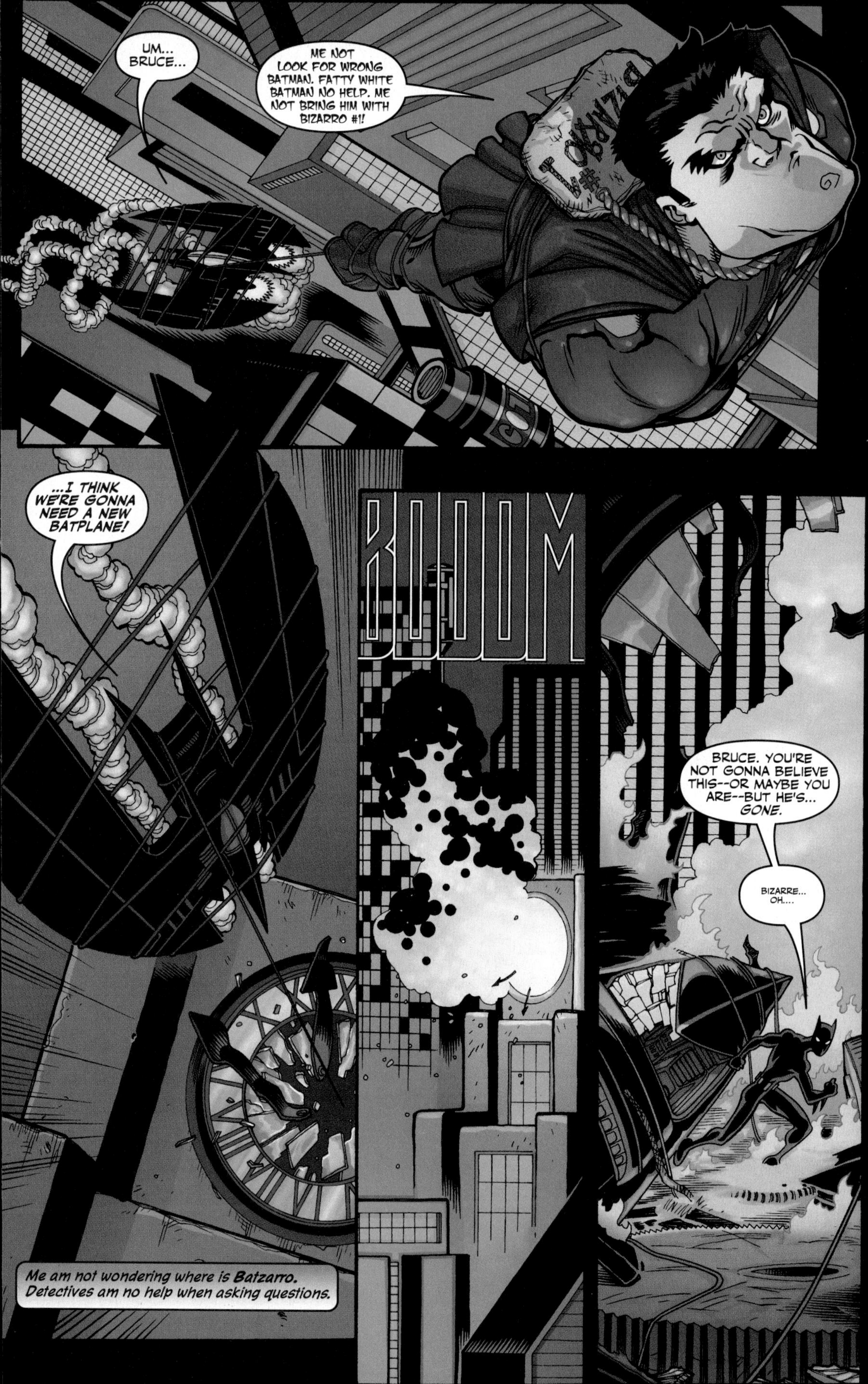
UM... BRUCE...
ME NOT LOOK FOR WRONG BATMAN. FATTY WHITE BATMAN NO HELP. ME NOT BRING HIM WITH BIZARRO #1!
BIZARRO #1
...I THINK WE'RE GONNA NEED A NEW BATPLANE!
Me am not wondering where is Batzarro. Detectives am no help when asking questions.
BOOOM
BRUCE. YOU'RE NOT GONNA BELIEVE THIS--OR MAYBE YOU ARE--BUT HE'S... GONE.
BIZARRE... OH....

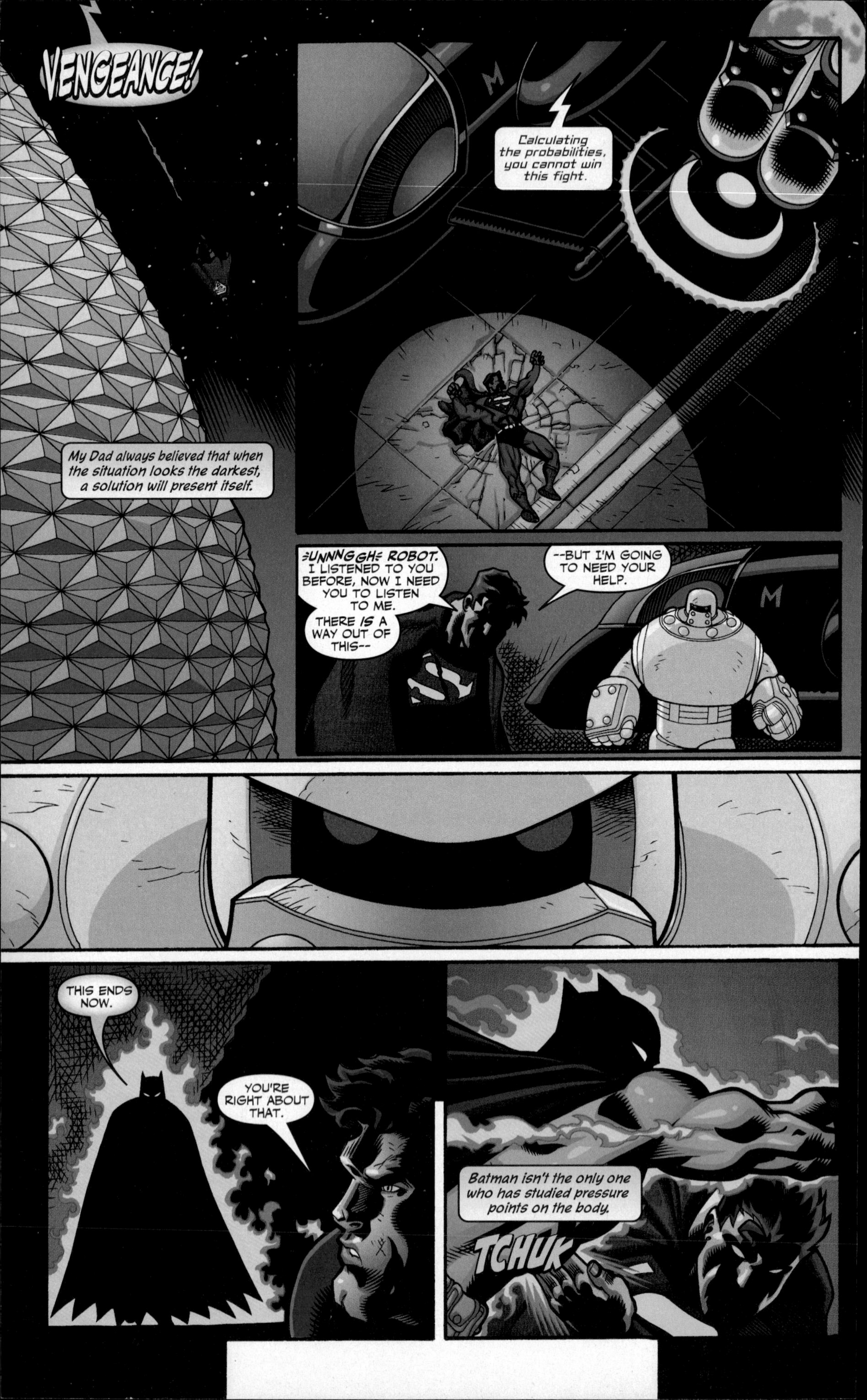
VENGEANCE!
Calculating the probabilities, you cannot win this fight.
My Dad always believed that when the situation looks the darkest, a solution will present itself.
=UNNGGH= ROBOT. I LISTENED TO YOU BEFORE, NOW I NEED YOU TO LISTEN TO ME.
THERE IS A WAY OUT OF THIS--
--BUT I'M GOING TO NEED YOUR HELP.
THIS ENDS NOW.
YOU'RE RIGHT ABOUT THAT.
Batman isn't the only one who has studied pressure points on the body.
TCHUK

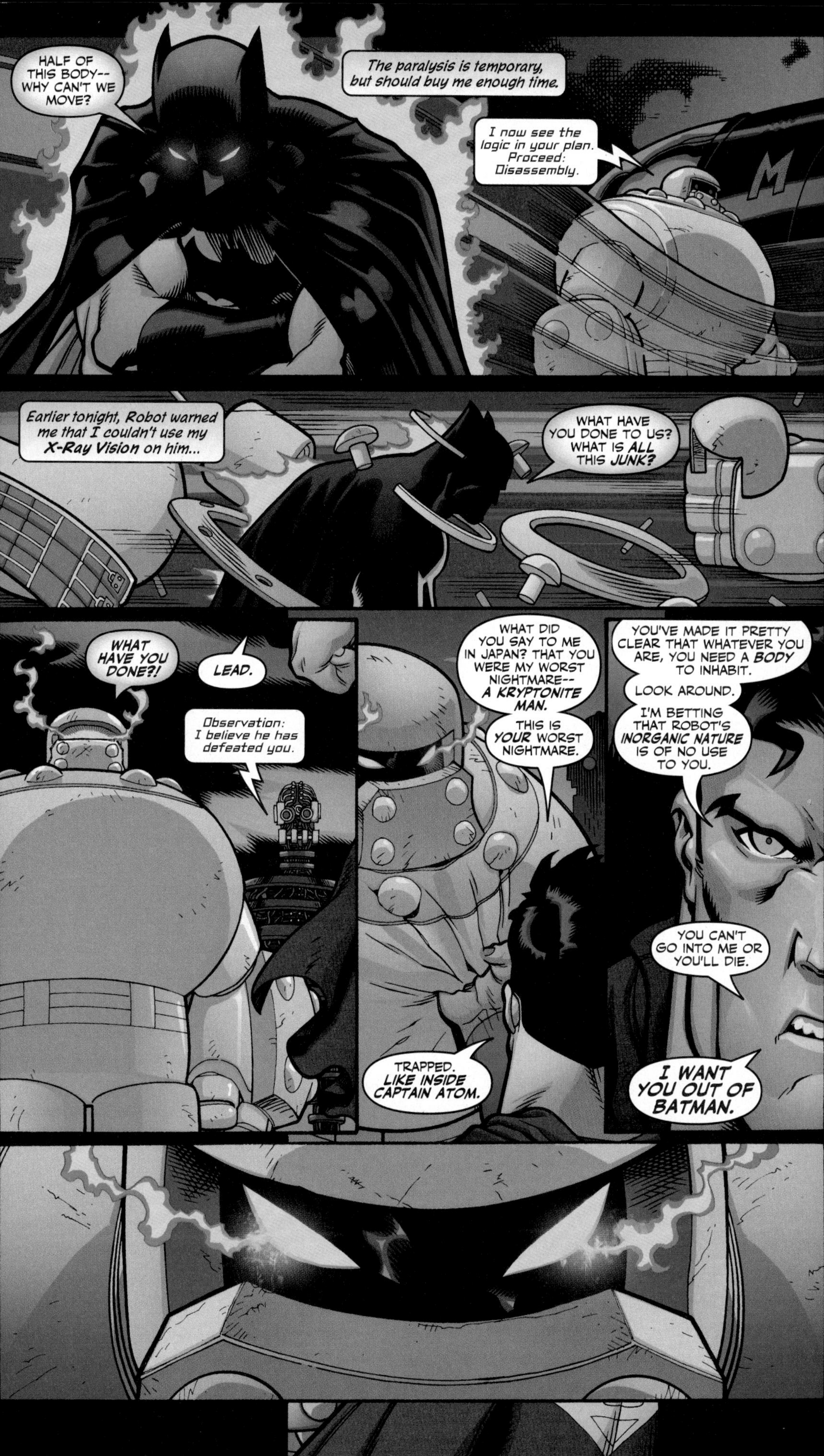
HALF OF THIS BODY-- WHY CAN'T WE MOVE?
The paralysis is temporary, but should buy me enough time.
I now see the logic in your plan. Proceed: Disassembly.
Earlier tonight, Robot warned me that I couldn't use my X-Ray Vision on him...
WHAT HAVE YOU DONE TO US? WHAT IS ALL THIS JUNK?
WHAT HAVE YOU DONE?!
LEAD.
Observation: I believe he has defeated you.
WHAT DID YOU SAY TO ME IN JAPAN? THAT YOU WERE MY WORST NIGHTMARE-- A KRYPTONITE MAN.
THIS IS YOUR WORST NIGHTMARE.
TRAPPED. LIKE INSIDE CAPTAIN ATOM.
YOU'VE MADE IT PRETTY CLEAR THAT WHATEVER YOU ARE, YOU NEED A BODY TO INHABIT.
LOOK AROUND.
I'M BETTING THAT ROBOT'S INORGANIC NATURE IS OF NO USE TO YOU.
YOU CAN'T GO INTO ME OR YOU'LL DIE.
I WANT YOU OUT OF BATMAN.

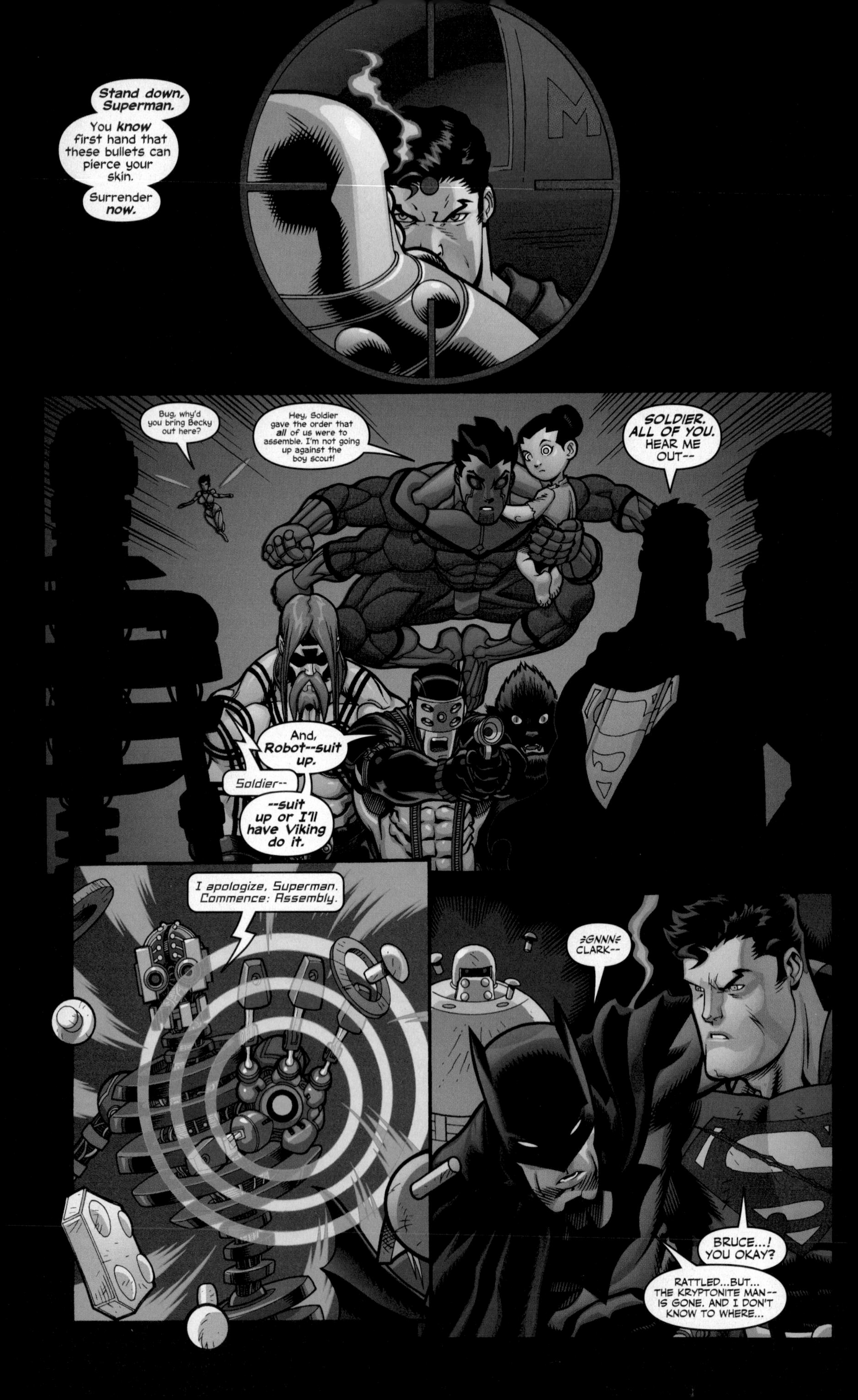

Stand down, Superman.
You know first hand that these bullets can pierce your skin.
Surrender now.
Bug, why'd you bring Becky out here?
Hey, Soldier gave the order that all of us were to assemble. I'm not going up against the boy scout!
SOLDIER. ALL OF YOU. HEAR ME OUT--
And, Robot--suit up.
Soldier--
--suit up or I'll have Viking do it.
I apologize, Superman. Commence: Assembly.
=GNNN= CLARK--
BRUCE...! YOU OKAY?
RATTLED...BUT... THE KRYPTONITE MAN--IS GONE. AND I DON'T KNOW TO WHERE...

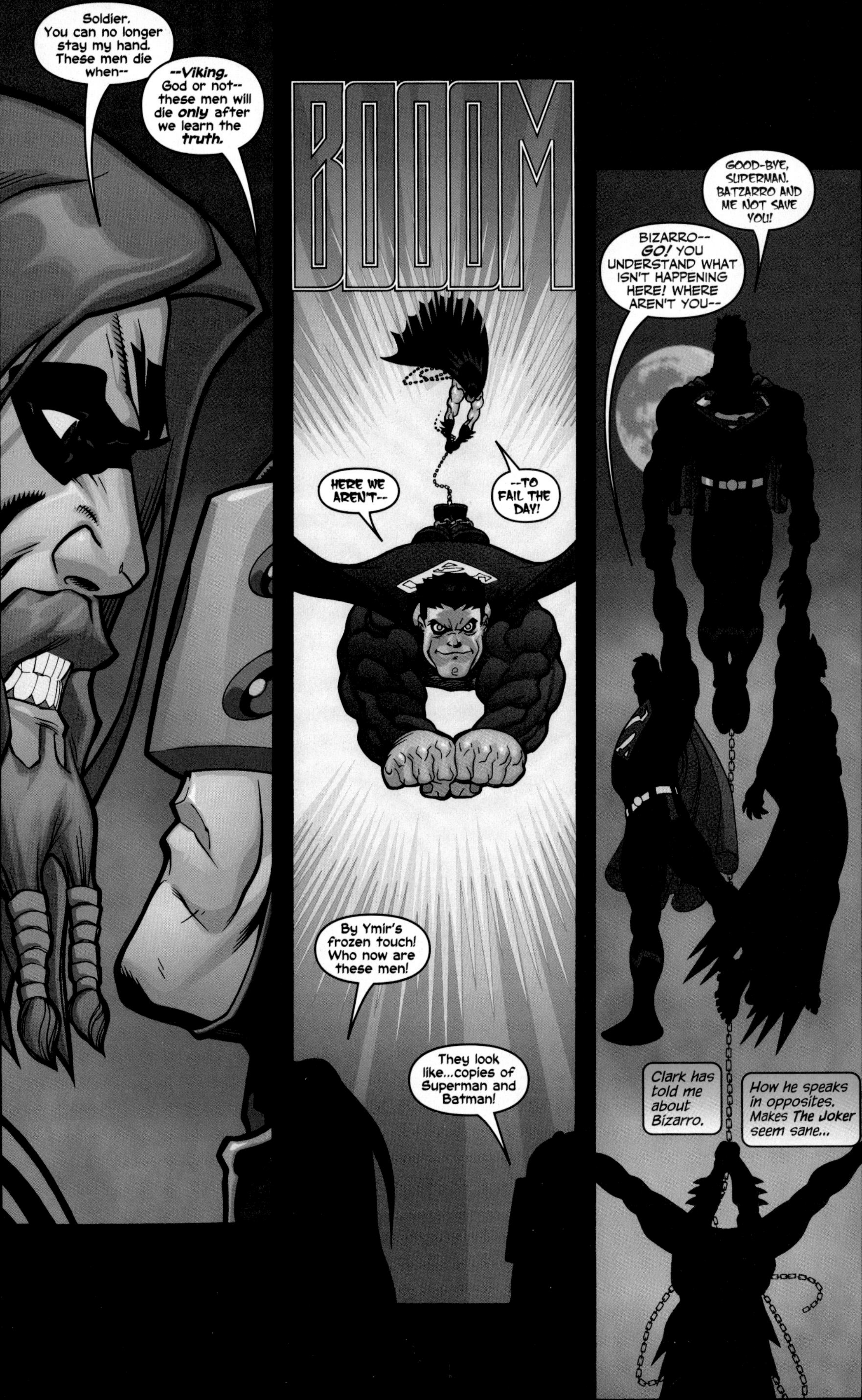
Soldier. You can no longer stay my hand. These men die when--
--Viking. God or not--these men will die only after we learn the truth.
BOOOM
HERE WE AREN'T--
--TO FAIL THE DAY!
By Ymir's frozen touch! Who now are these men!
They look like...copies of Superman and Batman!
GOOD-BYE, SUPERMAN. BATZARRO AND ME NOT SAVE YOU!
BIZARRO--GO! YOU UNDERSTAND WHAT ISN'T HAPPENING HERE! WHERE AREN'T YOU--
Clark has told me about Bizarro.
How he speaks in opposites. Makes The Joker seem sane...

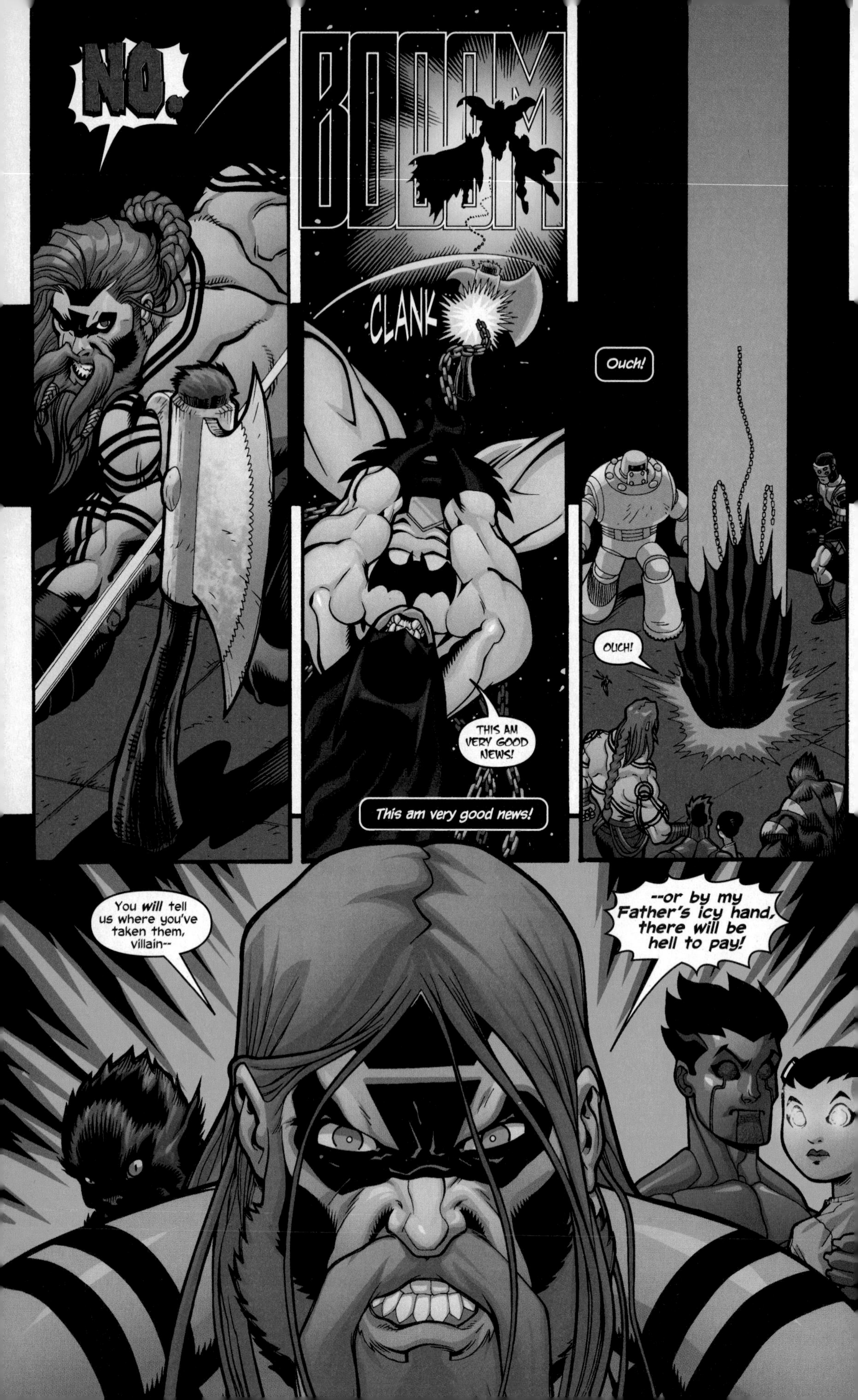
NO.
BOOOM
CLANK
THIS AM VERY GOOD NEWS!
This am very good news!
Ouch!
OUCH!
You will tell us where you've taken them, villain--
--or by my Father's icy hand, there will be hell to pay!

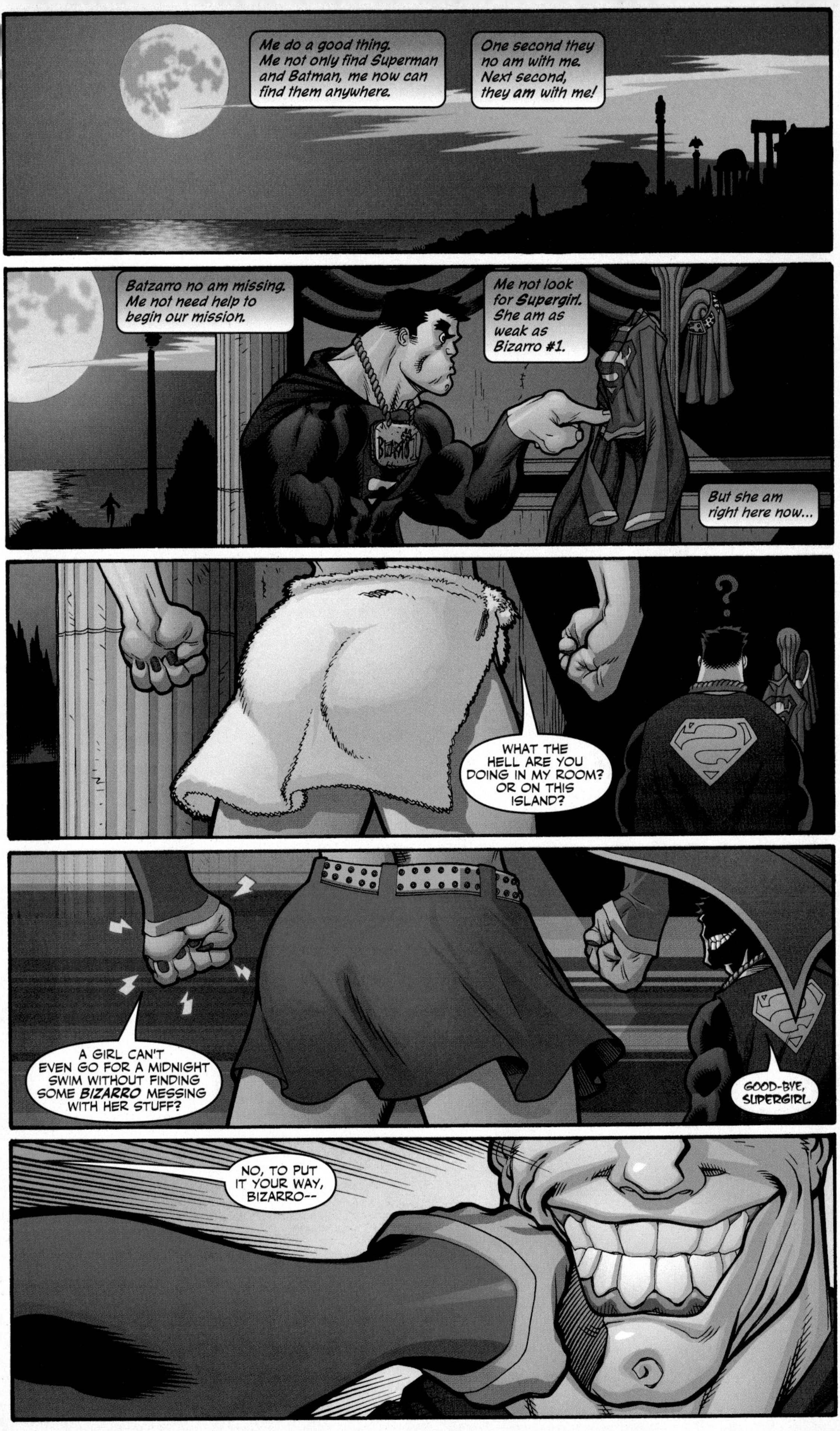
Me do a good thing.
Me not only find Superman and Batman, me now can find them anywhere.
One second they no am with me. Next second, they am with me!
Batzarro no am missing. Me not need help to begin our mission.
Me not look for Supergirl. She am as weak as Bizarro #1.
But she am right here now...
WHAT THE HELL ARE YOU DOING IN MY ROOM? OR ON THIS ISLAND?
A GIRL CAN'T EVEN GO FOR A MIDNIGHT SWIM WITHOUT FINDING SOME BIZARRO MESSING WITH HER STUFF?
GOOD-BYE, SUPERGIRL.
NO, TO PUT IT YOUR WAY, BIZARRO--

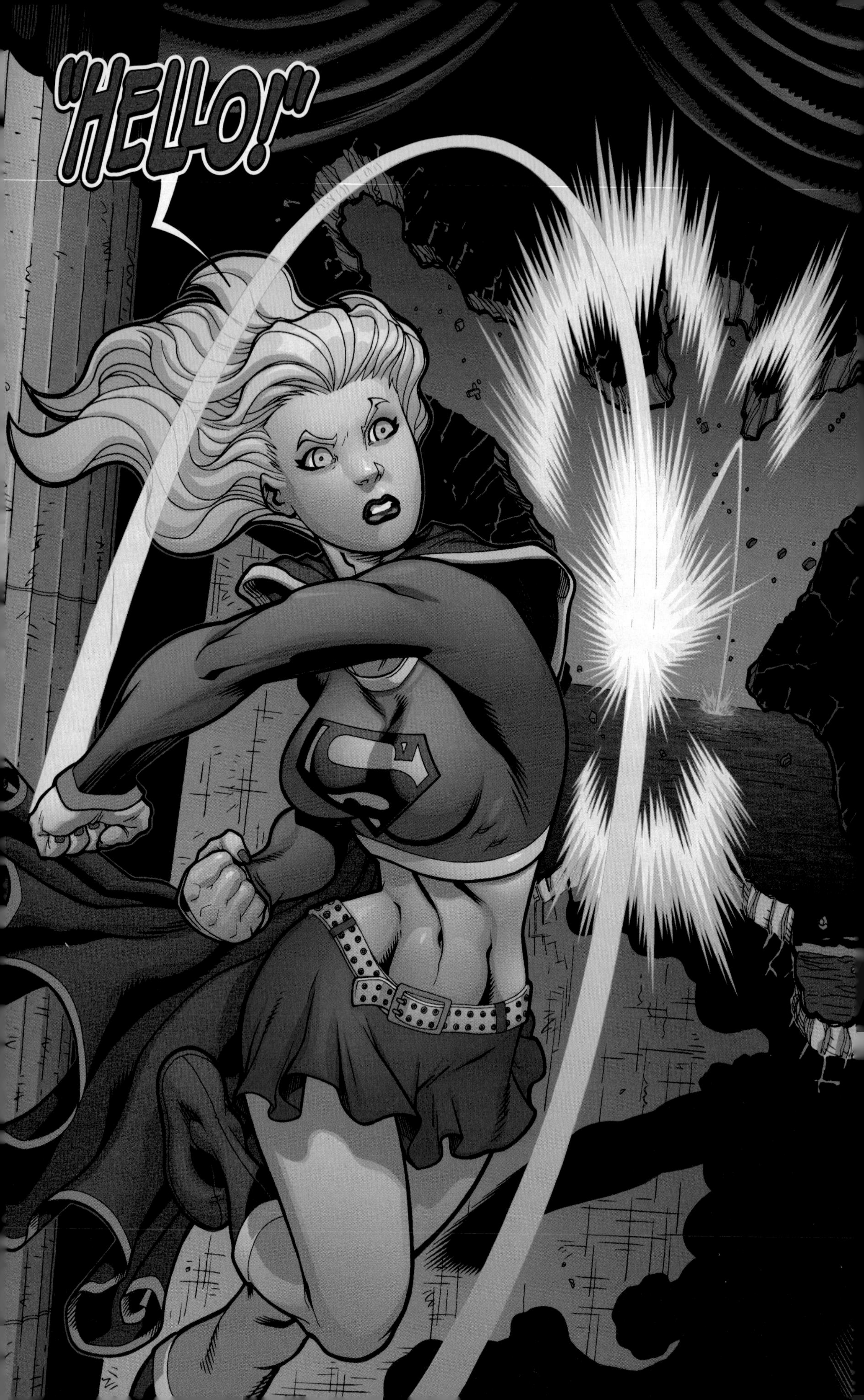
"HELLO!"

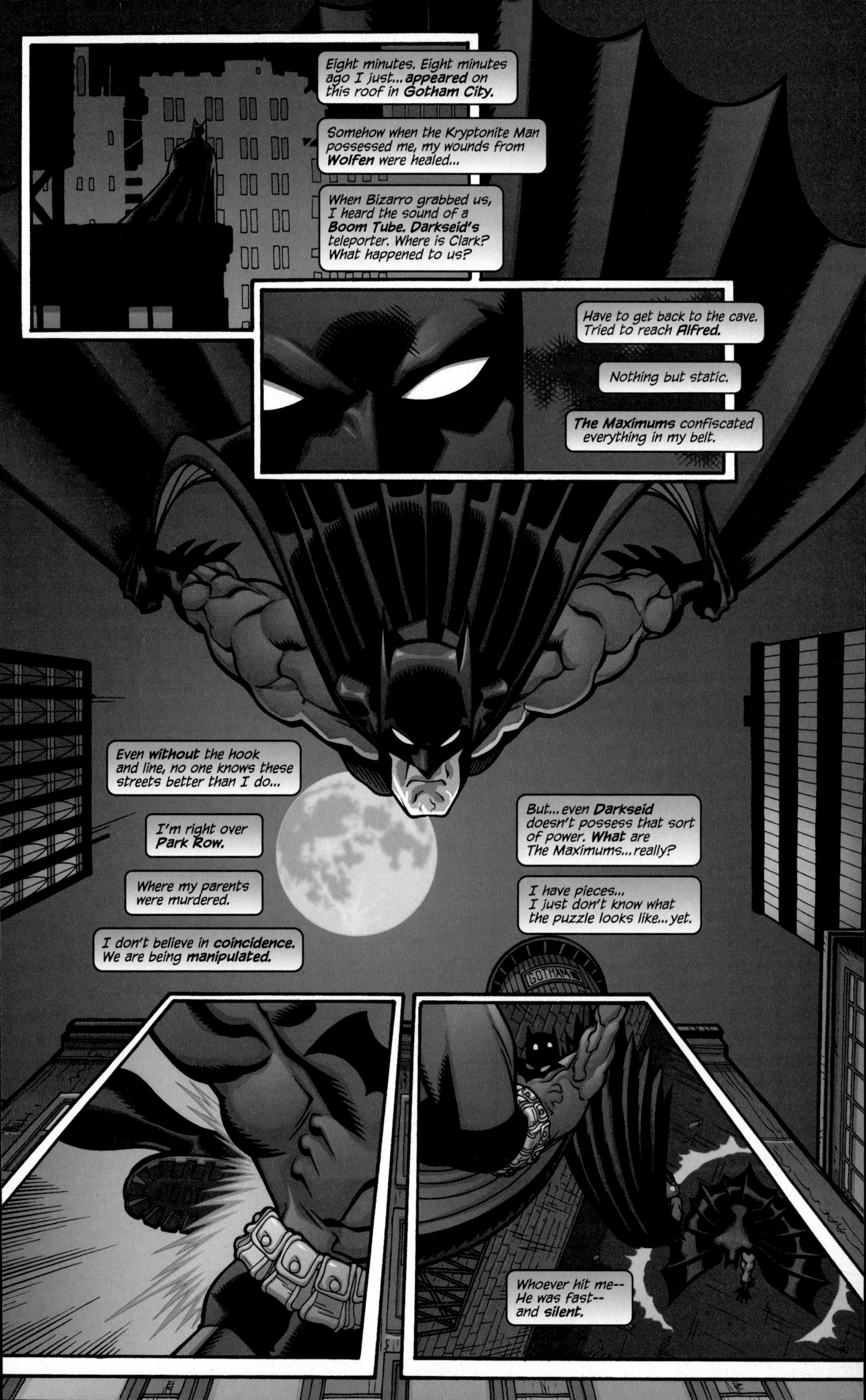
Eight minutes. Eight minutes ago I just... appeared on this roof in Gotham City.
Somehow when the Kryptonite Man possessed me, my wounds from Wolfen were healed...
When Bizarro grabbed us, I heard the sound of a Boom Tube. Darkseid's teleporter. Where is Clark? What happened to us?
Have to get back to the cave. Tried to reach Alfred.
Nothing but static.
The Maximums confiscated everything in my belt.
Even without the hook and line, no one knows these streets better than I do...
I'm right over Park Row.
Where my parents were murdered.
I don't believe in coincidence. We are being manipulated.
But... even Darkseid doesn't possess that sort of power. What are The Maximums... really?
I have pieces... I just don't know what the puzzle looks like... yet.
GOTHAM
Whoever hit me-- He was fast-- and silent.

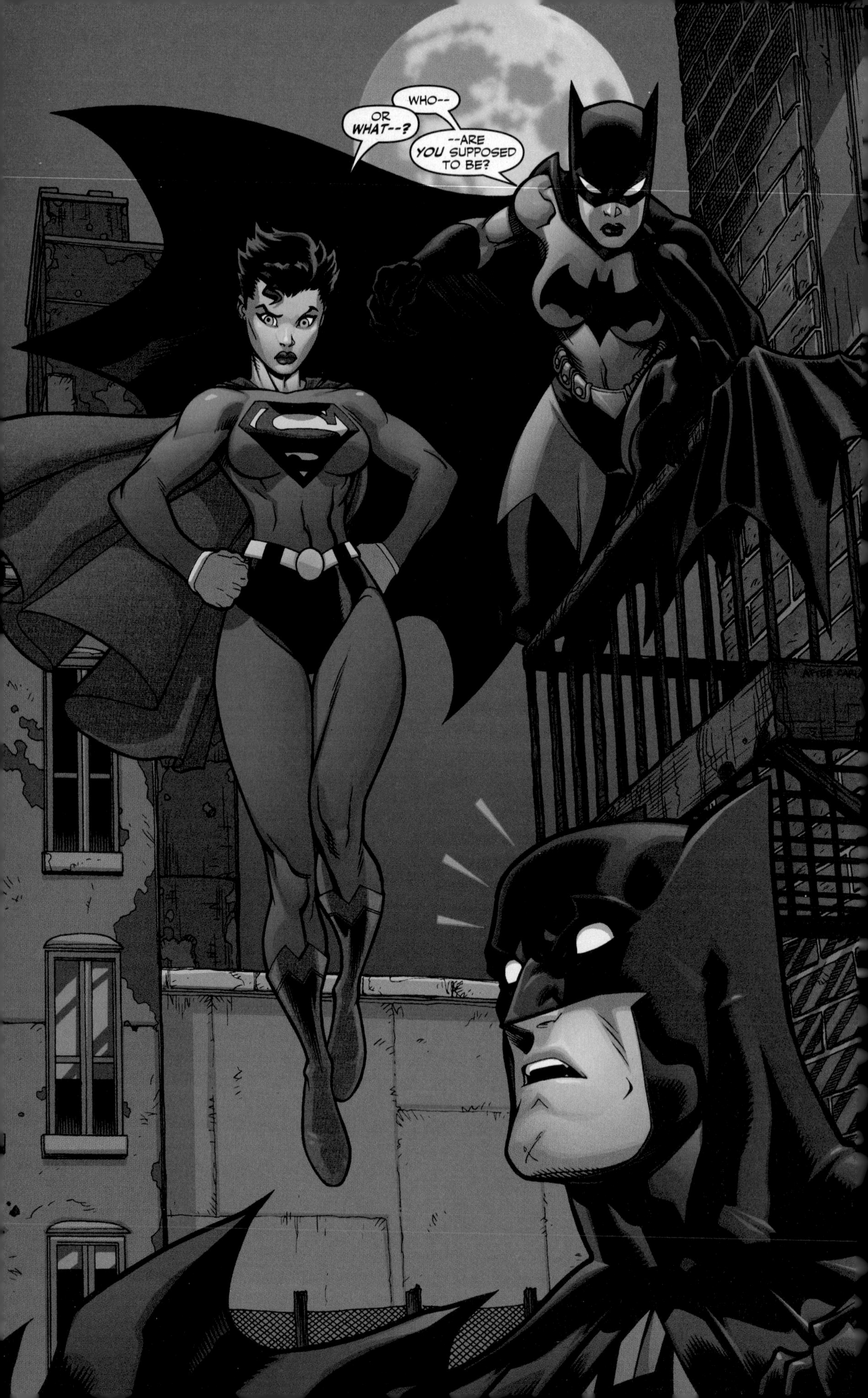
WHO--
--ARE YOU SUPPOSED TO BE?
OR WHAT--?

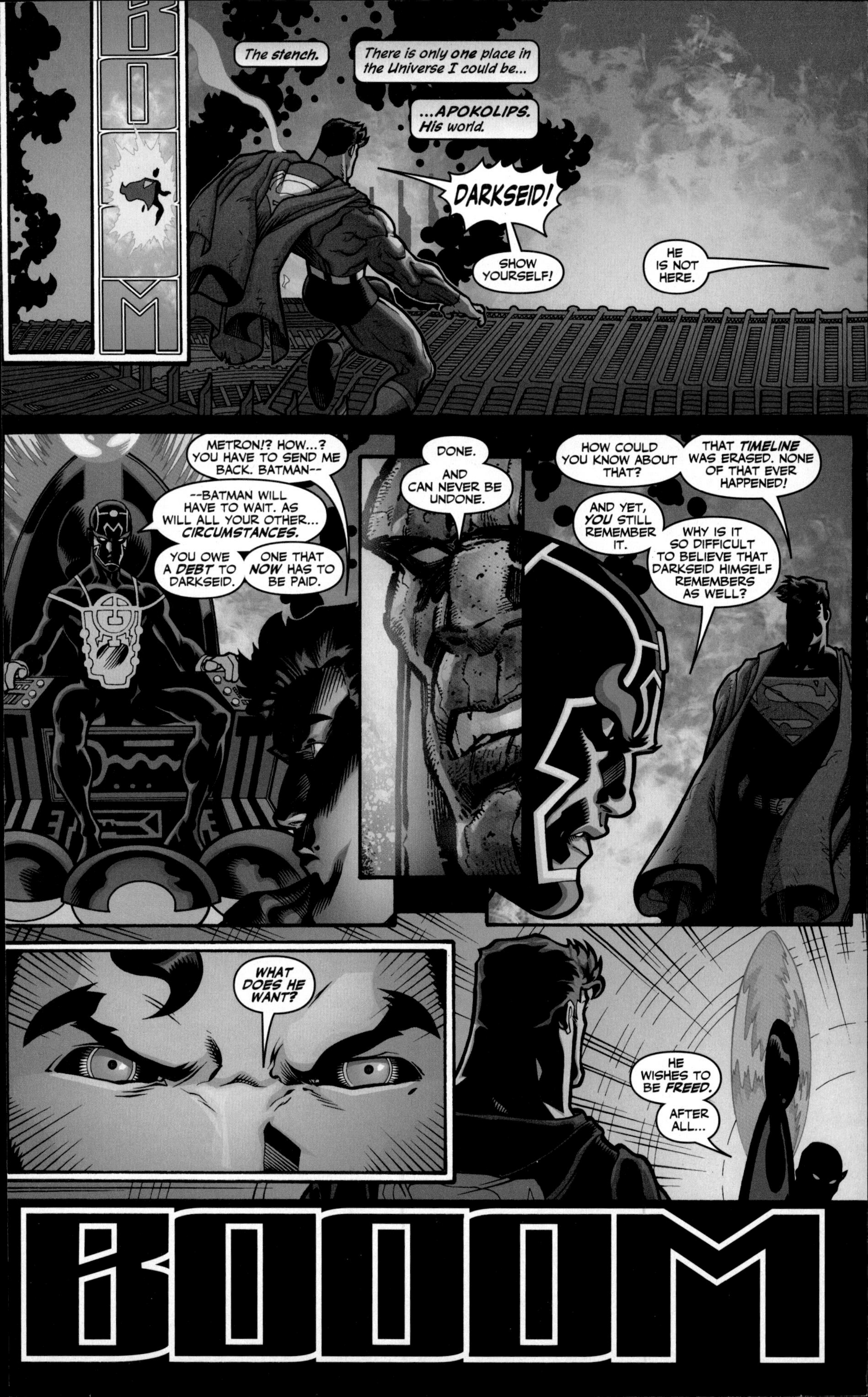
BOOM
The stench.
There is only one place in the Universe I could be...
...APOKOLIPS. His world.
DARKSEID!
SHOW YOURSELF!
HE IS NOT HERE.
METRON!? HOW...? YOU HAVE TO SEND ME BACK. BATMAN--
--BATMAN WILL HAVE TO WAIT. AS WILL ALL YOUR OTHER... CIRCUMSTANCES.
YOU OWE A DEBT TO DARKSEID.
ONE THAT NOW HAS TO BE PAID.
DONE.
AND CAN NEVER BE UNDONE.
HOW COULD YOU KNOW ABOUT THAT?
THAT TIMELINE WAS ERASED. NONE OF THAT EVER HAPPENED!
AND YET, YOU STILL REMEMBER IT.
WHY IS IT SO DIFFICULT TO BELIEVE THAT DARKSEID HIMSELF REMEMBERS AS WELL?
WHAT DOES HE WANT?
HE WISHES TO BE FREED.
AFTER ALL...
BOOM

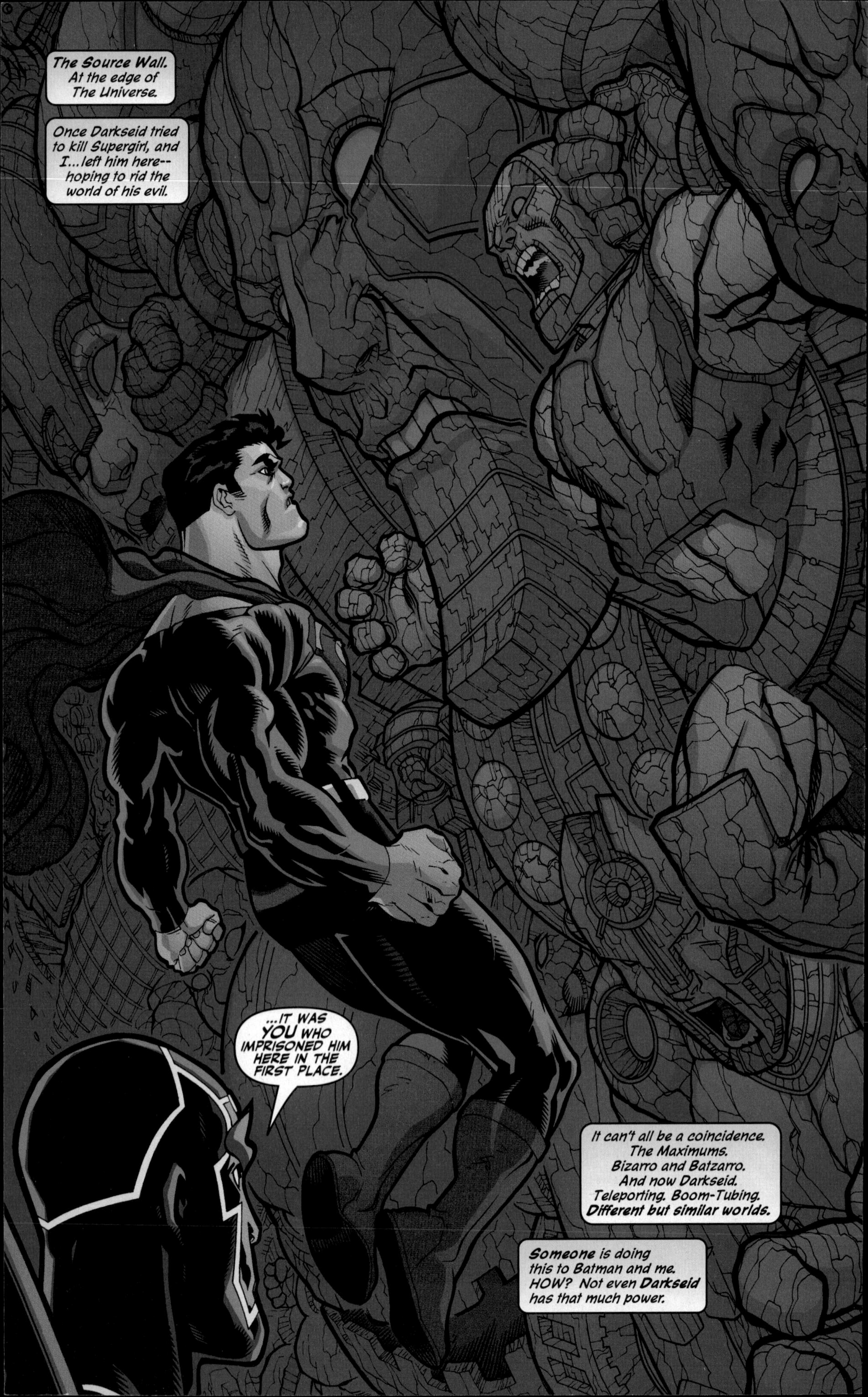

The Source Wall. At the edge of The Universe.
Once Darkseid tried to kill Supergirl, and I...left him here--hoping to rid the world of his evil.
...IT WAS YOU WHO IMPRISONED HIM HERE IN THE FIRST PLACE.
It can't all be a coincidence. The Maximums. Bizarro and Batzarro. And now Darkseid. Teleporting. Boom-Tubing. Different but similar worlds.
Someone is doing this to Batman and me. HOW? Not even Darkseid has that much power.

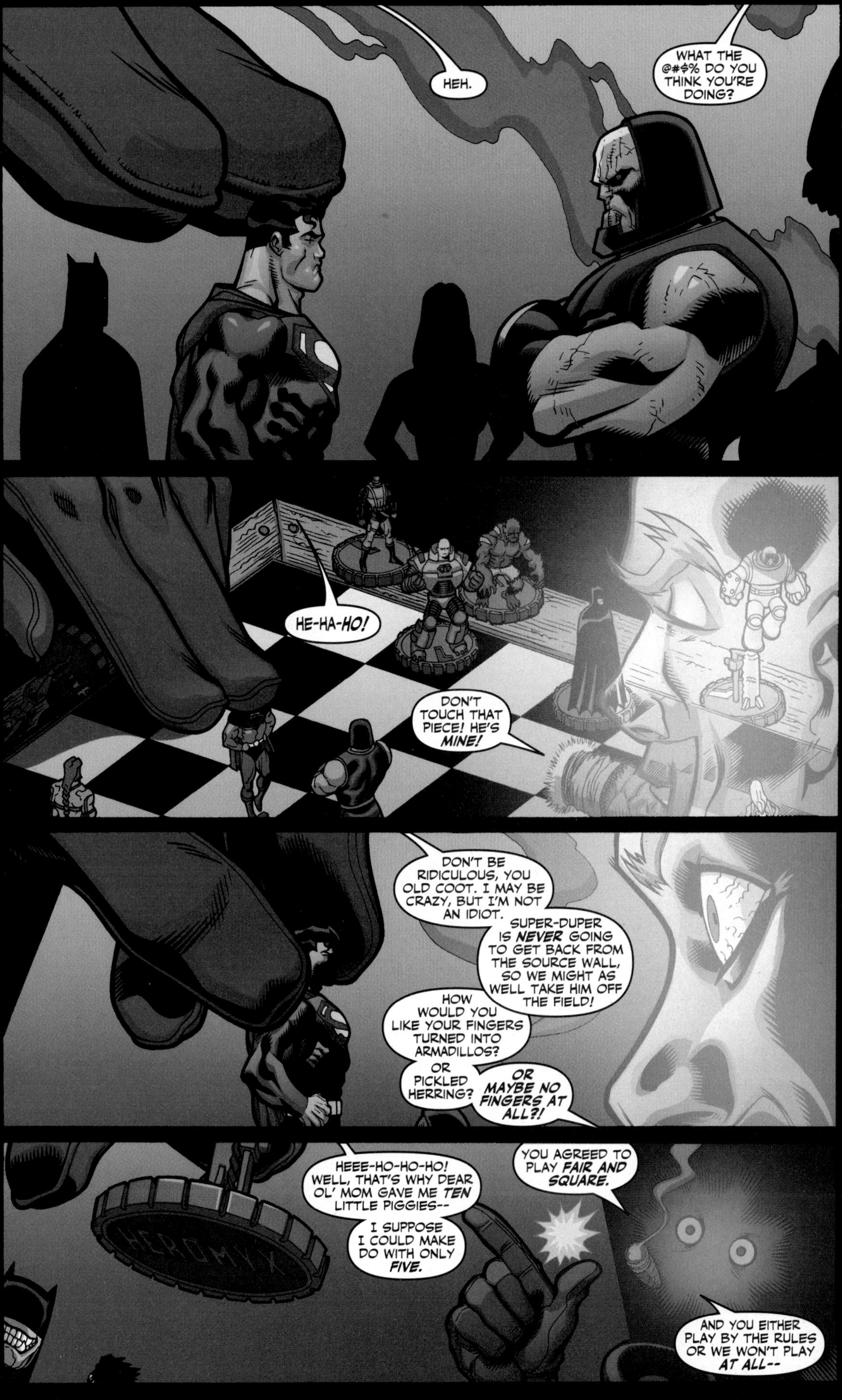

HEH.
WHAT THE @#$% DO YOU THINK YOU'RE DOING?
HE-HA-HO!
DON'T TOUCH THAT PIECE! HE'S MINE!
DON'T BE RIDICULOUS, YOU OLD COOT. I MAY BE CRAZY, BUT I'M NOT AN IDIOT.
SUPER-DUPER IS NEVER GOING TO GET BACK FROM THE SOURCE WALL, SO WE MIGHT AS WELL TAKE HIM OFF THE FIELD!
HOW WOULD YOU LIKE YOUR FINGERS TURNED INTO ARMADILLOS?
OR PICKLED HERRING?
OR MAYBE NO FINGERS AT ALL?!
HEEE-HO-HO-HO! WELL, THAT'S WHY DEAR OL' MOM GAVE ME TEN LITTLE PIGGIES--
I SUPPOSE I COULD MAKE DO WITH ONLY FIVE.
YOU AGREED TO PLAY FAIR AND SQUARE.
AND YOU EITHER PLAY BY THE RULES OR WE WON'T PLAY AT ALL--

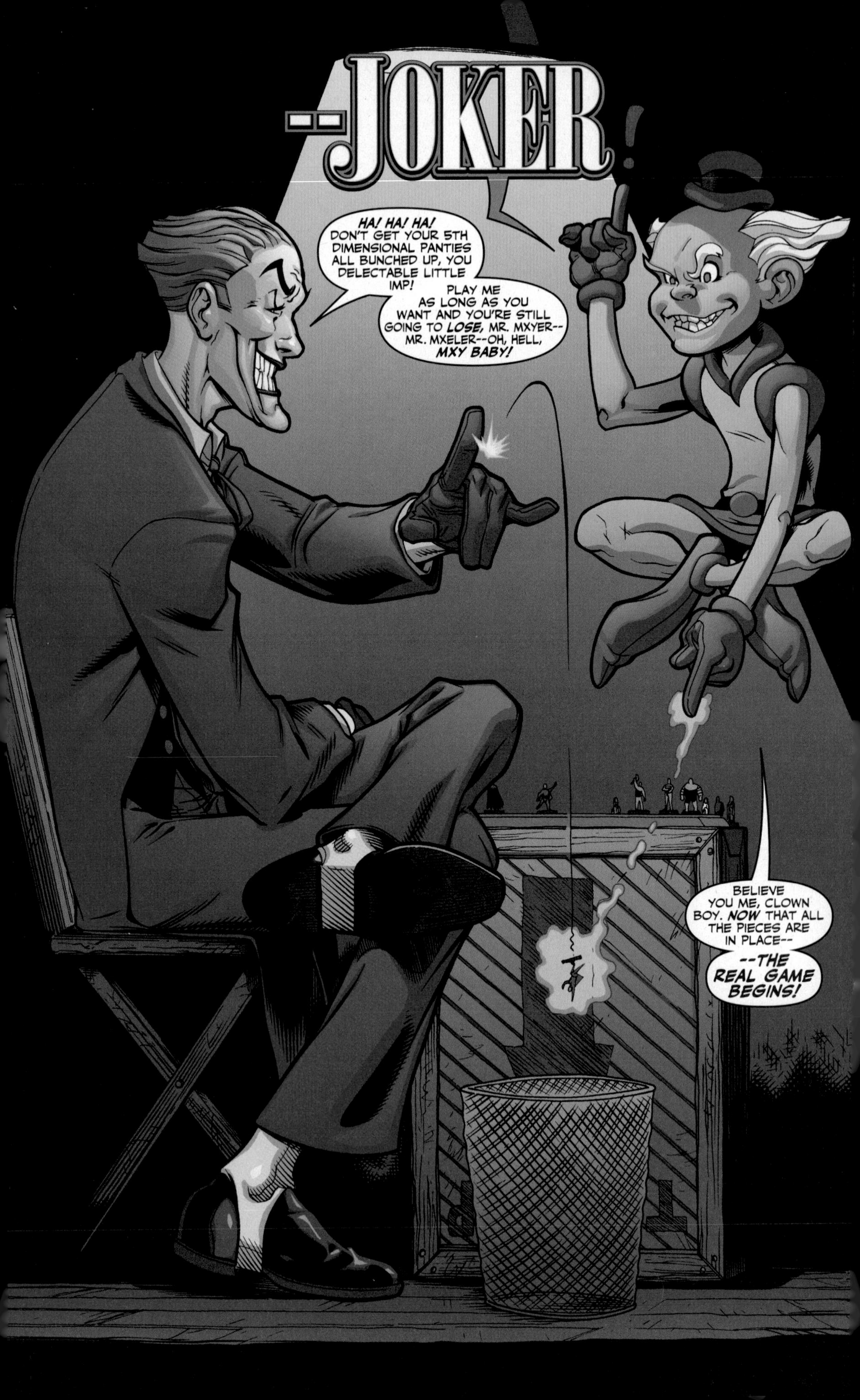
--JOKER!
HA! HA! HA! DON'T GET YOUR 5TH DIMENSIONAL PANTIES ALL BUNCHED UP, YOU DELECTABLE LITTLE IMP!
PLAY ME AS LONG AS YOU WANT AND YOU'RE STILL GOING TO LOSE, MR. MXYER-- MR. MXELER--OH, HELL, MXY BABY!
BELIEVE YOU ME, CLOWN BOY. NOW THAT ALL THE PIECES ARE IN PLACE--
--THE REAL GAME BEGINS!

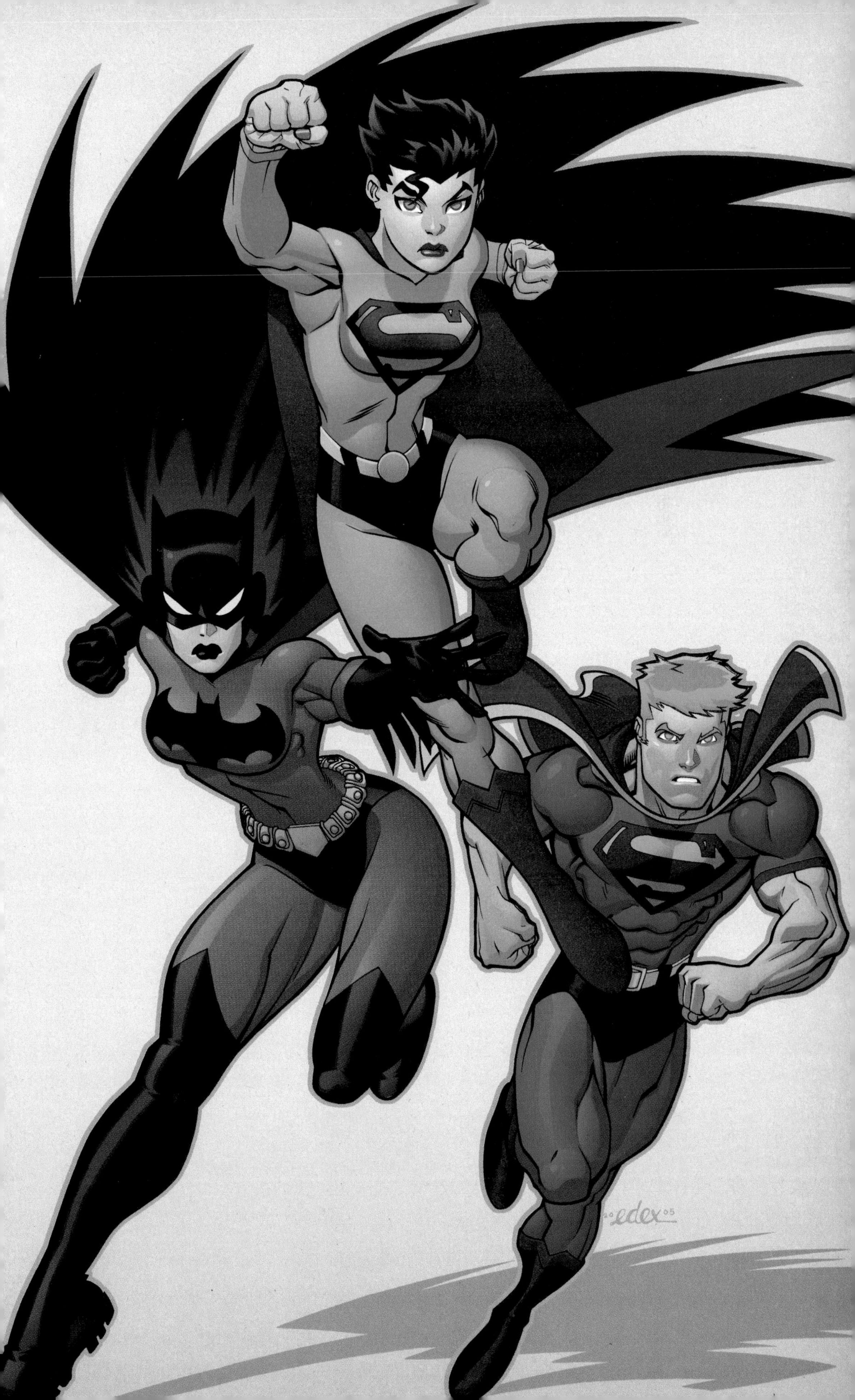
edex

"THE PRICE OF OUR SINS"

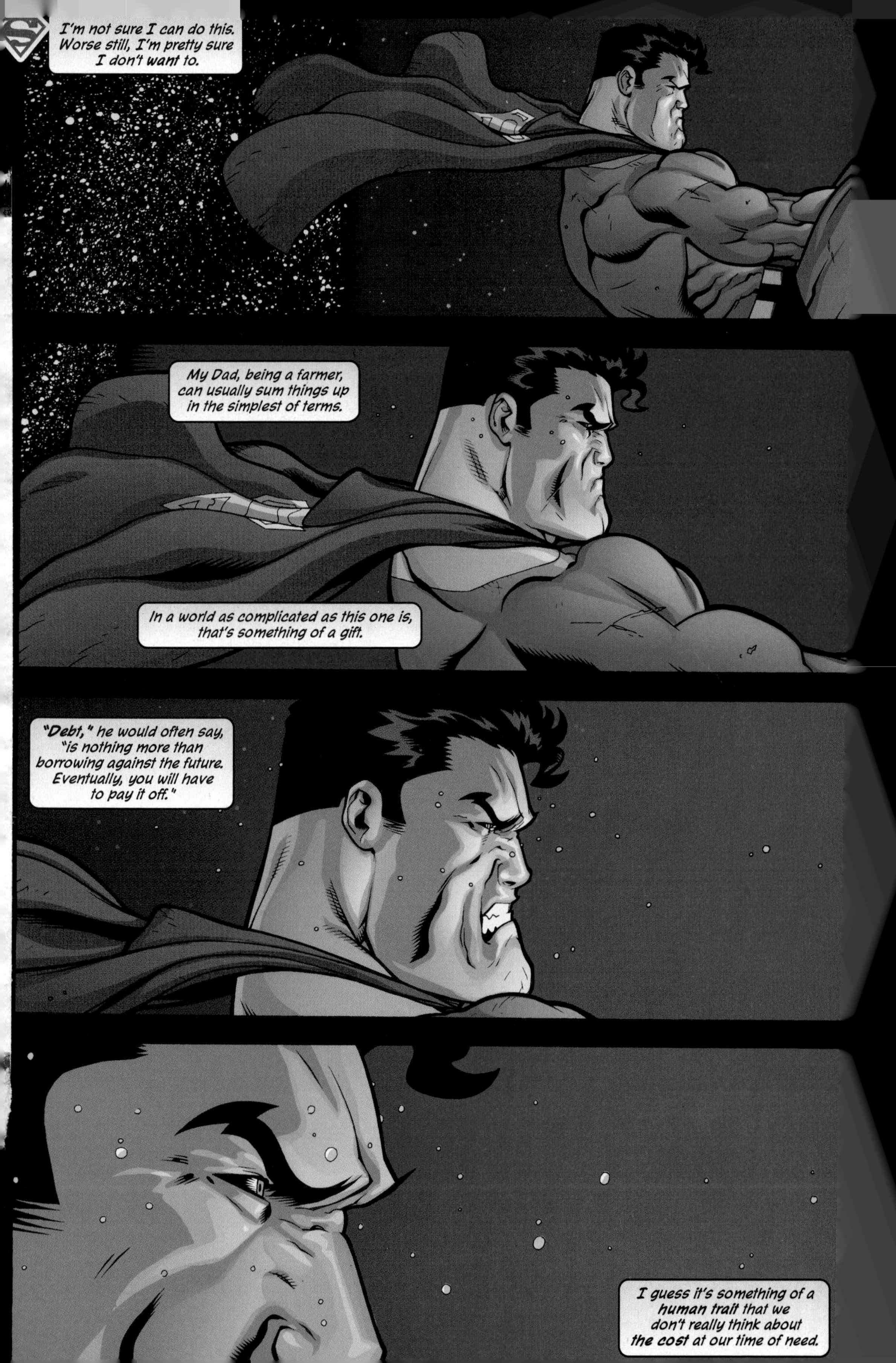
I'm not sure I can do this. Worse still, I'm pretty sure I don't want to.
My Dad, being a farmer, can usually sum things up in the simplest of terms.
In a world as complicated as this one is, that's something of a gift.
"Debt," he would often say, "is nothing more than borrowing against the future. Eventually, you will have to pay it off."
I guess it's something of a human trait that we don't really think about the cost at our time of need.

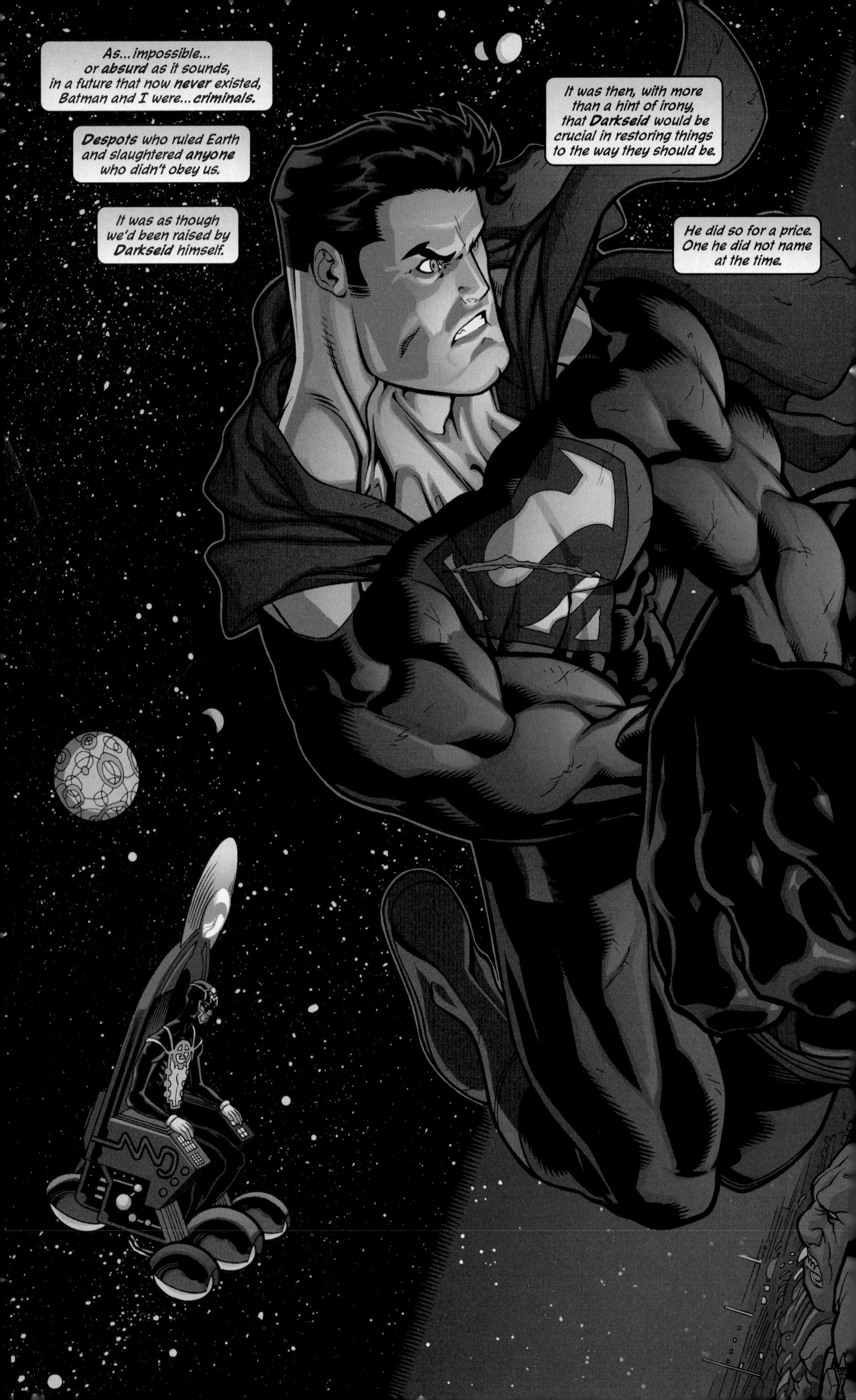
As...impossible... or absurd as it sounds, in a future that now never existed, Batman and I were...criminals.
Despots who ruled Earth and slaughtered anyone who didn't obey us.
It was as though we'd been raised by Darkseid himself.
It was then, with more than a hint of irony, that Darkseid would be crucial in restoring things to the way they should be.
He did so for a price. One he did not name at the time.

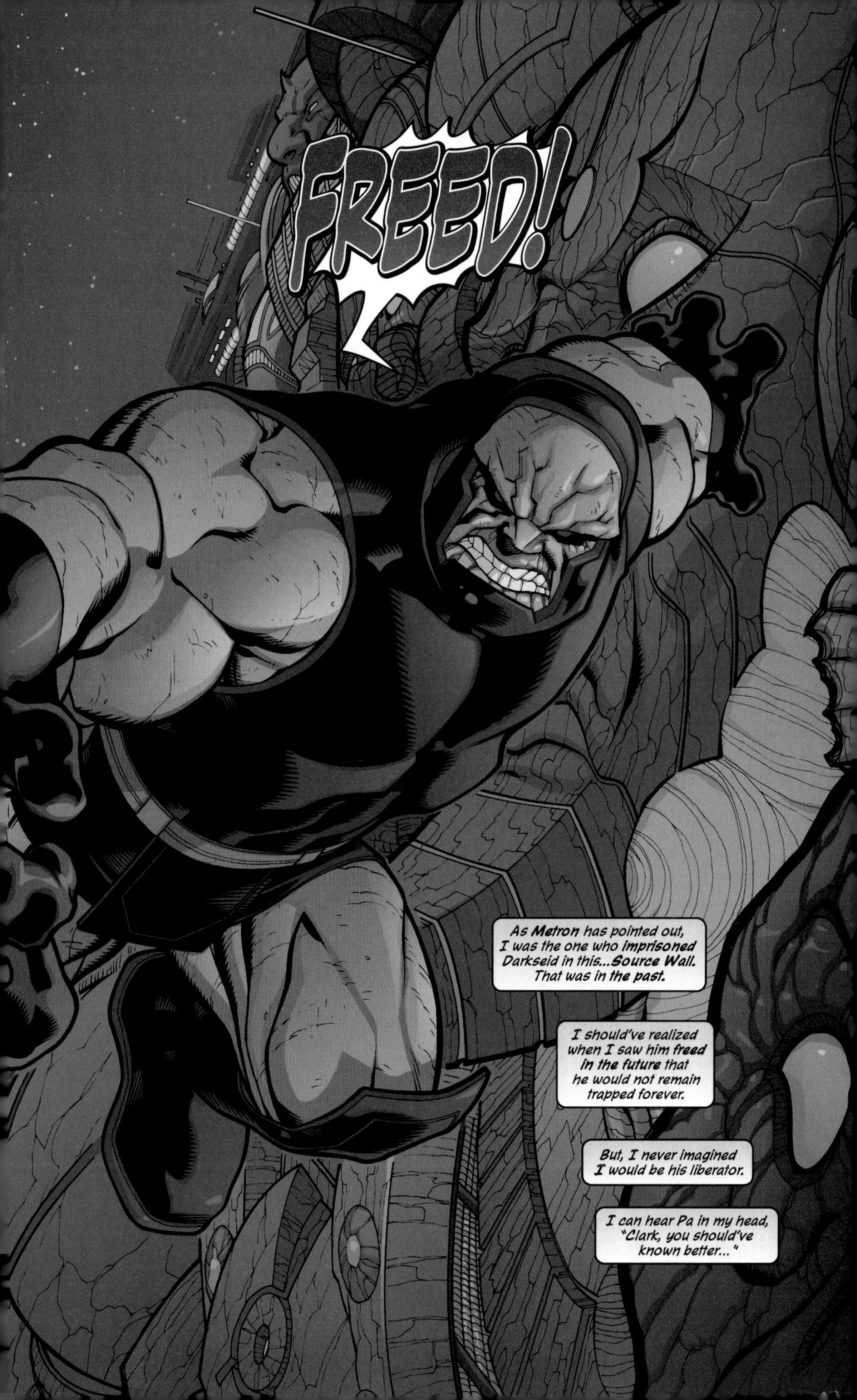
FREED!
As Metron has pointed out, I was the one who imprisoned Darkseid in this...Source Wall. That was in the past.
I should've realized when I saw him freed in the future that he would not remain trapped forever.
But, I never imagined I would be his liberator.
I can hear Pa in my head, "Clark, you should've known better..."

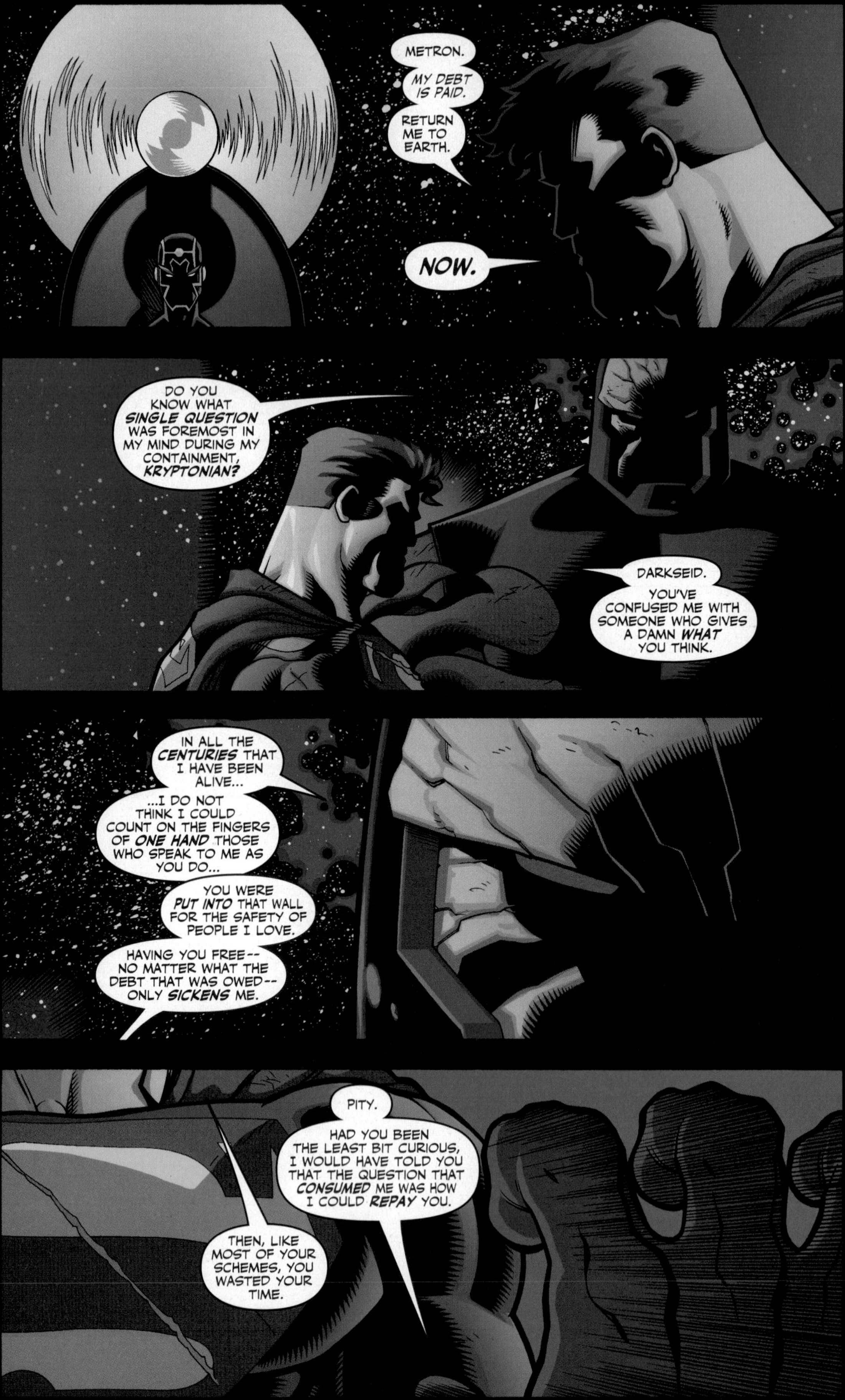

METRON.
MY DEBT IS PAID.
RETURN ME TO EARTH.
NOW.
DO YOU KNOW WHAT SINGLE QUESTION WAS FOREMOST IN MY MIND DURING MY CONTAINMENT, KRYPTONIAN?
DARKSEID.
YOU'VE CONFUSED ME WITH SOMEONE WHO GIVES A DAMN WHAT YOU THINK.
IN ALL THE CENTURIES THAT I HAVE BEEN ALIVE...
...I DO NOT THINK I COULD COUNT ON THE FINGERS OF ONE HAND THOSE WHO SPEAK TO ME AS YOU DO...
YOU WERE PUT INTO THAT WALL FOR THE SAFETY OF PEOPLE I LOVE.
HAVING YOU FREE-- NO MATTER WHAT THE DEBT THAT WAS OWED-- ONLY SICKENS ME.
PITY.
HAD YOU BEEN THE LEAST BIT CURIOUS, I WOULD HAVE TOLD YOU THAT THE QUESTION THAT CONSUMED ME WAS HOW I COULD REPAY YOU.
THEN, LIKE MOST OF YOUR SCHEMES, YOU WASTED YOUR TIME.

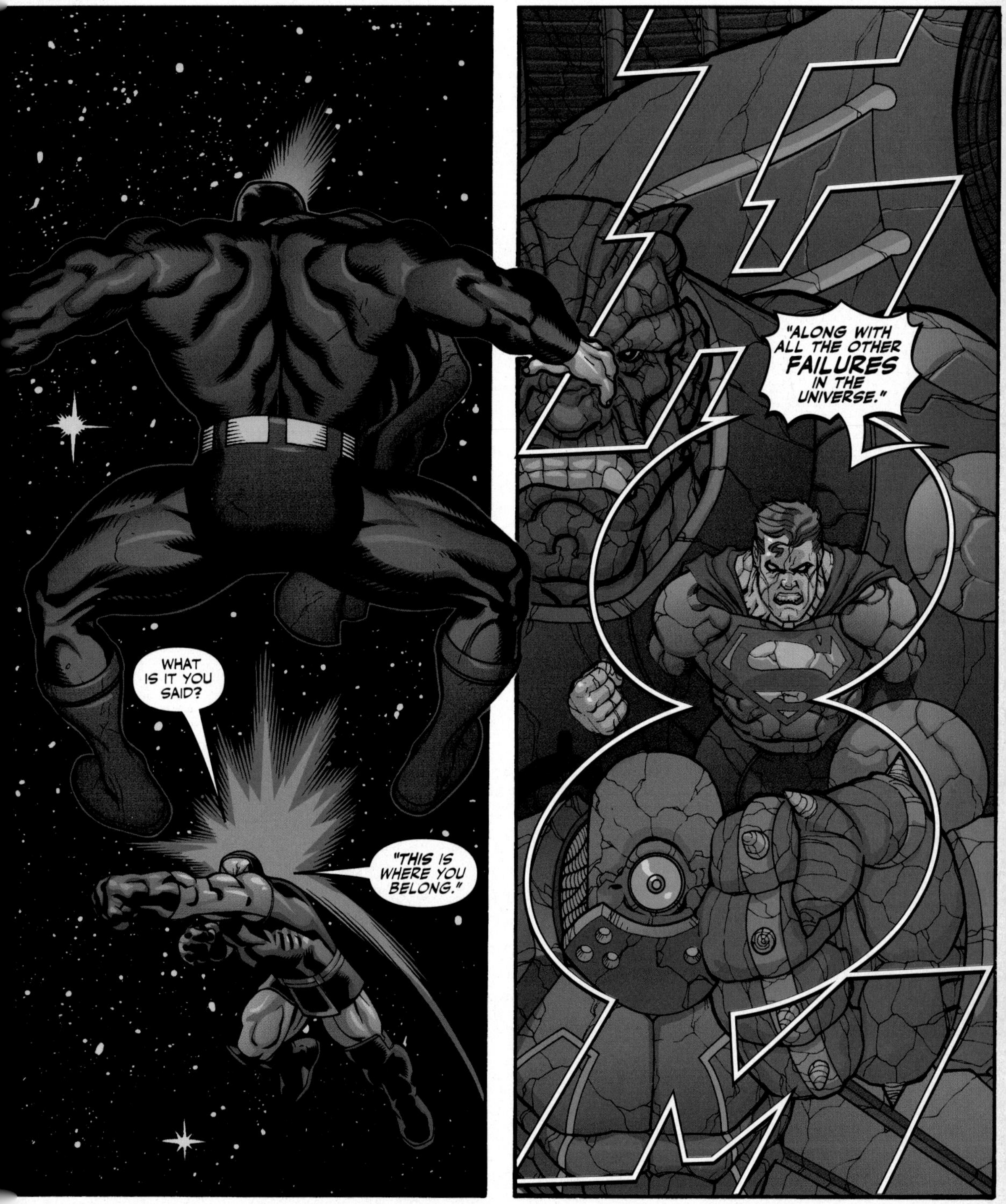
WHAT IS IT YOU SAID?
"THIS IS WHERE YOU BELONG."
"ALONG WITH ALL THE OTHER FAILURES IN THE UNIVERSE."

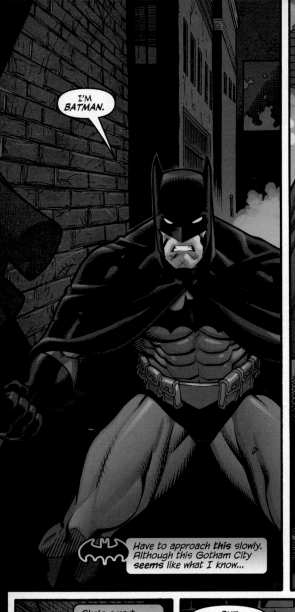

I'M BATMAN.

Have to approach **this** slowly. Although this Gotham City **seems** like what I know...

YOU SHOULD'VE DONE YOUR HOMEWORK, CHUM.

GOTHAM CITY ALREADY HAS HER OWN DARK KNIGHT...

...AND HER NAME IS BATWOMAN.

SUPERWOMAN...

...LET HIM SPEAK.

HE'S NOT GOING ANYWHERE.

We were traveling back from another world when I suddenly **appeared** here.

Where distaff versions of myself and Clark exist. **Where is Clark? What happened to him?**

NOTHING TO SAY...?

She's smart. Playing it **exactly** as I would.

ASSESSING THE SITUATION. ALLOWING YOUR OPPONENT TO SHOW HIS OR HER STRENGTHS AND WEAKNESSES.

EXACTLY AS I WOULD PLAY IT.

BUT YOU KNEW THAT, DIDN'T YOU?

RIGHT ABOUT NOW, YOU'RE WEIGHING YOUR OPTIONS FOR TAKING MY UTILITY BELT FROM ME--

--CLEARLY, **YOURS** WAS EMPTIED **BEFORE** YOU ARRIVED HERE AND I'M GUESSING **WITHOUT** YOUR PERMISSION.

Whatever is going on here... She is very good at this.

ASIDE FROM THE OBVIOUS, WHY DO YOU SEEM SO FAMILIAR?

ALMOST AS IF WE'D MET BEFORE...

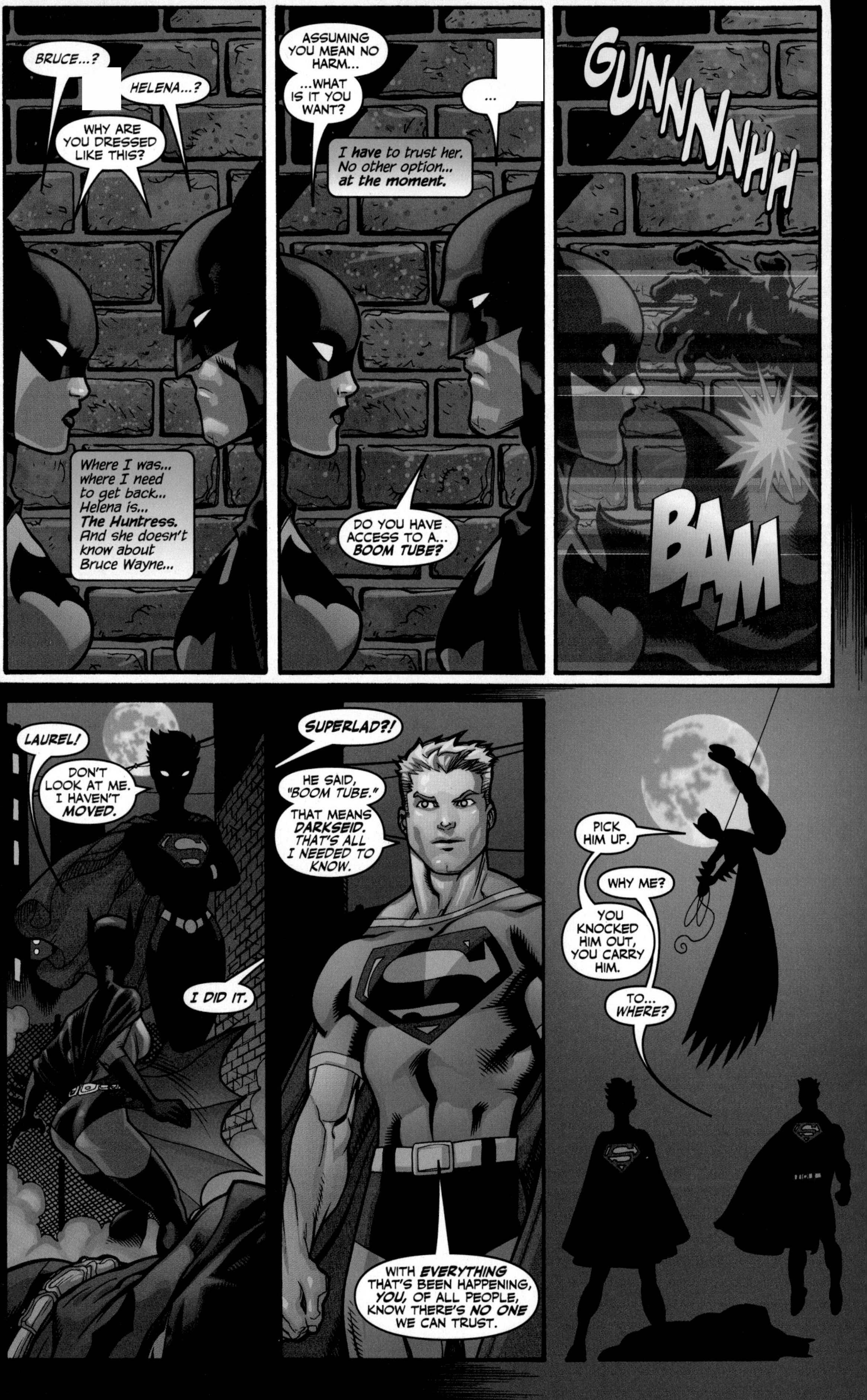
BRUCE...?
HELENA...?
WHY ARE YOU DRESSED LIKE THIS?
Where I was... where I need to get back... Helena is... The Huntress. And she doesn't know about Bruce Wayne...
ASSUMING YOU MEAN NO HARM...
...WHAT IS IT YOU WANT?
...
I have to trust her. No other option... at the moment.
DO YOU HAVE ACCESS TO A... BOOM TUBE?
GUNNNNHH
BAM
LAUREL!
DON'T LOOK AT ME. I HAVEN'T MOVED.
I DID IT.
SUPERLAD?!
HE SAID, "BOOM TUBE."
THAT MEANS DARKSEID. THAT'S ALL I NEEDED TO KNOW.
WITH EVERYTHING THAT'S BEEN HAPPENING, YOU, OF ALL PEOPLE, KNOW THERE'S NO ONE WE CAN TRUST.
PICK HIM UP.
WHY ME?
YOU KNOCKED HIM OUT, YOU CARRY HIM.
TO... WHERE?

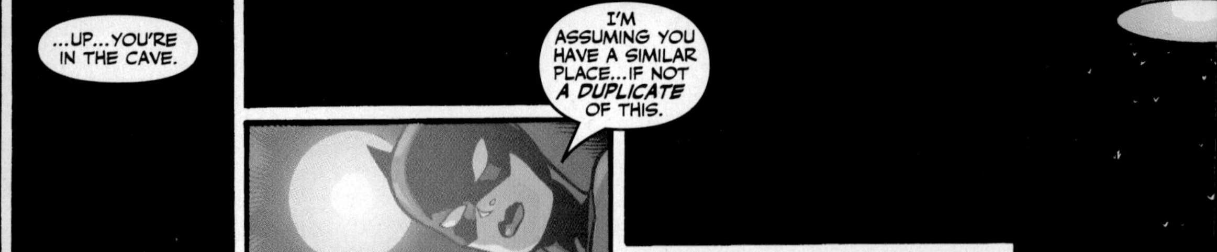
...UP...YOU'RE IN THE CAVE.
I'M ASSUMING YOU HAVE A SIMILAR PLACE...IF NOT A DUPLICATE OF THIS.

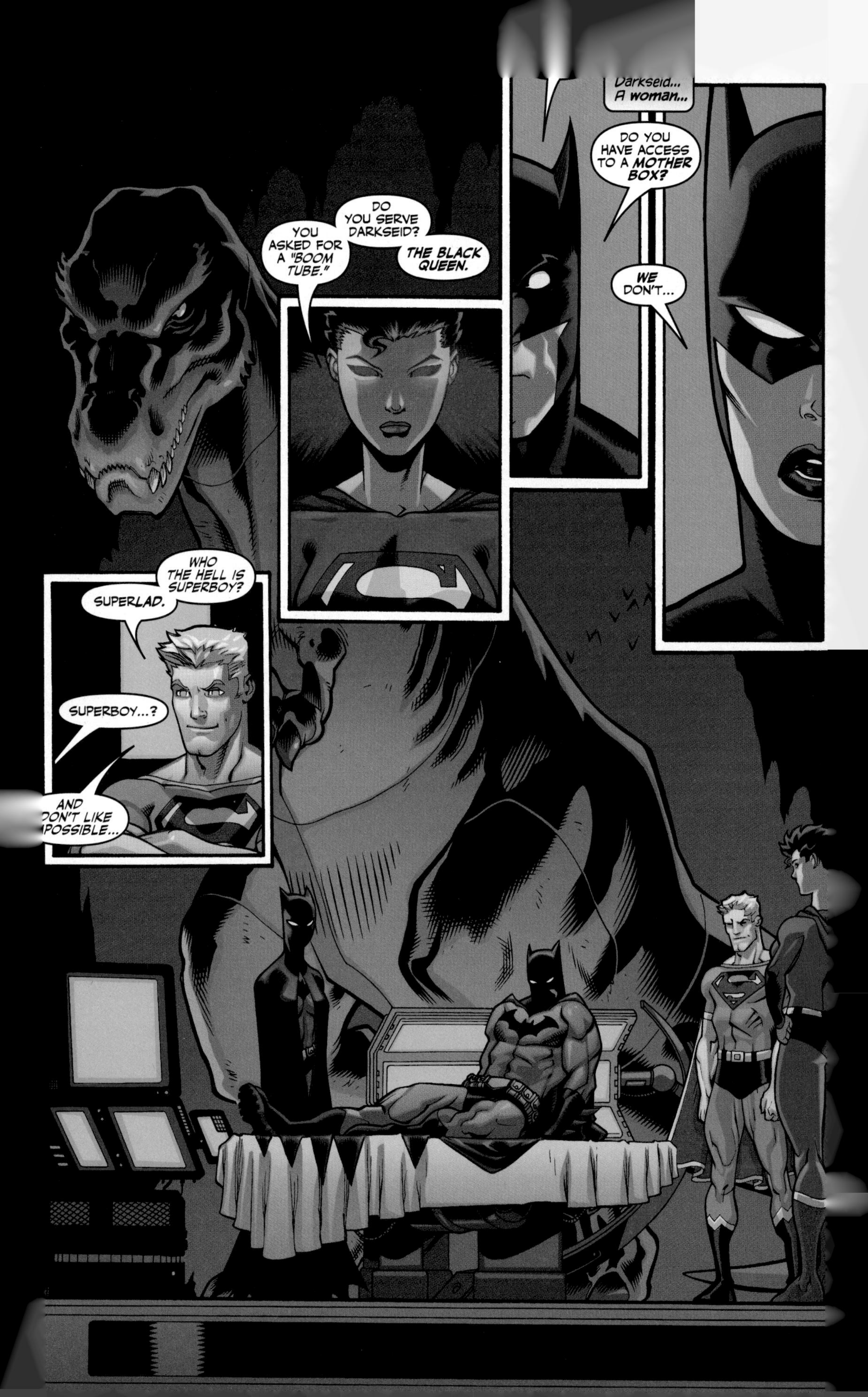

Darkseid...
A woman...
DO YOU HAVE ACCESS TO A MOTHER BOX?
WE DON'T...
YOU ASKED FOR A "BOOM TUBE."
DO YOU SERVE DARKSEID?
THE BLACK QUEEN.
WHO THE HELL IS SUPERBOY?
SUPERLAD.
SUPERBOY...?
AND DON'T LIKE POSSIBLE...

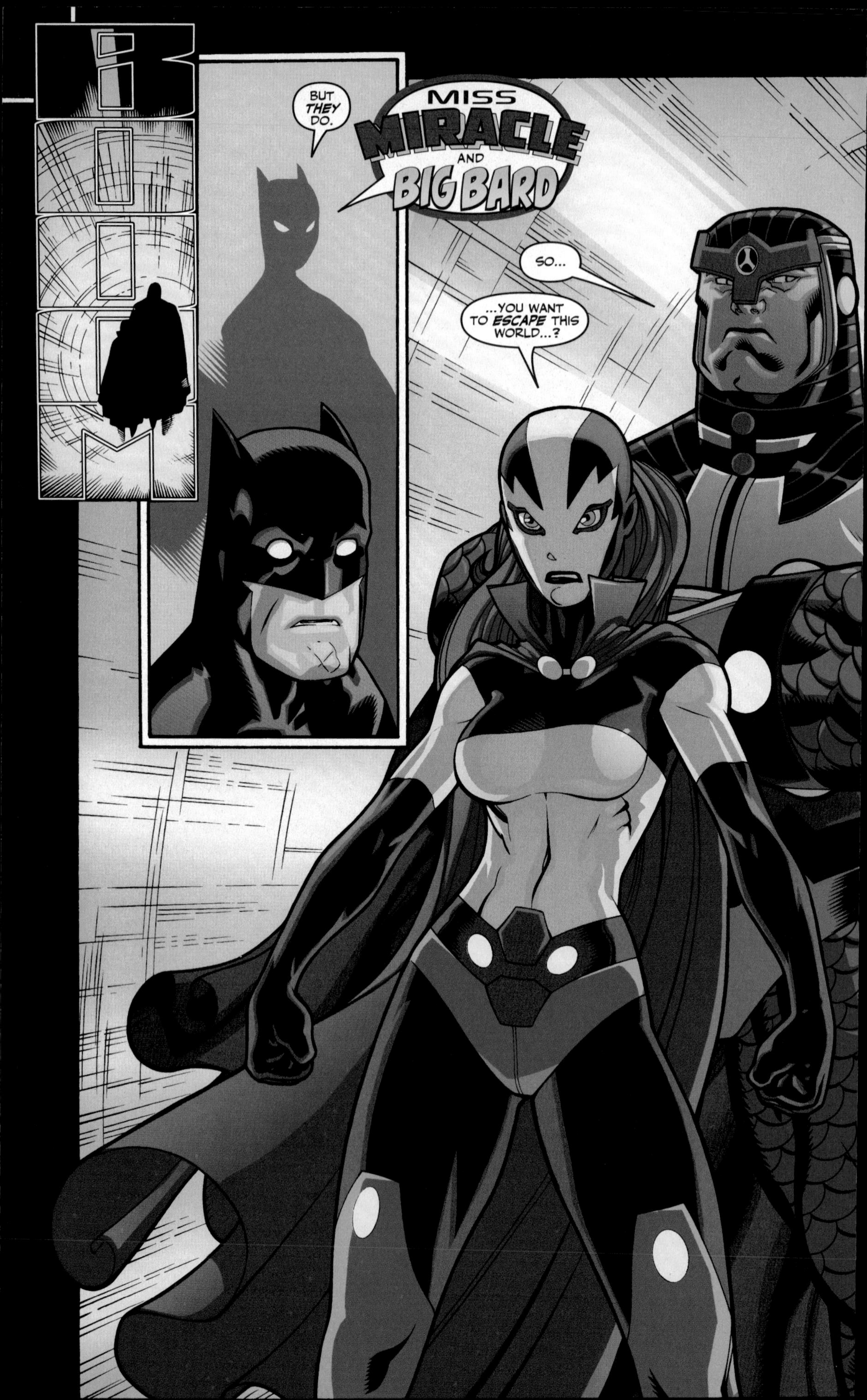BOOOM
BUT THEY DO.
MISS MIRACLE AND BIG BARD
SO...
...YOU WANT TO ESCAPE THIS WORLD...?

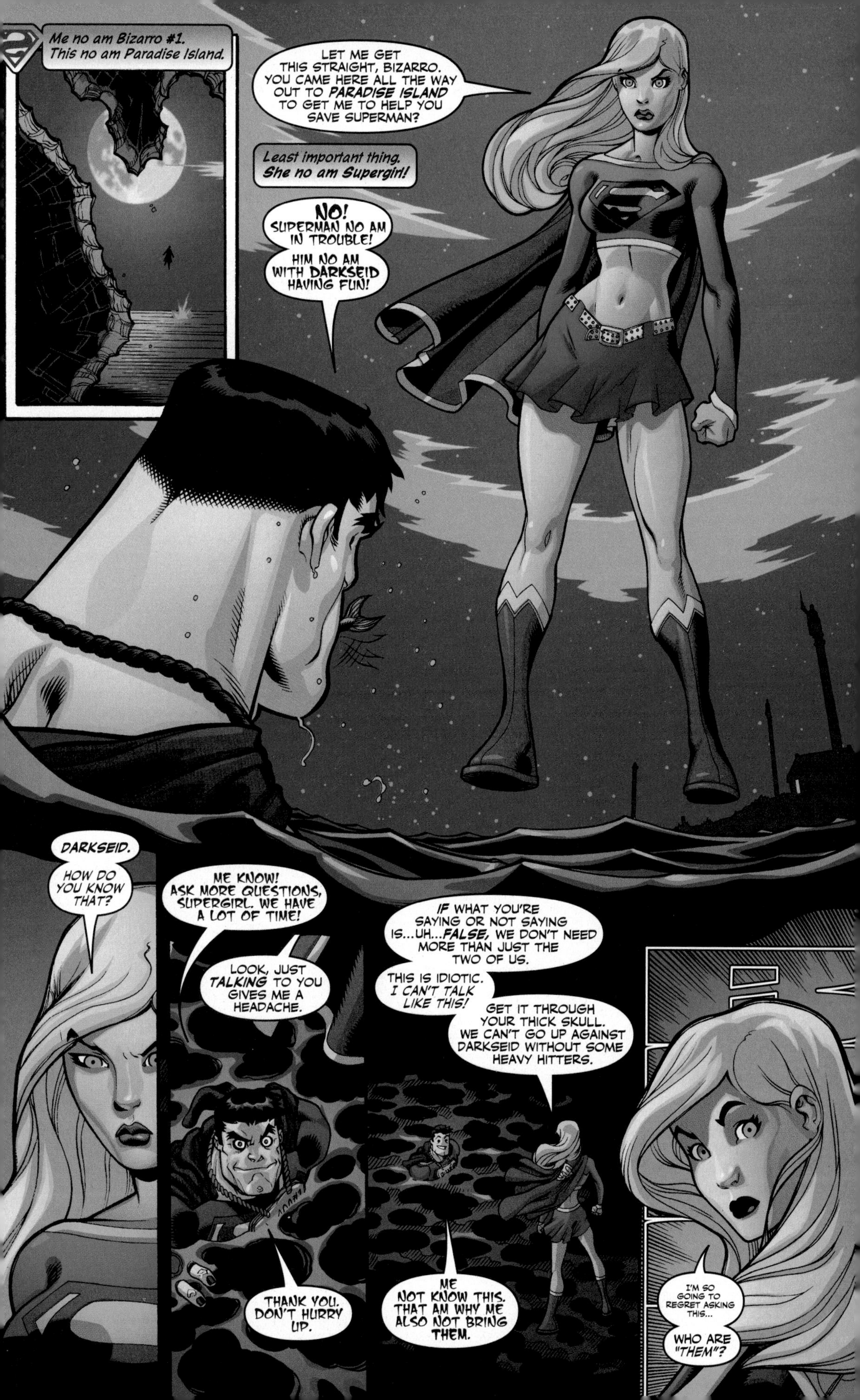

Me no am Bizarro #1. This no am Paradise Island.
LET ME GET THIS STRAIGHT, BIZARRO. YOU CAME HERE ALL THE WAY OUT TO PARADISE ISLAND TO GET ME TO HELP YOU SAVE SUPERMAN?
Least important thing. She no am Supergirl!
NO! SUPERMAN NO AM IN TROUBLE!
HIM NO AM WITH DARKSEID HAVING FUN!
DARKSEID.
HOW DO YOU KNOW THAT?
ME KNOW! ASK MORE QUESTIONS, SUPERGIRL. WE HAVE A LOT OF TIME!
LOOK, JUST TALKING TO YOU GIVES ME A HEADACHE.
THANK YOU. DON'T HURRY UP.
IF WHAT YOU'RE SAYING OR NOT SAYING IS...UH...FALSE, WE DON'T NEED MORE THAN JUST THE TWO OF US.
THIS IS IDIOTIC. I CAN'T TALK LIKE THIS!
GET IT THROUGH YOUR THICK SKULL. WE CAN'T GO UP AGAINST DARKSEID WITHOUT SOME HEAVY HITTERS.
ME NOT KNOW THIS. THAT AM WHY ME ALSO NOT BRING THEM.
I'M SO GOING TO REGRET ASKING THIS...
WHO ARE "THEM"?

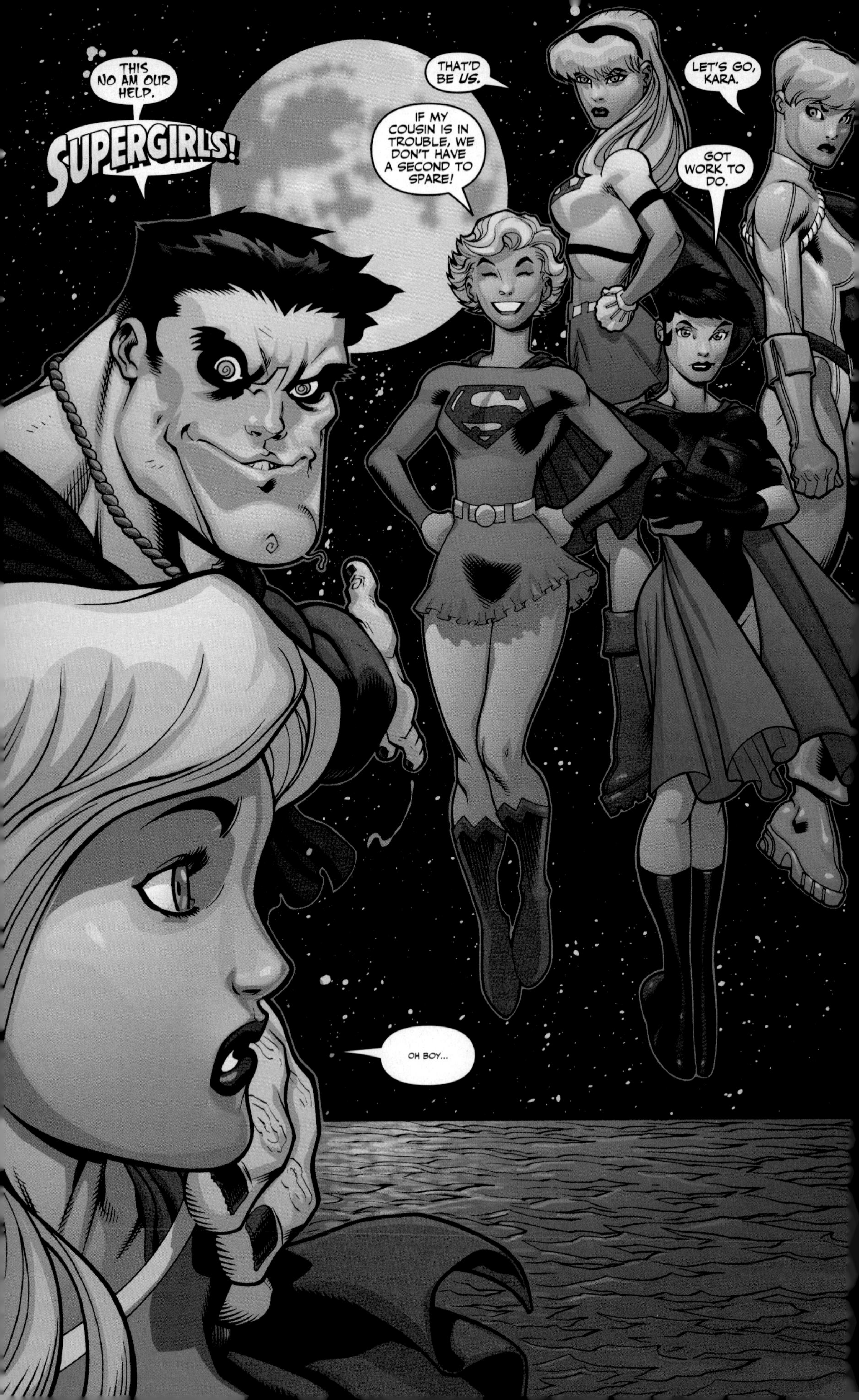
THIS NO AM OUR HELP.
SUPERGIRLS!
THAT'D BE US.
IF MY COUSIN IS IN TROUBLE, WE DON'T HAVE A SECOND TO SPARE!
LET'S GO, KARA.
GOT WORK TO DO.
OH BOY...

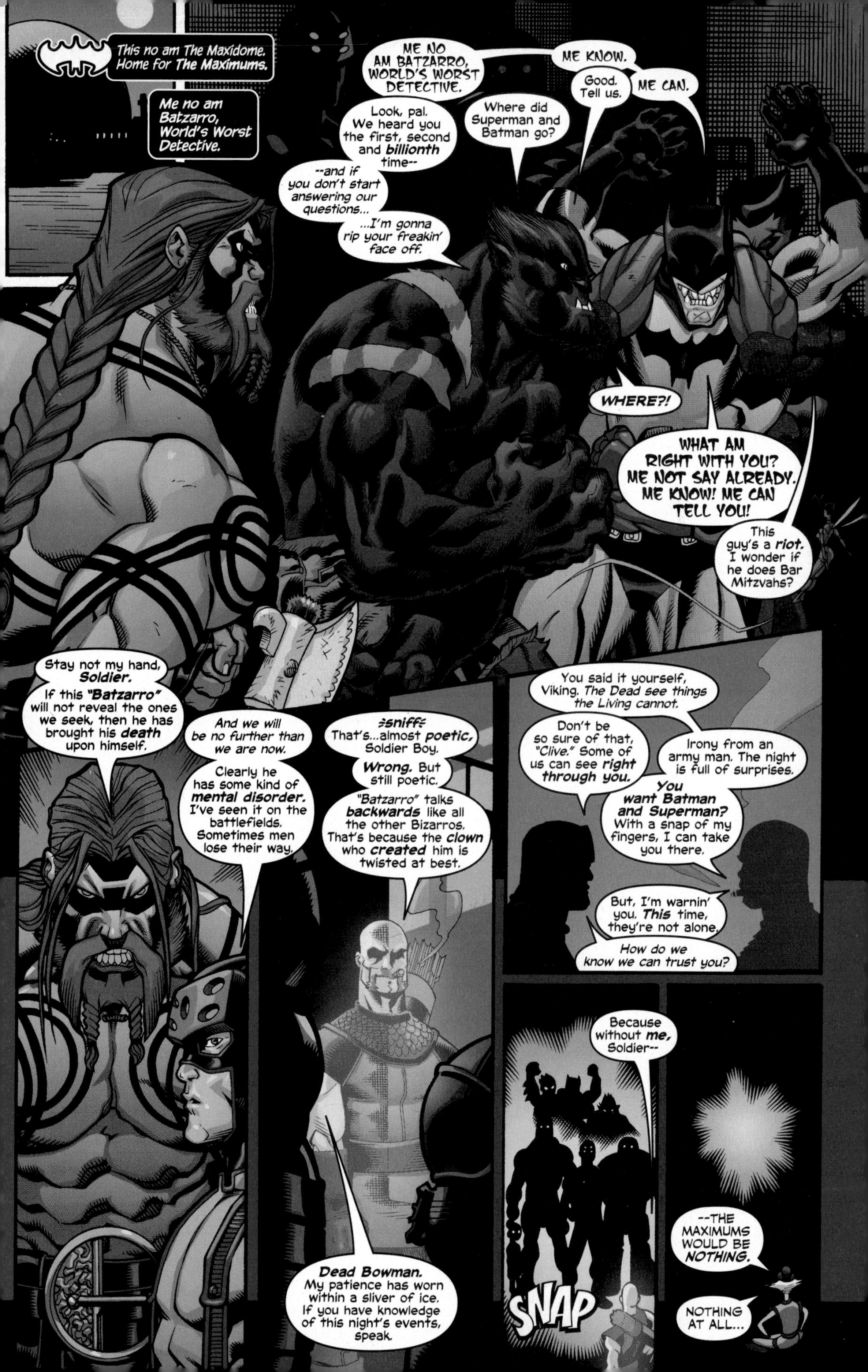
This no am The Maxidome. Home for The Maximums.
Me no am Batzarro, World's Worst Detective.
ME NO AM BATZARRO, WORLD'S WORST DETECTIVE.
ME KNOW.
Good. Tell us.
ME CAN.
Look, pal. We heard you the first, second and billionth time--
Where did Superman and Batman go?
--and if you don't start answering our questions...
...I'm gonna rip your freakin' face off.
WHERE?!
WHAT AM RIGHT WITH YOU? ME NOT SAY ALREADY. ME KNOW! ME CAN TELL YOU!
This guy's a riot. I wonder if he does Bar Mitzvahs?
Stay not my hand, Soldier.
If this "Batzarro" will not reveal the ones we seek, then he has brought his death upon himself.
And we will be no further than we are now.
Clearly he has some kind of mental disorder. I've seen it on the battlefields. Sometimes men lose their way.
sniff That's...almost poetic, Soldier Boy.
Wrong. But still poetic.
"Batzarro" talks backwards like all the other Bizarros. That's because the clown who created him is twisted at best.
Dead Bowman. My patience has worn within a sliver of ice. If you have knowledge of this night's events, speak.
You said it yourself, Viking. The Dead see things the Living cannot.
Don't be so sure of that, "Clive." Some of us can see right through you.
Irony from an army man. The night is full of surprises.
You want Batman and Superman? With a snap of my fingers, I can take you there.
But, I'm warnin' you. This time, they're not alone.
How do we know we can trust you?
Because without me, Soldier--
SNAP
--THE MAXIMUMS WOULD BE NOTHING.
NOTHING AT ALL...

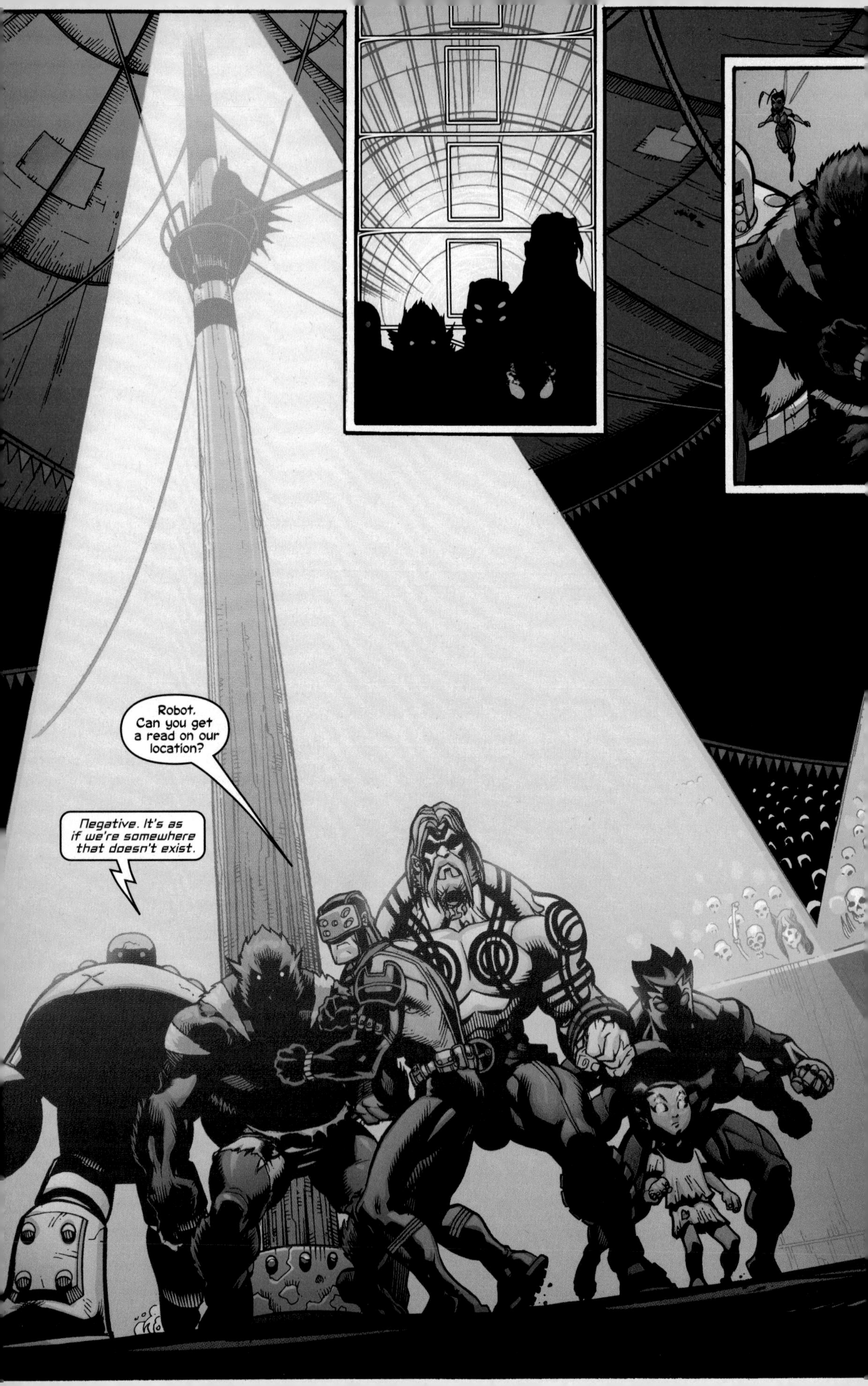
Robot. Can you get a read on our location?
Negative. It's as if we're somewhere that doesn't exist.

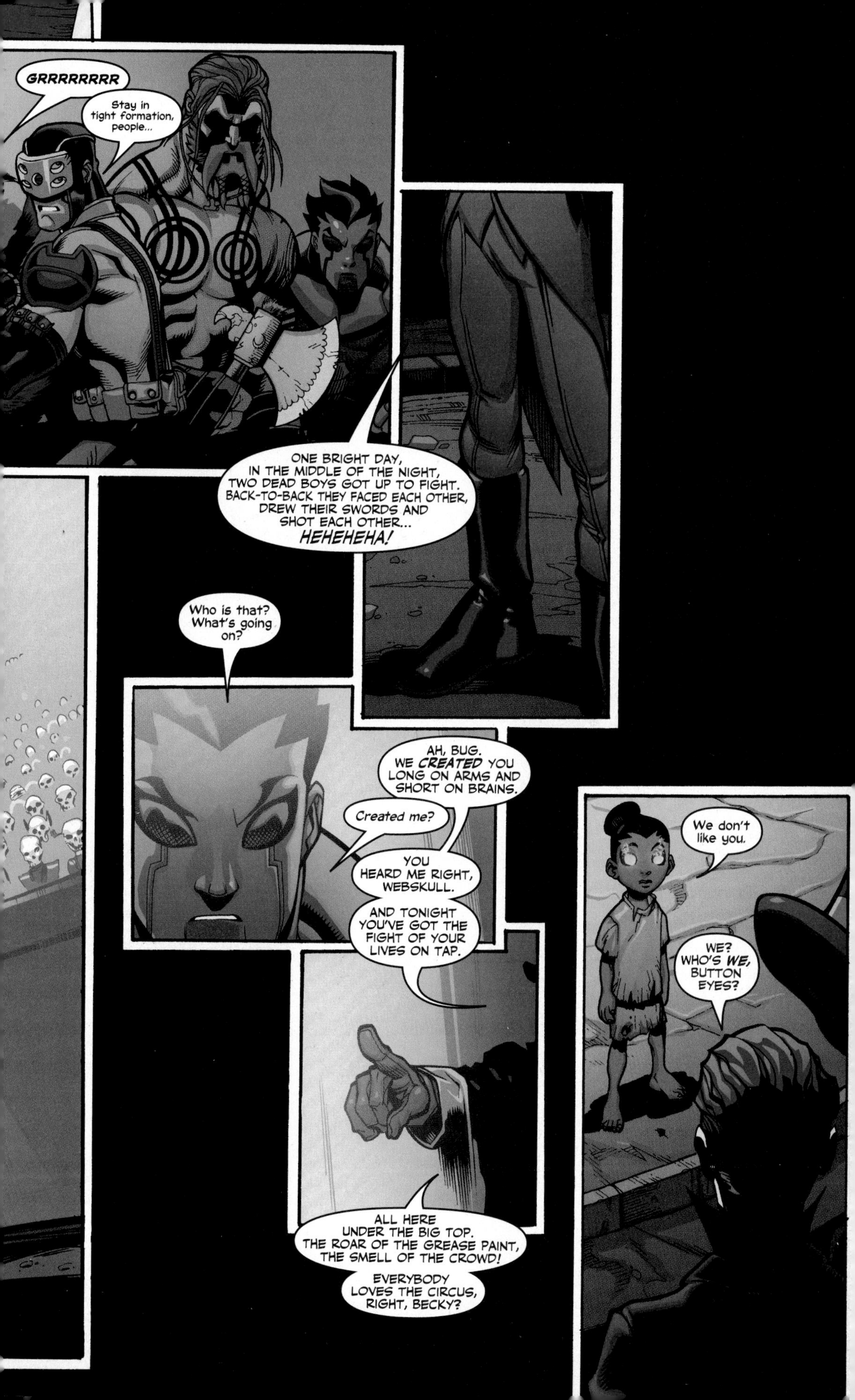
GRRRRRRRR
Stay in tight formation, people...
ONE BRIGHT DAY, IN THE MIDDLE OF THE NIGHT, TWO DEAD BOYS GOT UP TO FIGHT. BACK-TO-BACK THEY FACED EACH OTHER, DREW THEIR SWORDS AND SHOT EACH OTHER... HEHEHEHA!
Who is that? What's going on?
AH, BUG. WE CREATED YOU LONG ON ARMS AND SHORT ON BRAINS.
Created me?
YOU HEARD ME RIGHT, WEBSKULL.
AND TONIGHT YOU'VE GOT THE FIGHT OF YOUR LIVES ON TAP.
ALL HERE UNDER THE BIG TOP. THE ROAR OF THE GREASE PAINT, THE SMELL OF THE CROWD!
EVERYBODY LOVES THE CIRCUS, RIGHT, BECKY?
We don't like you.
WE? WHO'S WE, BUTTON EYES?

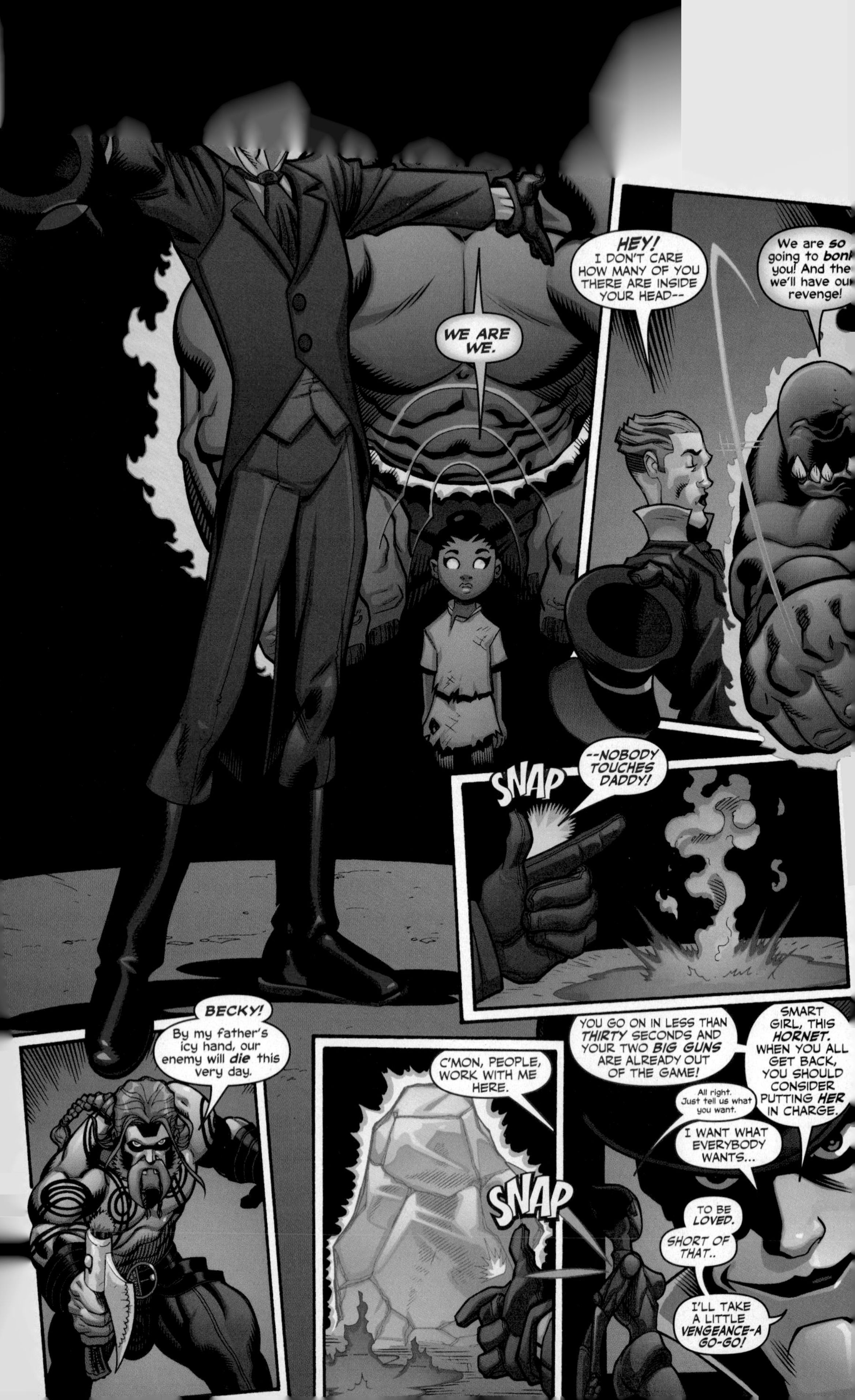
WE ARE WE.
HEY! I DON'T CARE HOW MANY OF YOU THERE ARE INSIDE YOUR HEAD--
We are so going to bonk you! And then we'll have our revenge!
SNAP
--NOBODY TOUCHES DADDY!
BECKY! By my father's icy hand, our enemy will die this very day.
C'MON, PEOPLE, WORK WITH ME HERE.
SNAP
YOU GO ON IN LESS THAN THIRTY SECONDS AND YOUR TWO BIG GUNS ARE ALREADY OUT OF THE GAME!
SMART GIRL, THIS HORNET. WHEN YOU ALL GET BACK, YOU SHOULD CONSIDER PUTTING HER IN CHARGE.
All right. Just tell us what you want.
I WANT WHAT EVERYBODY WANTS...
TO BE LOVED.
SHORT OF THAT..
I'LL TAKE A LITTLE VENGEANCE-A GO-GO!

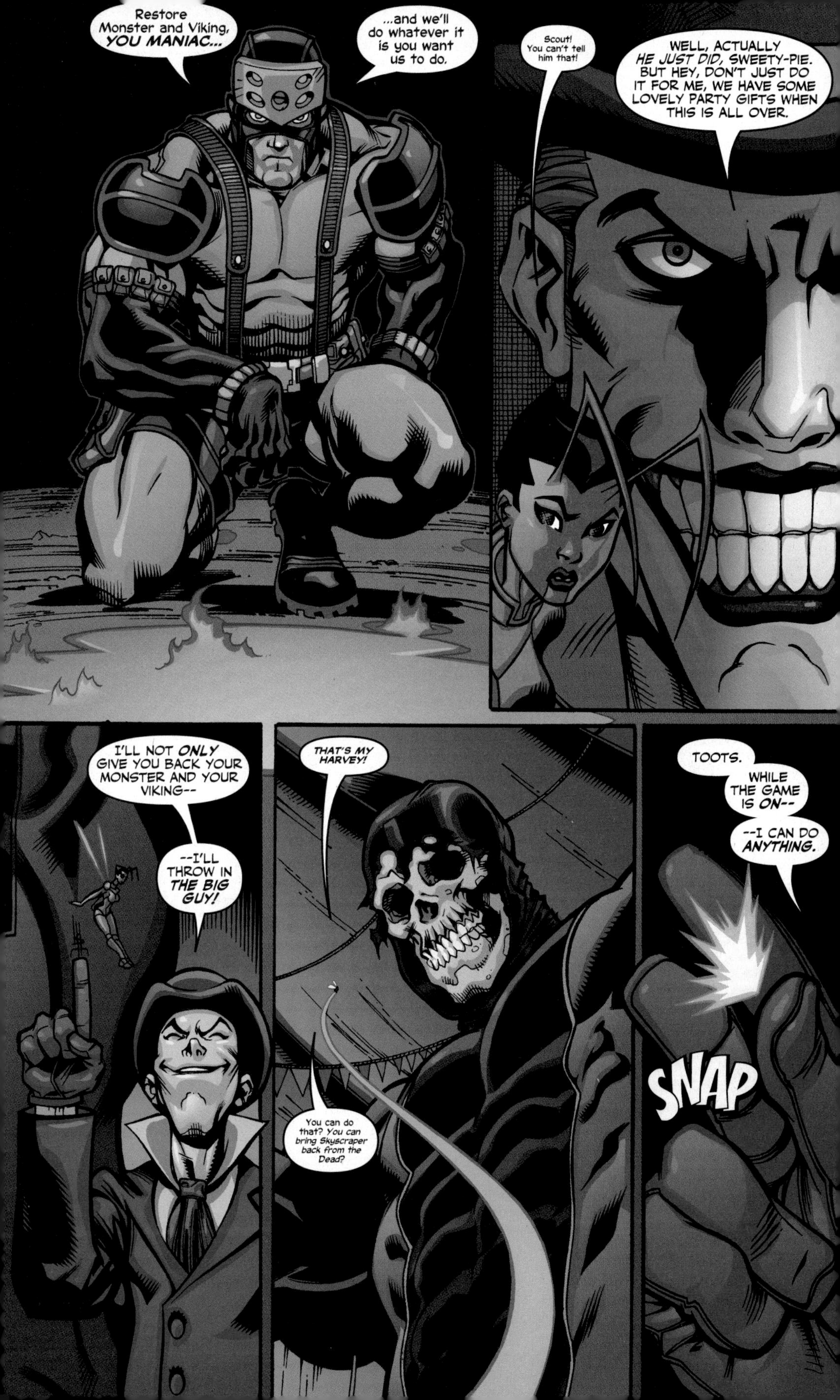

Restore Monster and Viking, YOU MANIAC...
...and we'll do whatever it is you want us to do.
Scout! You can't tell him that!
WELL, ACTUALLY HE JUST DID, SWEETY-PIE. BUT HEY, DON'T JUST DO IT FOR ME, WE HAVE SOME LOVELY PARTY GIFTS WHEN THIS IS ALL OVER.
I'LL NOT ONLY GIVE YOU BACK YOUR MONSTER AND YOUR VIKING--
--I'LL THROW IN THE BIG GUY!
THAT'S MY HARVEY!
You can do that? You can bring Skyscraper back from the Dead?
TOOTS.
WHILE THE GAME IS ON--
--I CAN DO ANYTHING.
SNAP

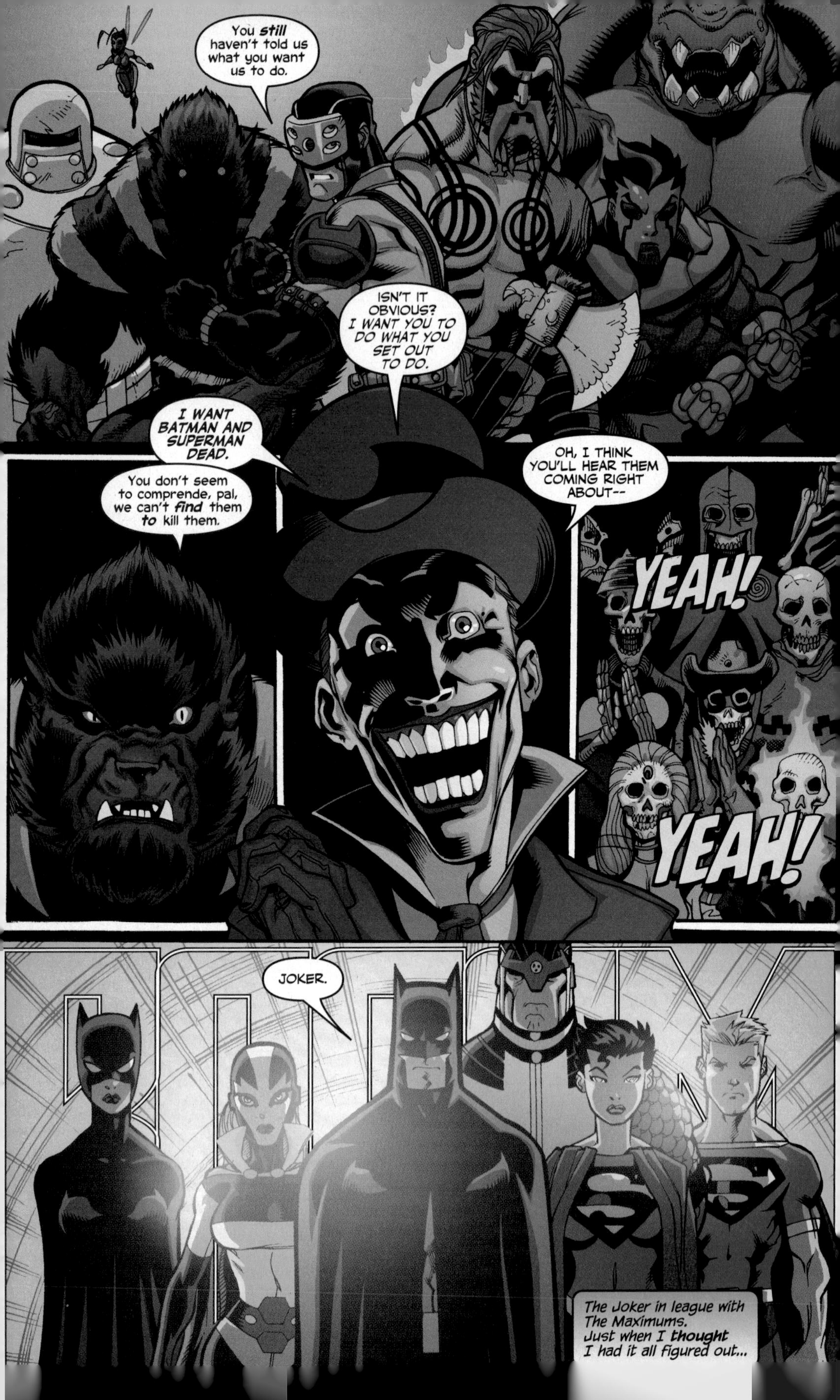
You still haven't told us what you want us to do.
ISN'T IT OBVIOUS? I WANT YOU TO DO WHAT YOU SET OUT TO DO.
I WANT BATMAN AND SUPERMAN DEAD.
You don't seem to comprende, pal, we can't find them to kill them.
OH, I THINK YOU'LL HEAR THEM COMING RIGHT ABOUT--
YEAH!
YEAH!
JOKER.
The Joker in league with The Maximums. Just when I thought I had it all figured out...

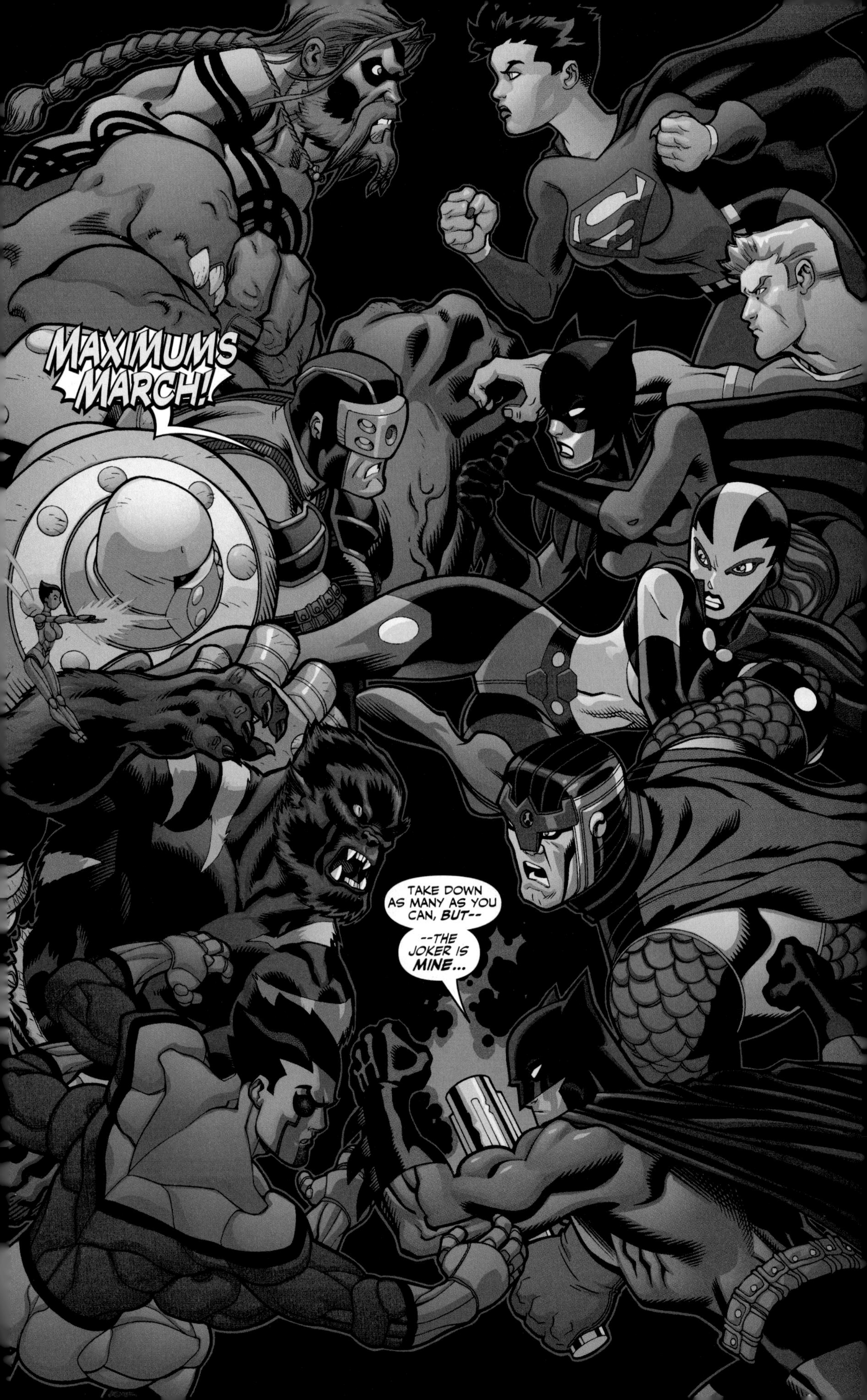
MAXIMUMS MARCH!
TAKE DOWN AS MANY AS YOU CAN, BUT--
--THE JOKER IS MINE...

THIS IS WHAT HAPPENS WHEN YOU TRY TO PUT TOGETHER YOUR OWN *PERSONAL CRISIS*.

YOU GET ALL THESE PEOPLE INVOLVED AND EVERYBODY HAS THEIR OWN OPINIONS.

FEH.

BUT LIKE MOM ALWAYS SAID...

...IF YOU WANT SOMETHING DONE RIGHT...

...YOU HAVE TO MURDER THEM YOURSELF!

ALTHOUGH IT CERTAINLY IS HELPFUL WHEN YOUR VICTIM WEARS A NICE BIG *TARGET* ON HIS CHEST.

BANG

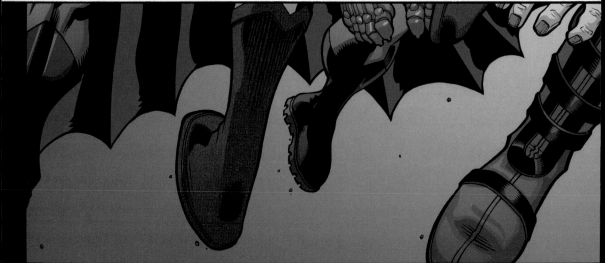

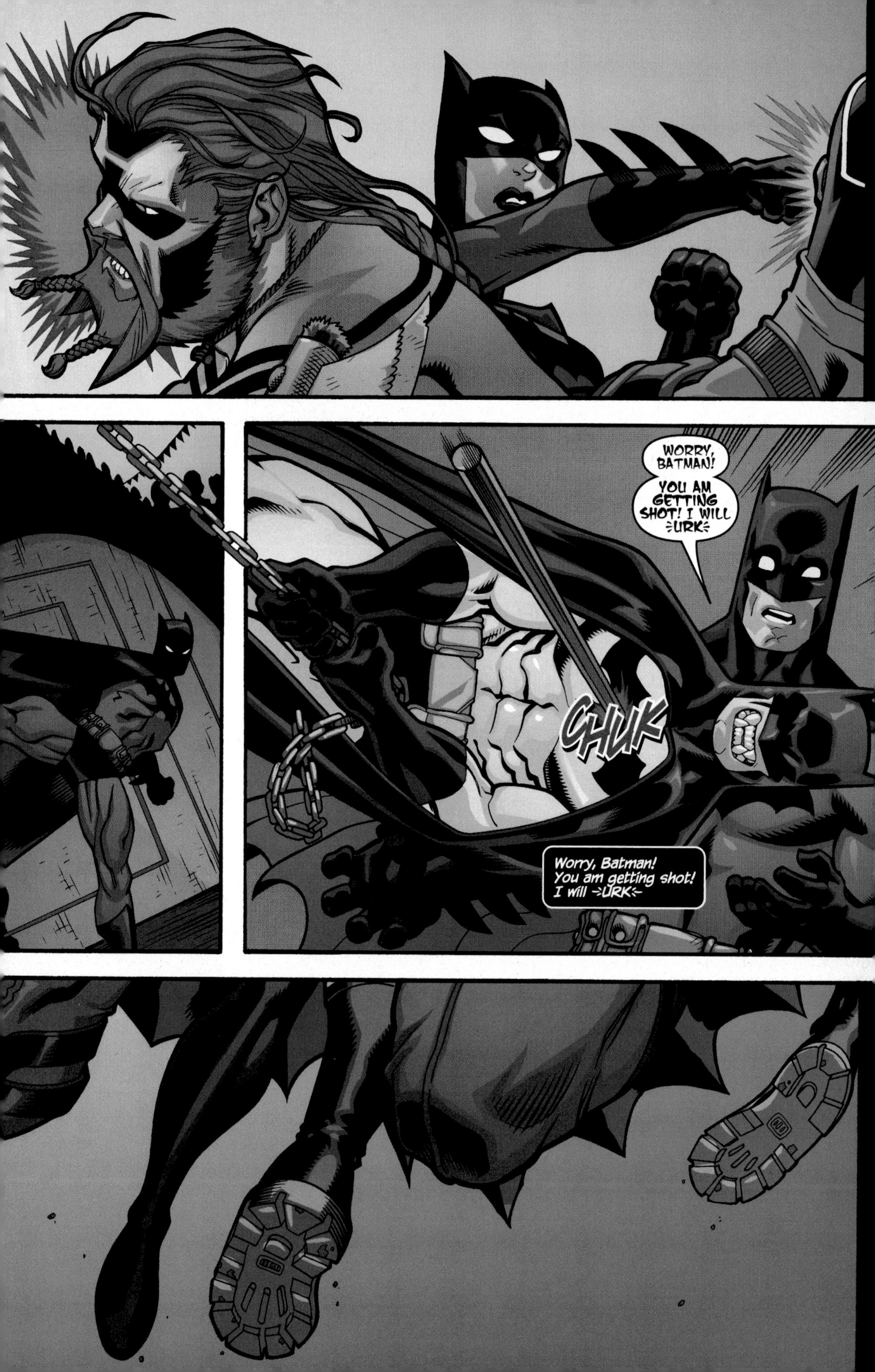 WORRY, BATMAN!
YOU AM GETTING SHOT! I WILL =URK=
CHUK
Worry, Batman! You am getting shot! I will =URK=

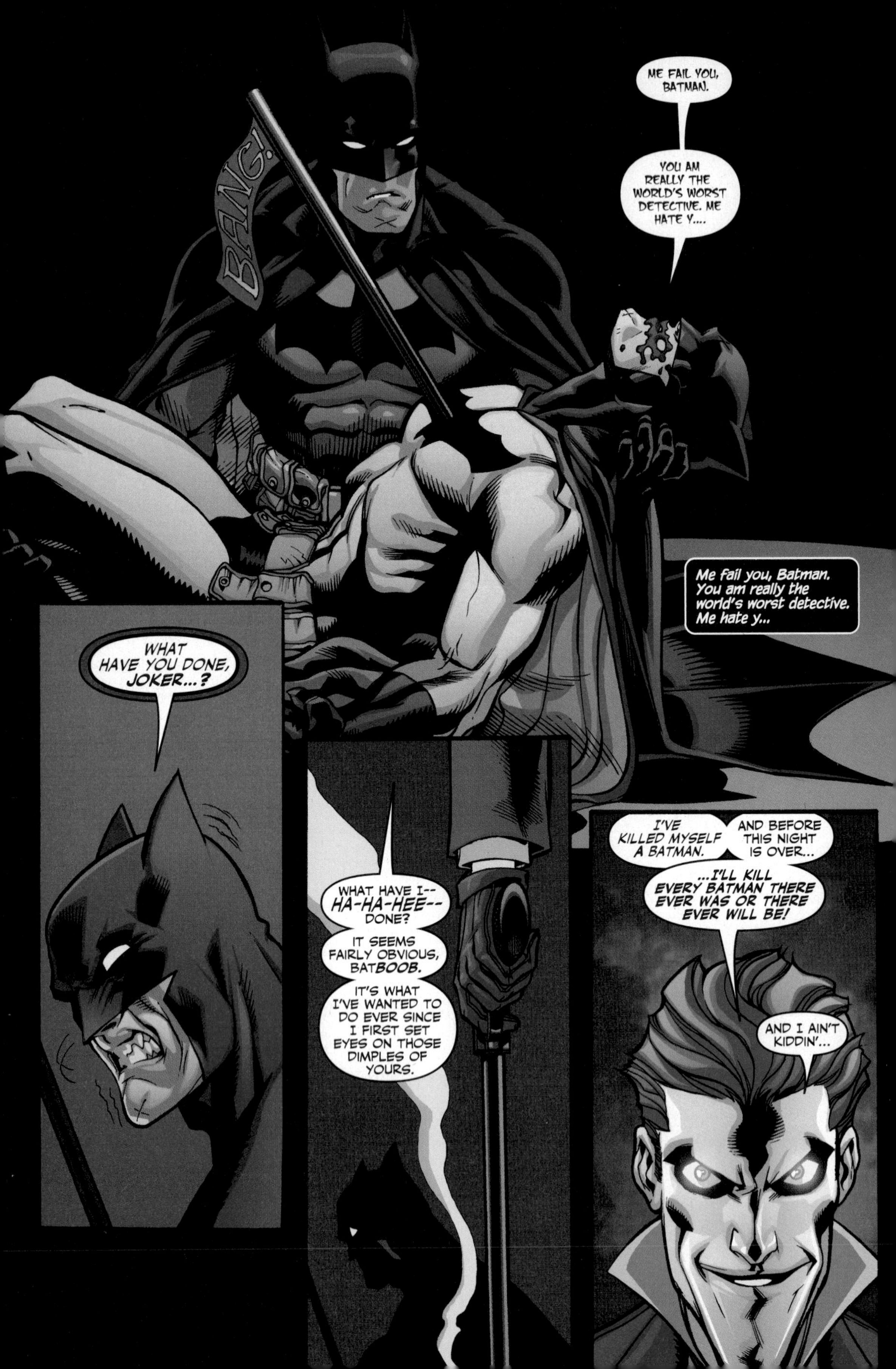
BANG!
ME FAIL YOU, BATMAN.
YOU AM REALLY THE WORLD'S WORST DETECTIVE. ME HATE Y....
Me fail you, Batman. You am really the world's worst detective. Me hate y...
WHAT HAVE YOU DONE, JOKER...?
WHAT HAVE I-- HA-HA-HEE-- DONE?
IT SEEMS FAIRLY OBVIOUS, BATBOOB.
IT'S WHAT I'VE WANTED TO DO EVER SINCE I FIRST SET EYES ON THOSE DIMPLES OF YOURS.
I'VE KILLED MYSELF A BATMAN.
AND BEFORE THIS NIGHT IS OVER...
...I'LL KILL EVERY BATMAN THERE EVER WAS OR THERE EVER WILL BE!
AND I AIN'T KIDDIN'...

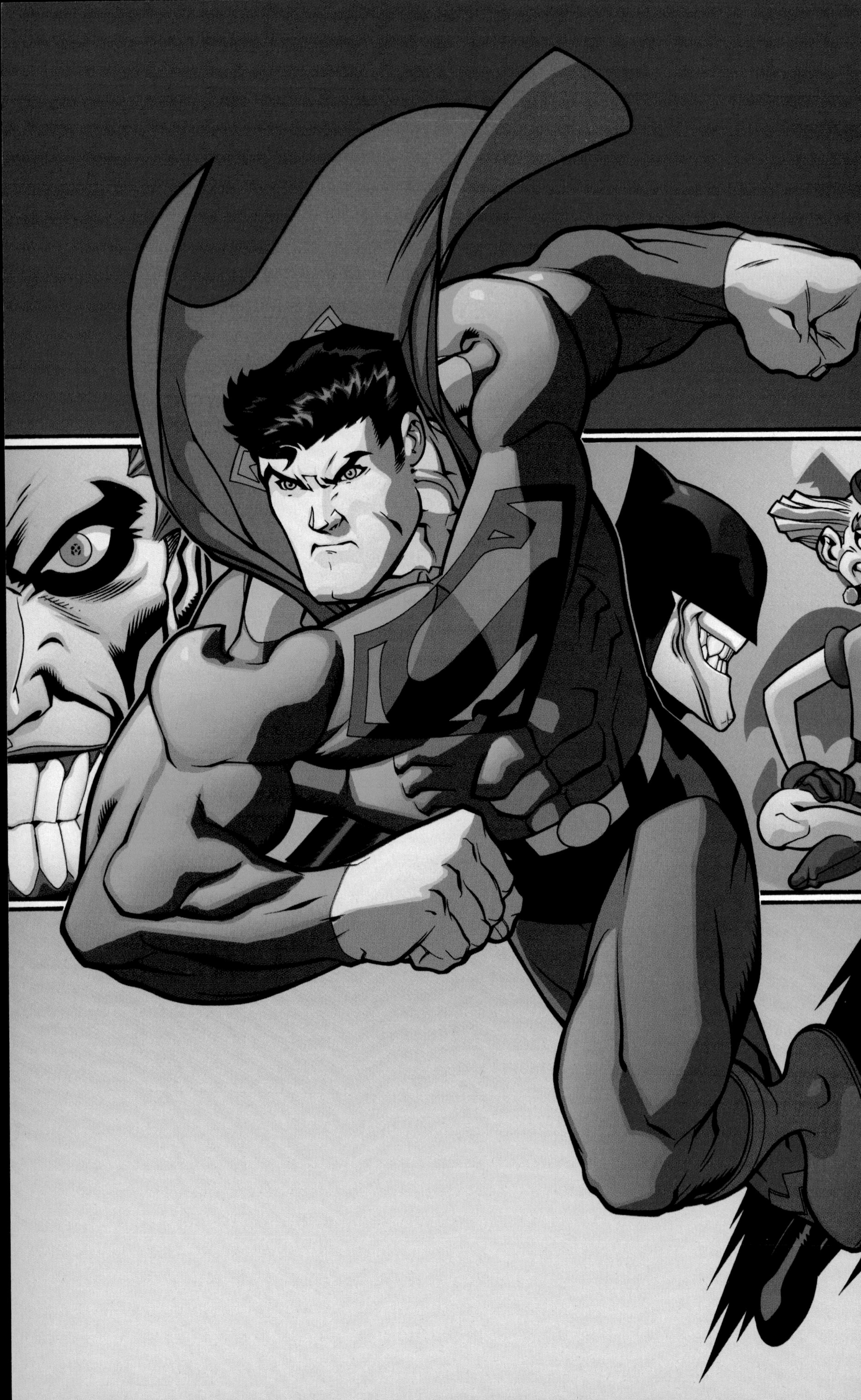

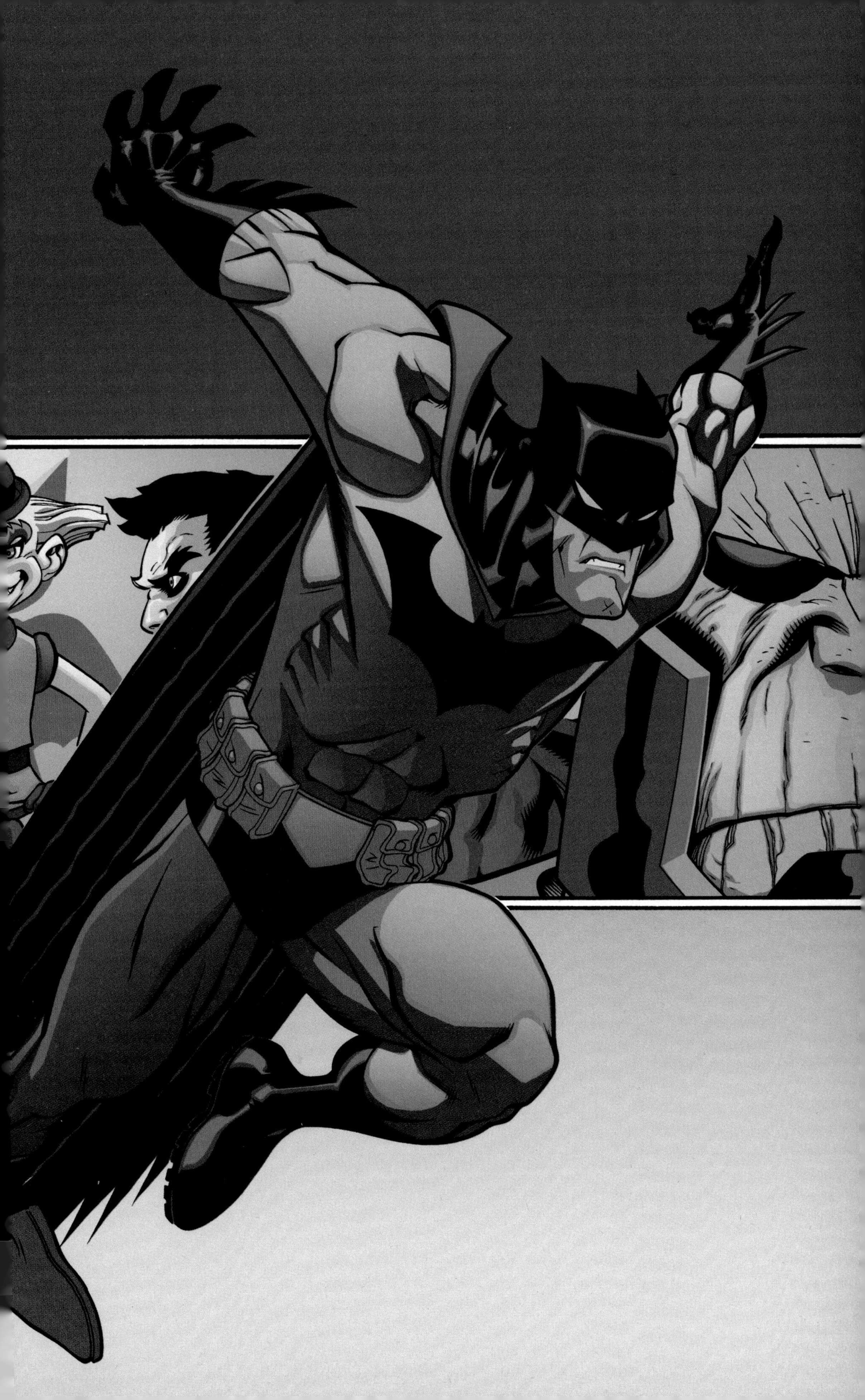

"SUPERMEN / BATMEN"

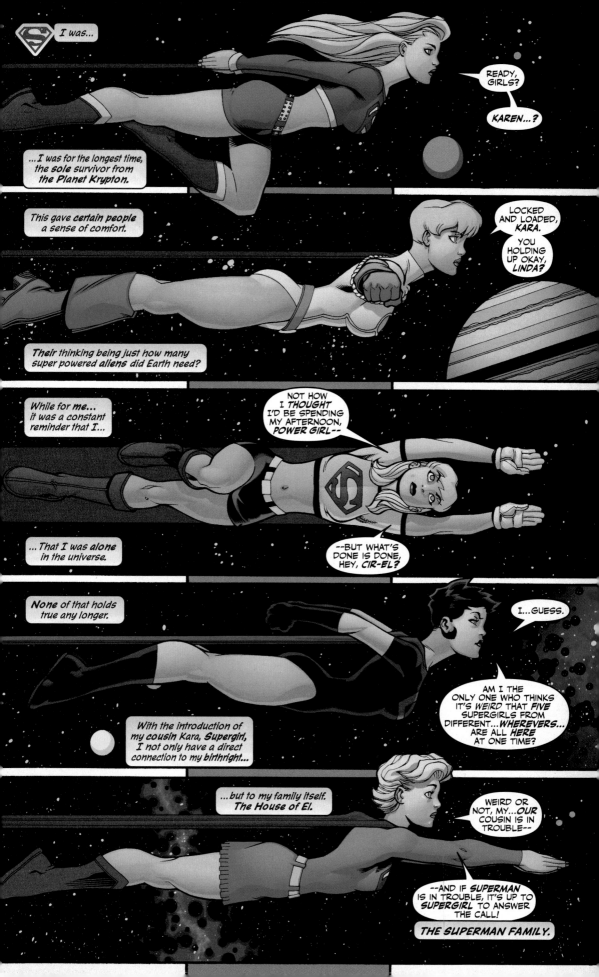

I was...

READY, GIRLS?

KAREN...?

...I was for the longest time, the sole survivor from the Planet Krypton.

This gave certain people a sense of comfort.

LOCKED AND LOADED, KARA.

YOU HOLDING UP OKAY, LINDA?

Their thinking being just how many super powered aliens did Earth need?

While for me... it was a constant reminder that I...

NOT HOW I THOUGHT I'D BE SPENDING MY AFTERNOON, POWER GIRL--

...That I was alone in the universe.

--BUT WHAT'S DONE IS DONE, HEY, CIR-EL?

None of that holds true any longer.

I...GUESS.

AM I THE ONLY ONE WHO THINKS IT'S WEIRD THAT FIVE SUPERGIRLS FROM DIFFERENT...WHEREVERS... ARE ALL HERE AT ONE TIME?

With the introduction of my cousin Kara, Supergirl, I not only have a direct connection to my birthright...

...but to my family itself. The House of El.

WEIRD OR NOT, MY...OUR COUSIN IS IN TROUBLE--

--AND IF SUPERMAN IS IN TROUBLE, IT'S UP TO SUPERGIRL TO ANSWER THE CALL!

THE SUPERMAN FAMILY.

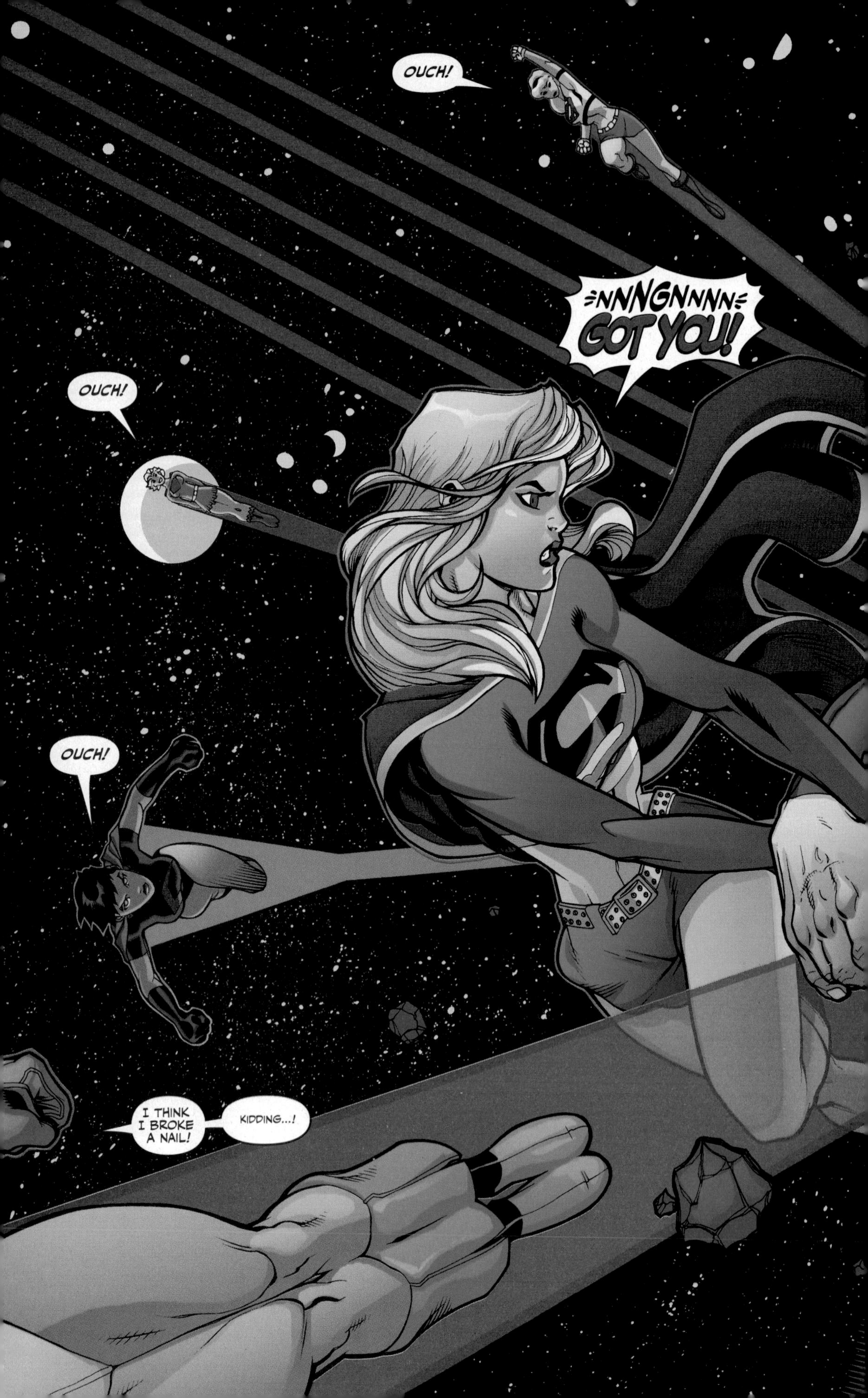
OUCH!
NNNGNNNN GOT YOU!
OUCH!
OUCH!
I THINK I BROKE A NAIL!
KIDDING...!

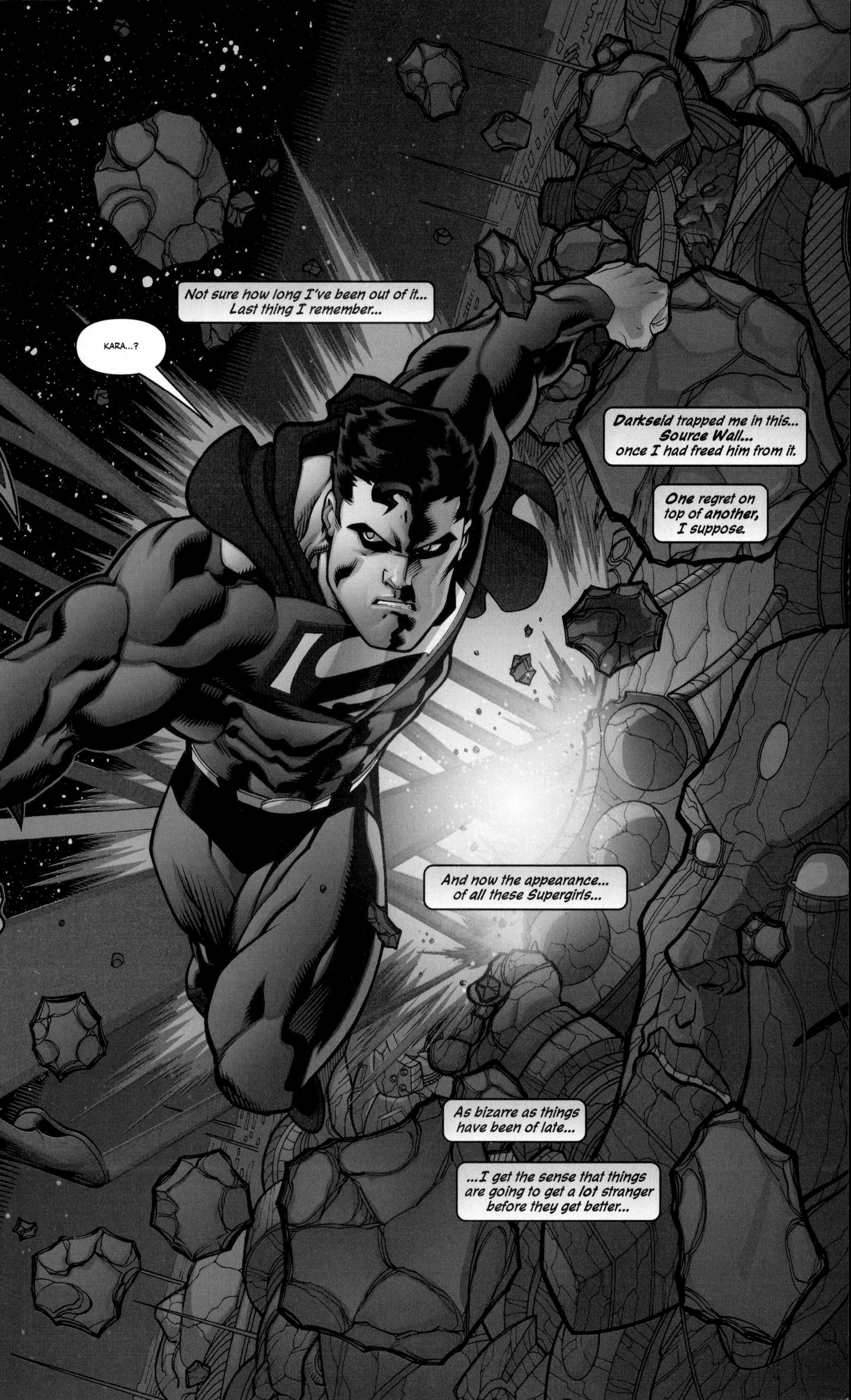
Not sure how long I've been out of it... Last thing I remember...
KARA...?
Darkseid trapped me in this... Source Wall... once I had freed him from it.
One regret on top of another, I suppose.
And now the appearance... of all these Supergirls...
As bizarre as things have been of late...
...I get the sense that things are going to get a lot stranger before they get better...

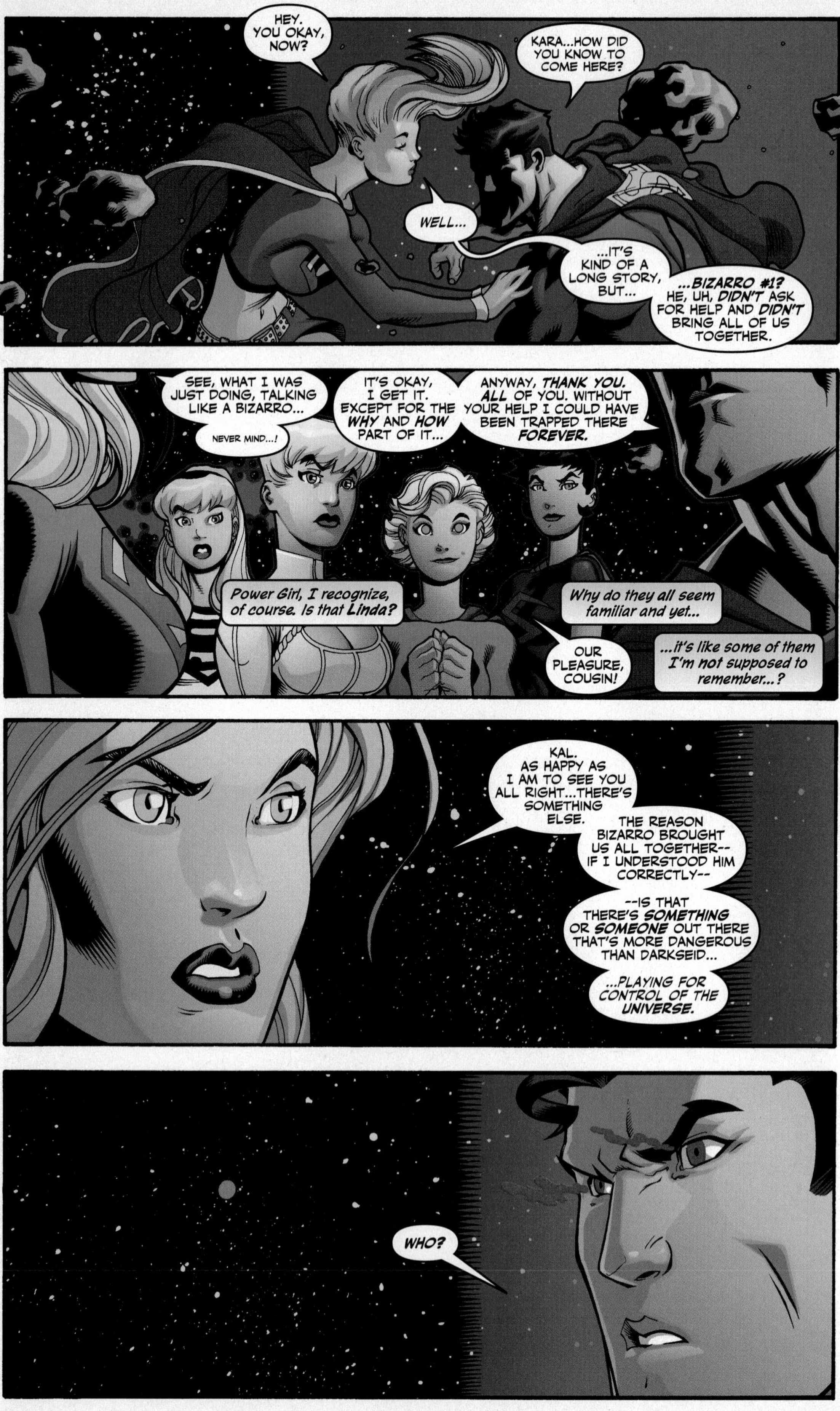
HEY. YOU OKAY, NOW?
KARA...HOW DID YOU KNOW TO COME HERE?
WELL...
...IT'S KIND OF A LONG STORY, BUT...
...BIZARRO #1? HE, UH, DIDN'T ASK FOR HELP AND DIDN'T BRING ALL OF US TOGETHER.
SEE, WHAT I WAS JUST DOING, TALKING LIKE A BIZARRO...
NEVER MIND...!
IT'S OKAY, I GET IT. EXCEPT FOR THE WHY AND HOW PART OF IT...
ANYWAY, THANK YOU. ALL OF YOU. WITHOUT YOUR HELP I COULD HAVE BEEN TRAPPED THERE FOREVER.
Power Girl, I recognize, of course. Is that Linda?
Why do they all seem familiar and yet...
OUR PLEASURE, COUSIN!
...it's like some of them I'm not supposed to remember...?
KAL. AS HAPPY AS I AM TO SEE YOU ALL RIGHT...THERE'S SOMETHING ELSE.
THE REASON BIZARRO BROUGHT US ALL TOGETHER--IF I UNDERSTOOD HIM CORRECTLY--
--IS THAT THERE'S SOMETHING OR SOMEONE OUT THERE THAT'S MORE DANGEROUS THAN DARKSEID...
...PLAYING FOR CONTROL OF THE UNIVERSE.
WHO?

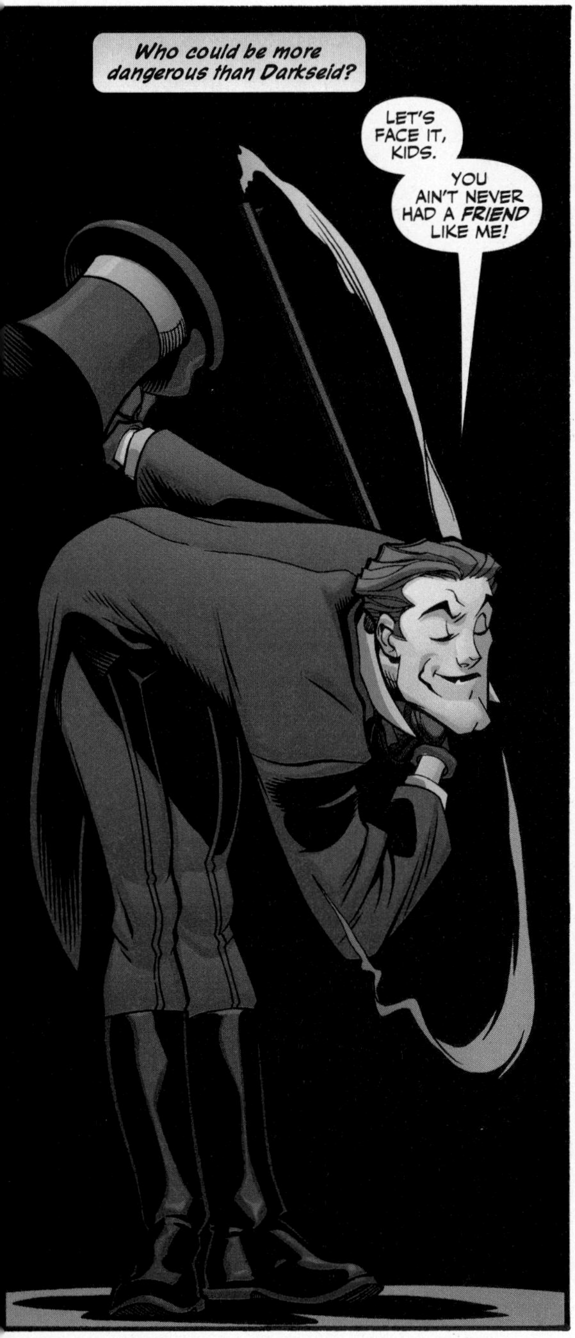
Who could be more dangerous than Darkseid?
LET'S FACE IT, KIDS.
YOU AIN'T NEVER HAD A FRIEND LIKE ME!

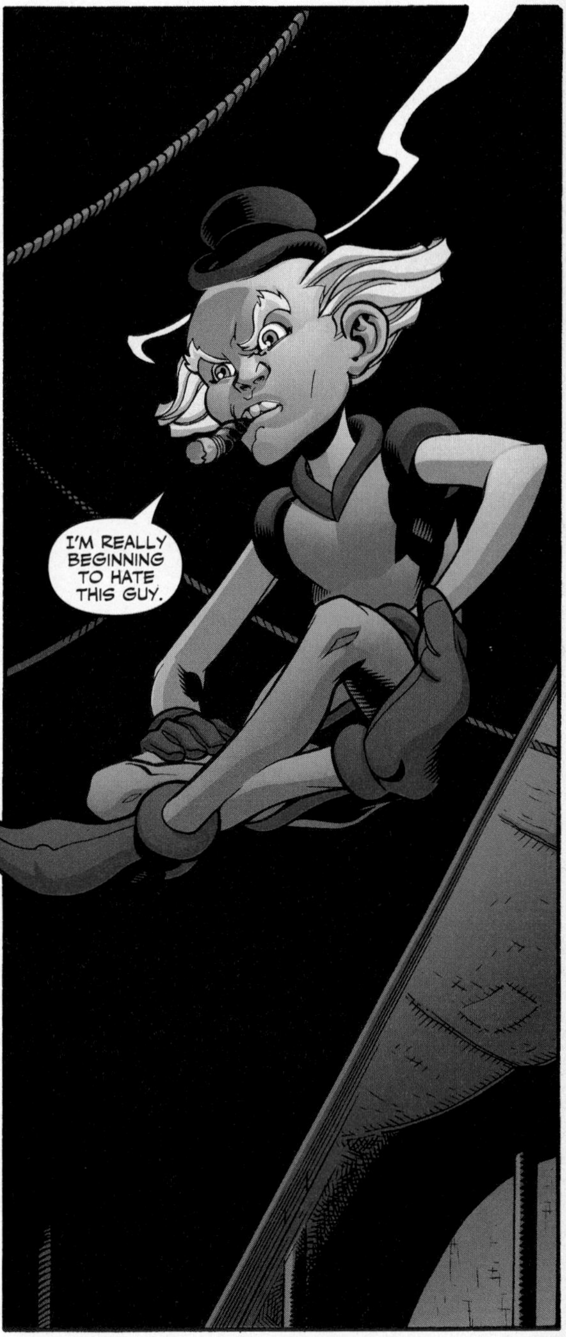
I'M REALLY BEGINNING TO HATE THIS GUY.

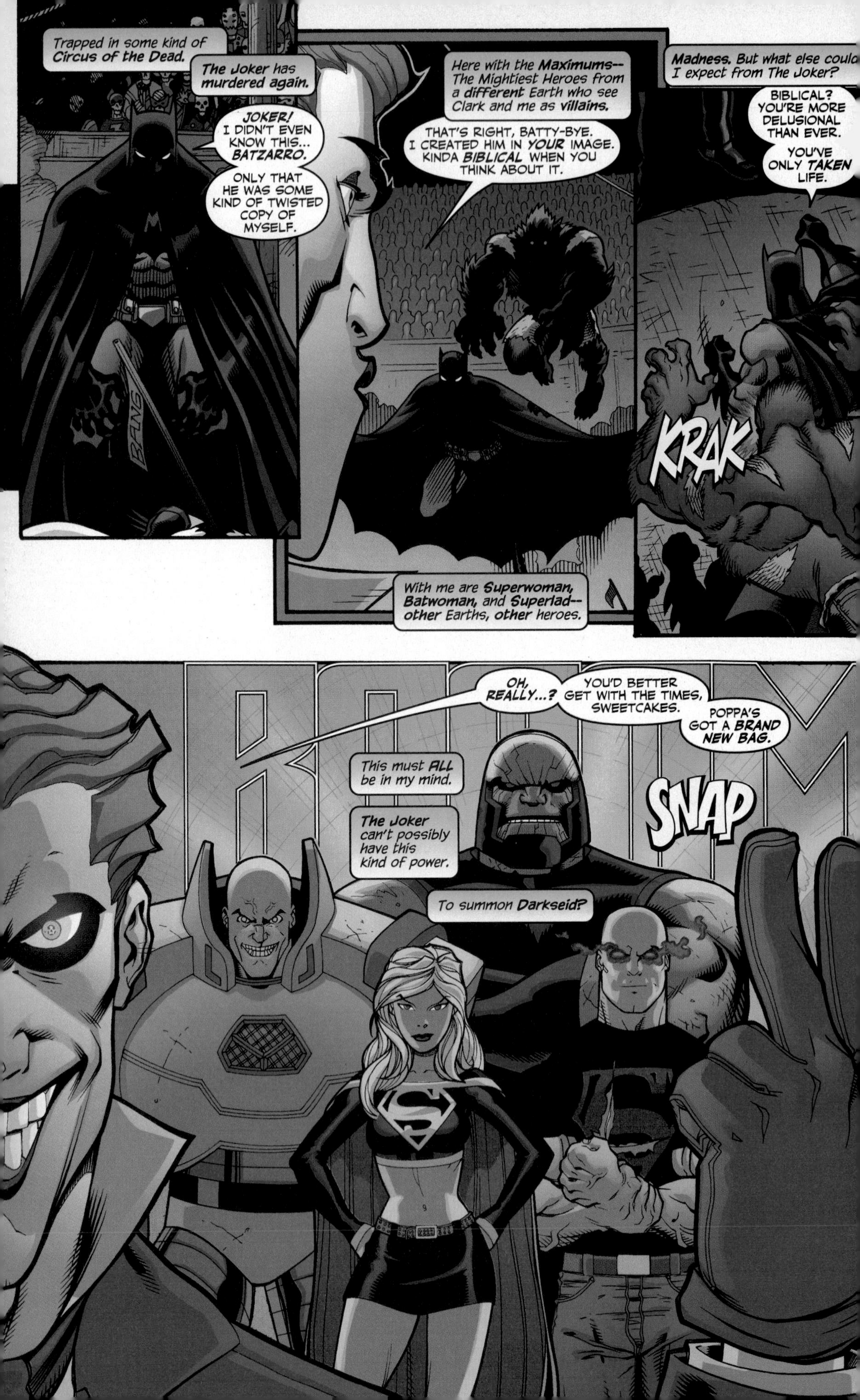

Trapped in some kind of Circus of the Dead.
The Joker has murdered again.
JOKER! I DIDN'T EVEN KNOW THIS... BATZARRO.
ONLY THAT HE WAS SOME KIND OF TWISTED COPY OF MYSELF.
BANG
Here with the Maximums-- The Mightiest Heroes from a different Earth who see Clark and me as villains.
THAT'S RIGHT, BATTY-BYE. I CREATED HIM IN YOUR IMAGE. KINDA BIBLICAL WHEN YOU THINK ABOUT IT.
With me are Superwoman, Batwoman, and Superlad-- other Earths, other heroes.
Madness. But what else could I expect from The Joker?
BIBLICAL? YOU'RE MORE DELUSIONAL THAN EVER.
YOU'VE ONLY TAKEN LIFE.
KRAK
OH, REALLY...?
YOU'D BETTER GET WITH THE TIMES, SWEETCAKES.
POPPA'S GOT A BRAND NEW BAG.
This must ALL be in my mind.
The Joker can't possibly have this kind of power.
To summon Darkseid?
SNAP

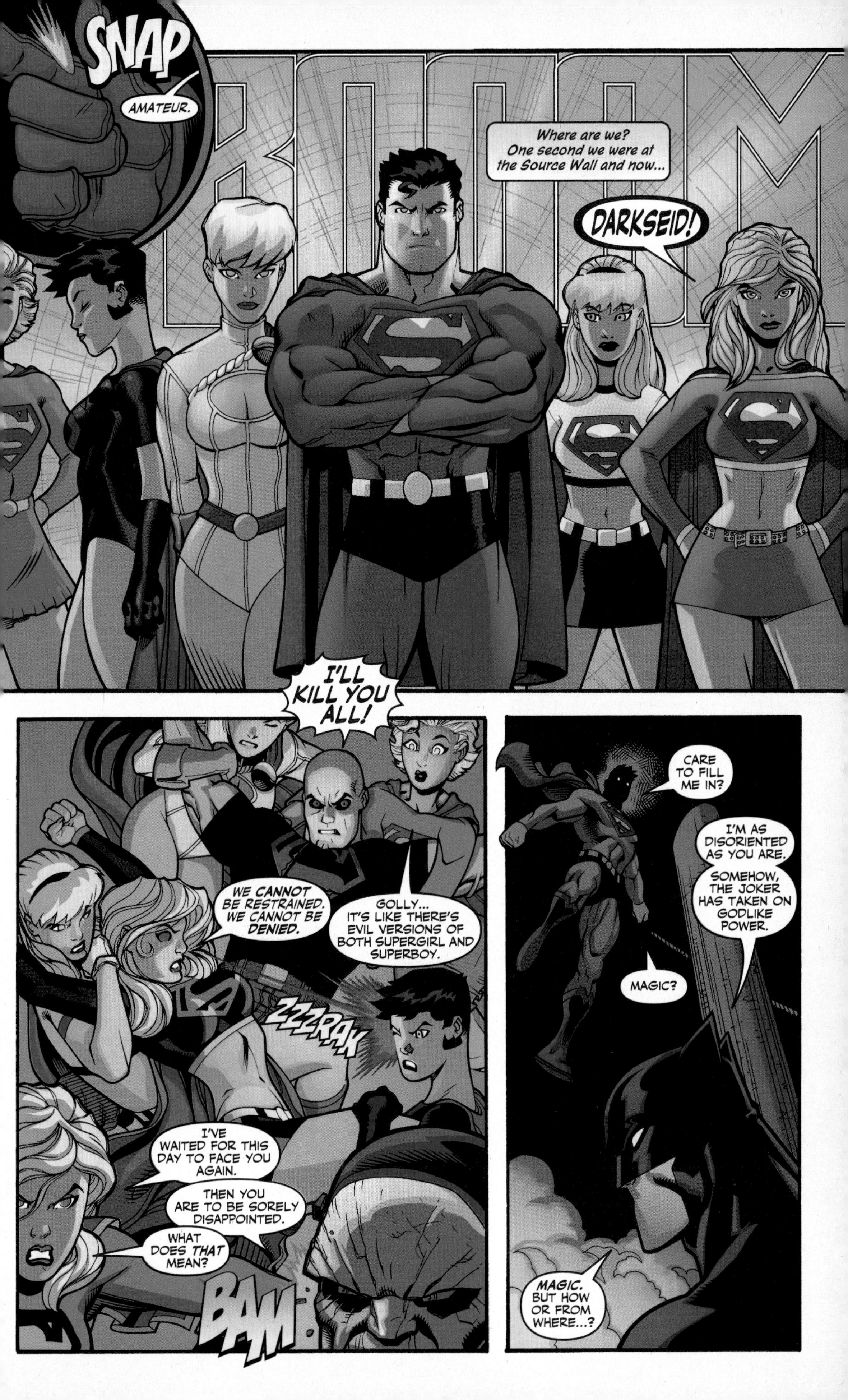
SNAP
AMATEUR.
BOOM
Where are we? One second we were at the Source Wall and now...
DARKSEID!
I'LL KILL YOU ALL!
WE CANNOT BE RESTRAINED. WE CANNOT BE DENIED.
GOLLY... IT'S LIKE THERE'S EVIL VERSIONS OF BOTH SUPERGIRL AND SUPERBOY.
ZZZRAK
I'VE WAITED FOR THIS DAY TO FACE YOU AGAIN.
THEN YOU ARE TO BE SORELY DISAPPOINTED.
WHAT DOES THAT MEAN?
BAM
CARE TO FILL ME IN?
I'M AS DISORIENTED AS YOU ARE.
SOMEHOW, THE JOKER HAS TAKEN ON GODLIKE POWER.
MAGIC?
MAGIC. BUT HOW OR FROM WHERE...?

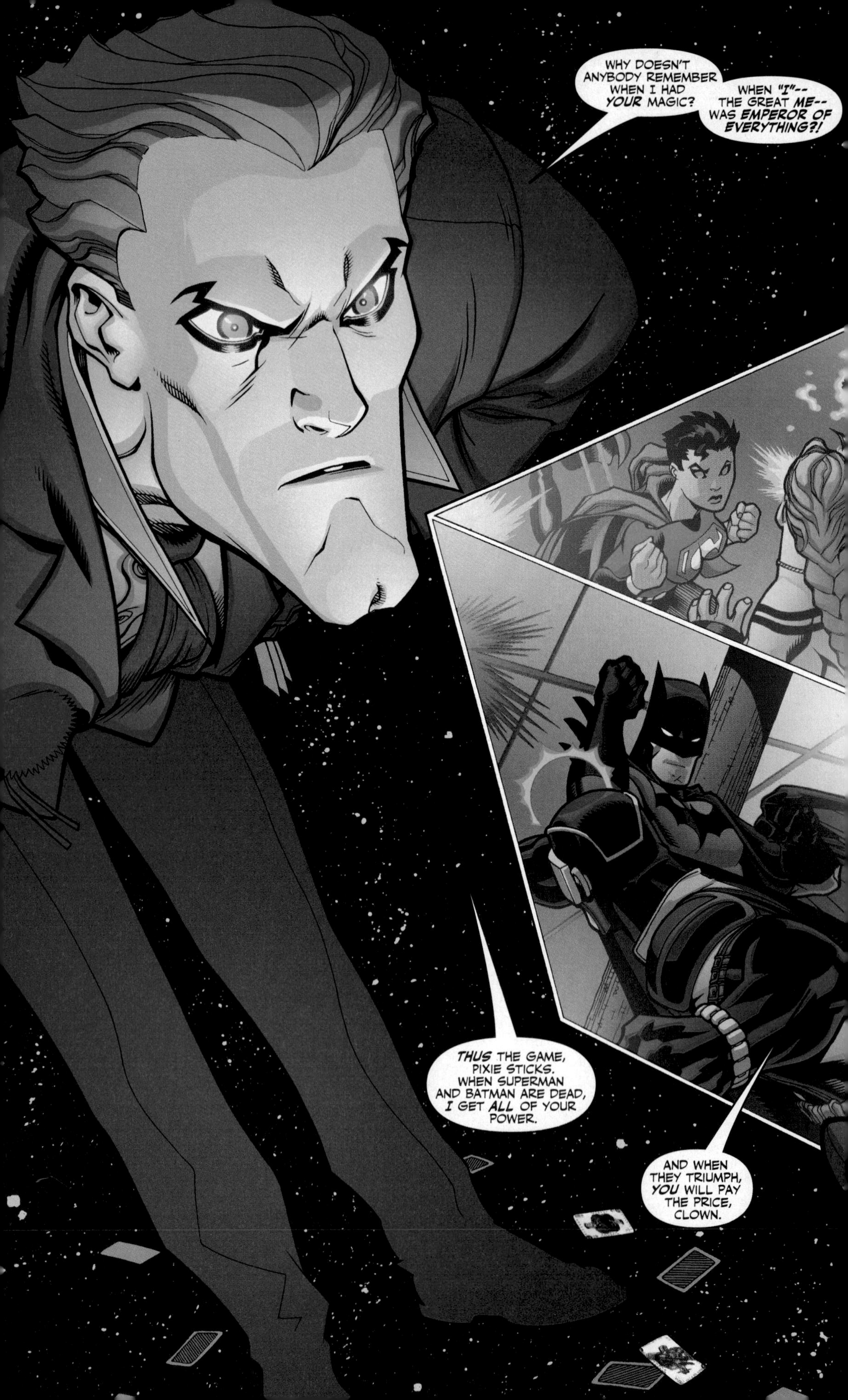
WHY DOESN'T ANYBODY REMEMBER WHEN I HAD *YOUR* MAGIC?
WHEN *"I"*-- THE GREAT *ME*-- WAS *EMPEROR OF EVERYTHING?!*
THUS THE GAME, PIXIE STICKS. WHEN SUPERMAN AND BATMAN ARE DEAD, *I* GET *ALL* OF YOUR POWER.
AND WHEN THEY TRIUMPH, *YOU* WILL PAY THE PRICE, CLOWN.

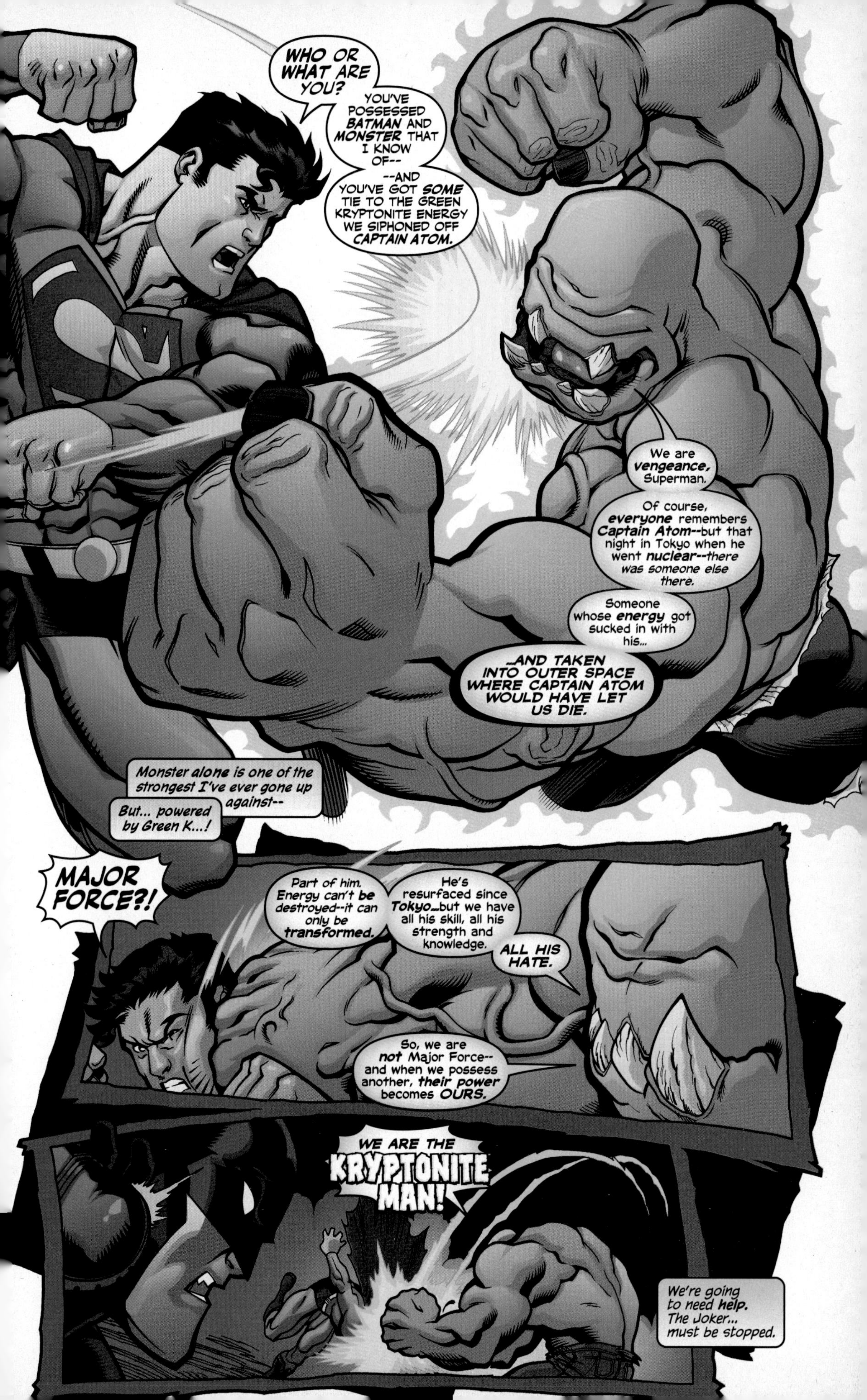
WHO OR WHAT ARE YOU?
YOU'VE POSSESSED BATMAN AND MONSTER THAT I KNOW OF--
--AND YOU'VE GOT SOME TIE TO THE GREEN KRYPTONITE ENERGY WE SIPHONED OFF CAPTAIN ATOM.
We are vengeance, Superman.
Of course, everyone remembers Captain Atom--but that night in Tokyo when he went nuclear--there was someone else there.
Someone whose energy got sucked in with his...
...AND TAKEN INTO OUTER SPACE WHERE CAPTAIN ATOM WOULD HAVE LET US DIE.
Monster alone is one of the strongest I've ever gone up against--
But... powered by Green K...!
MAJOR FORCE?!
Part of him. Energy can't be destroyed--it can only be transformed.
He's resurfaced since Tokyo...but we have all his skill, all his strength and knowledge.
ALL HIS HATE.
So, we are not Major Force--and when we possess another, their power becomes OURS.
WE ARE THE KRYPTONITE MAN!
We're going to need help. The Joker... must be stopped.

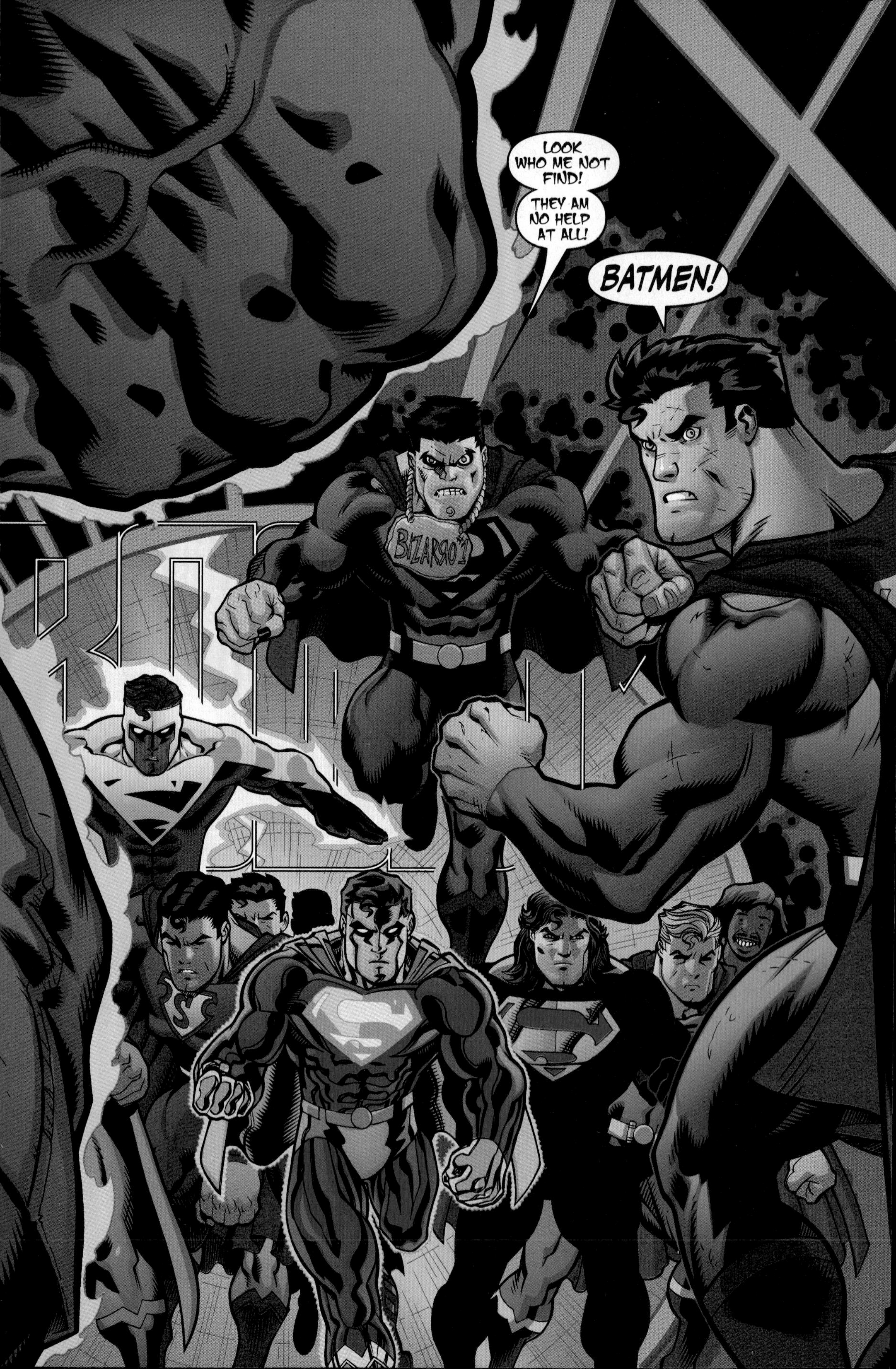
LOOK WHO ME NOT FIND!
THEY AM NO HELP AT ALL!
BATMEN!
BIZARRO 1

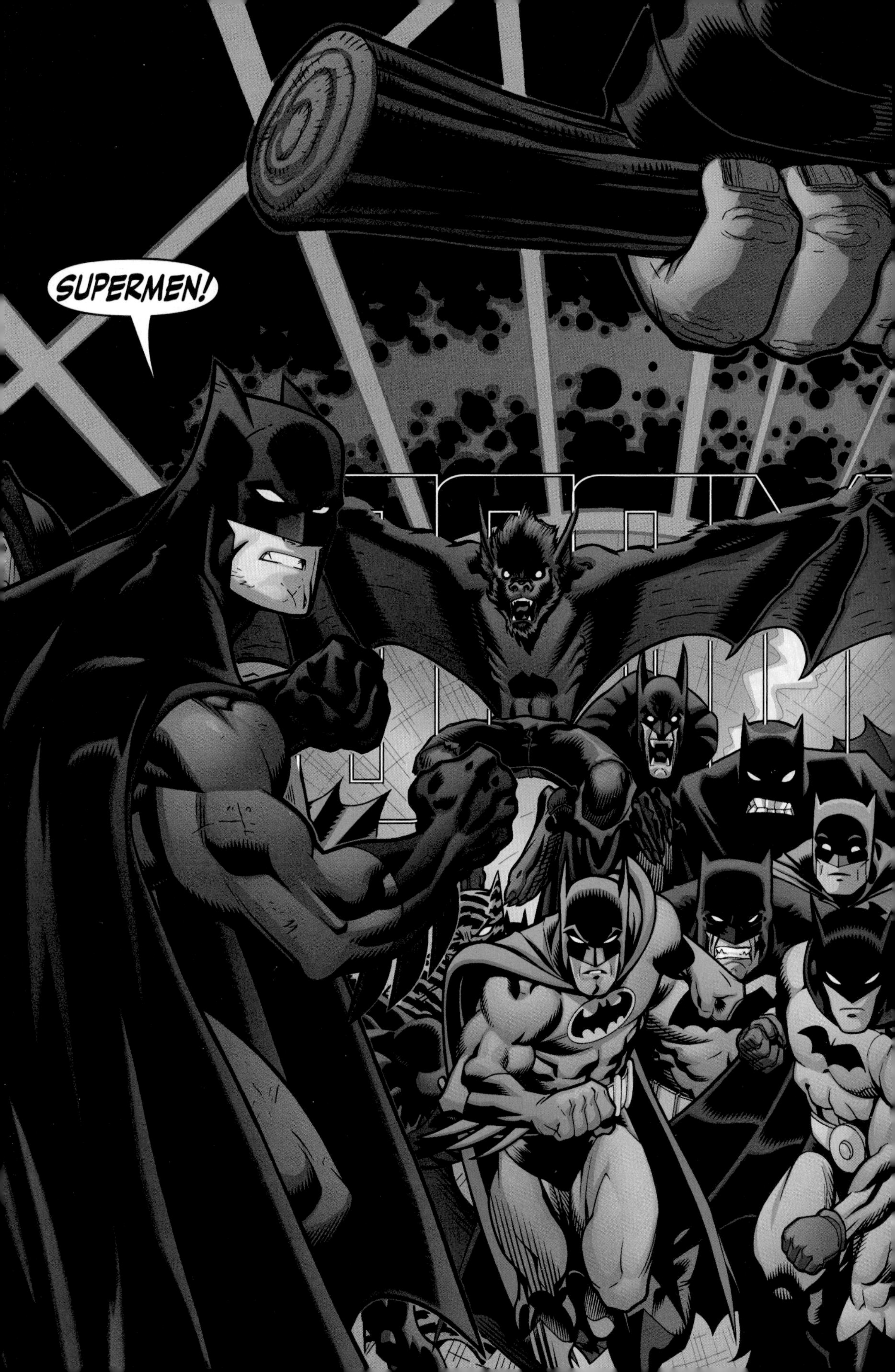
SUPERMEN!

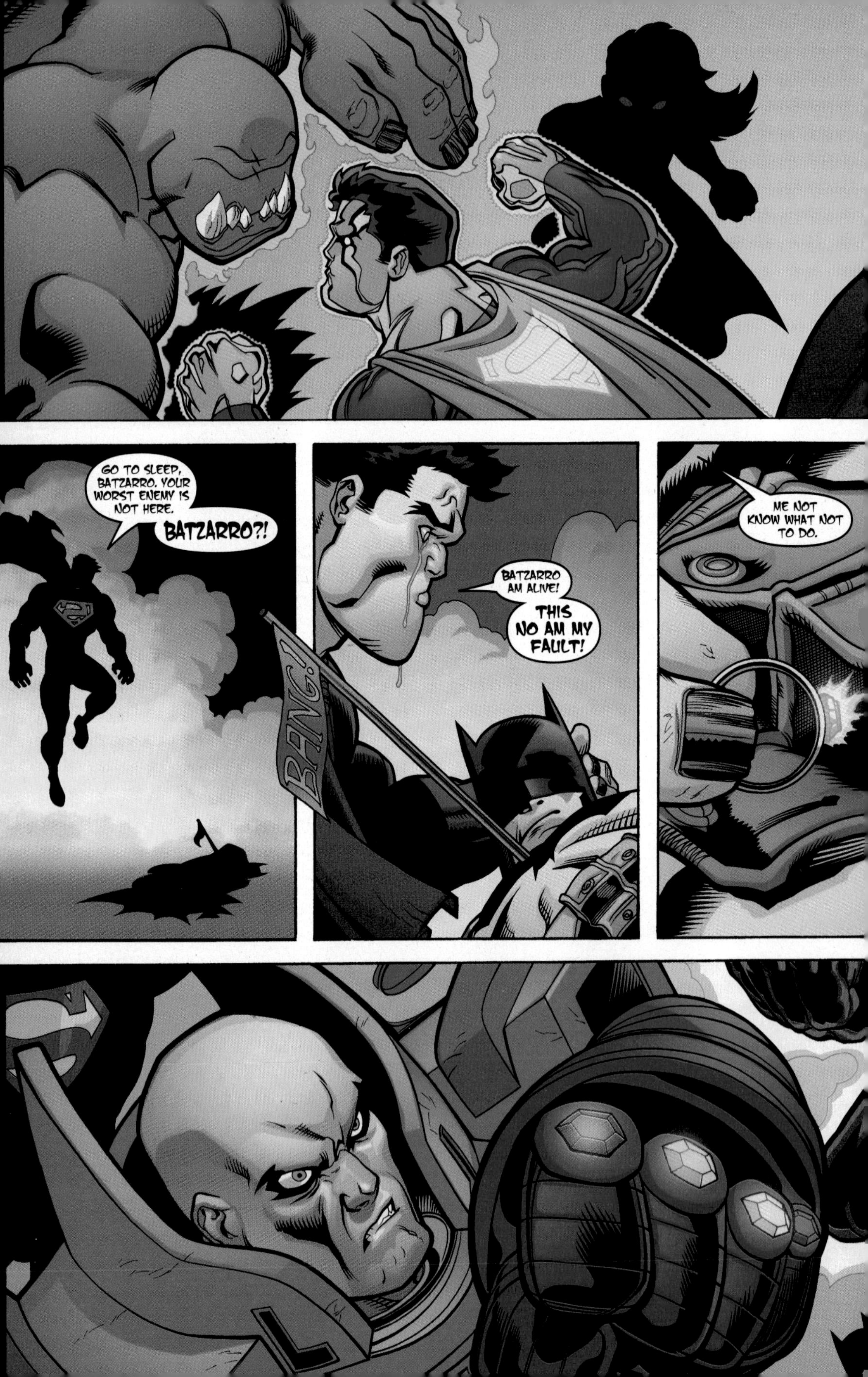
GO TO SLEEP, BATZARRO. YOUR WORST ENEMY IS NOT HERE.
BATZARRO?!
BATZARRO AM ALIVE!
THIS NO AM MY FAULT!
BANG!
ME NOT KNOW WHAT NOT TO DO.

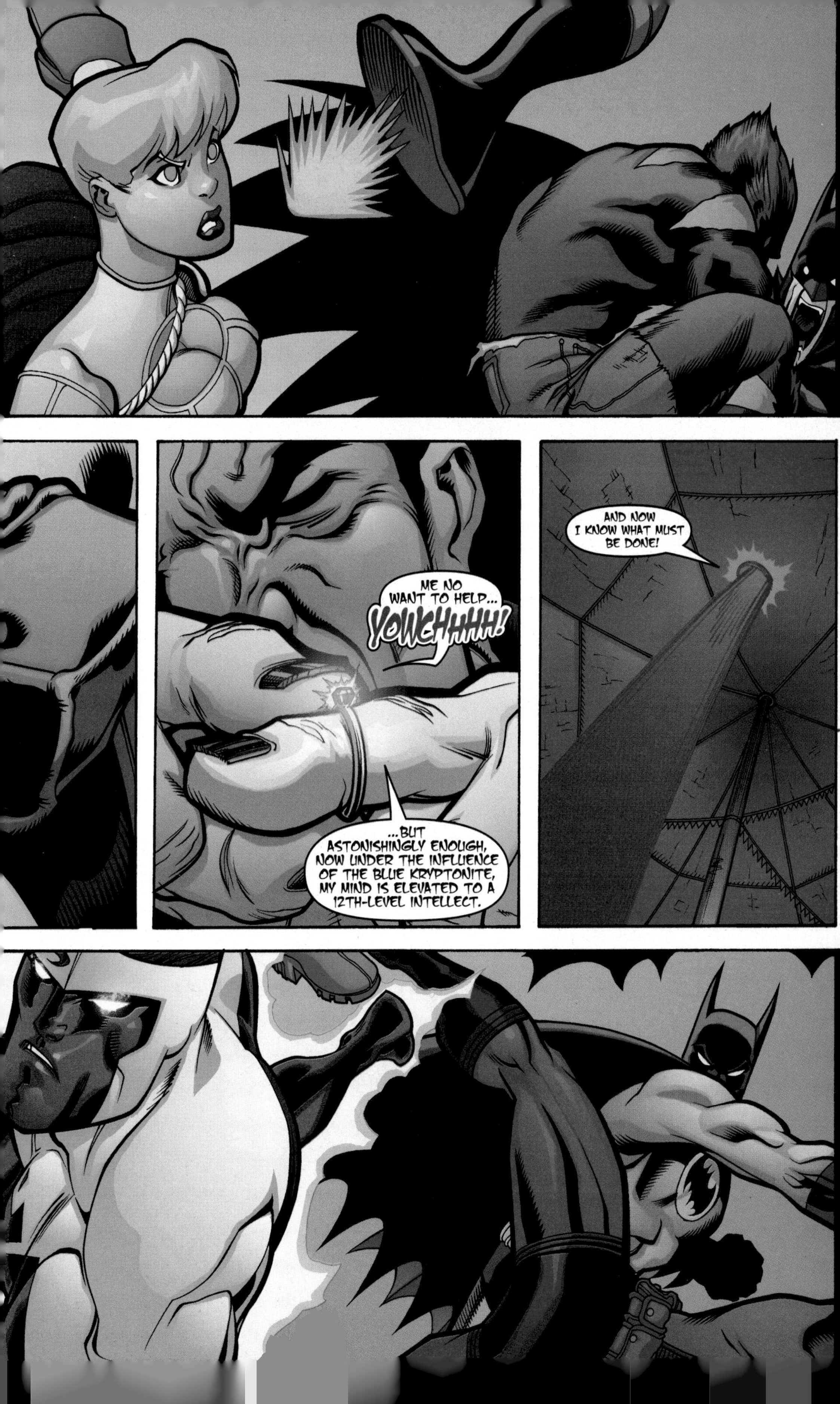
ME NO WANT TO HELP... YOWCHHHH!
...BUT ASTONISHINGLY ENOUGH, NOW UNDER THE INFLUENCE OF THE BLUE KRYPTONITE, MY MIND IS ELEVATED TO A 12TH-LEVEL INTELLECT.
AND NOW I KNOW WHAT MUST BE DONE!

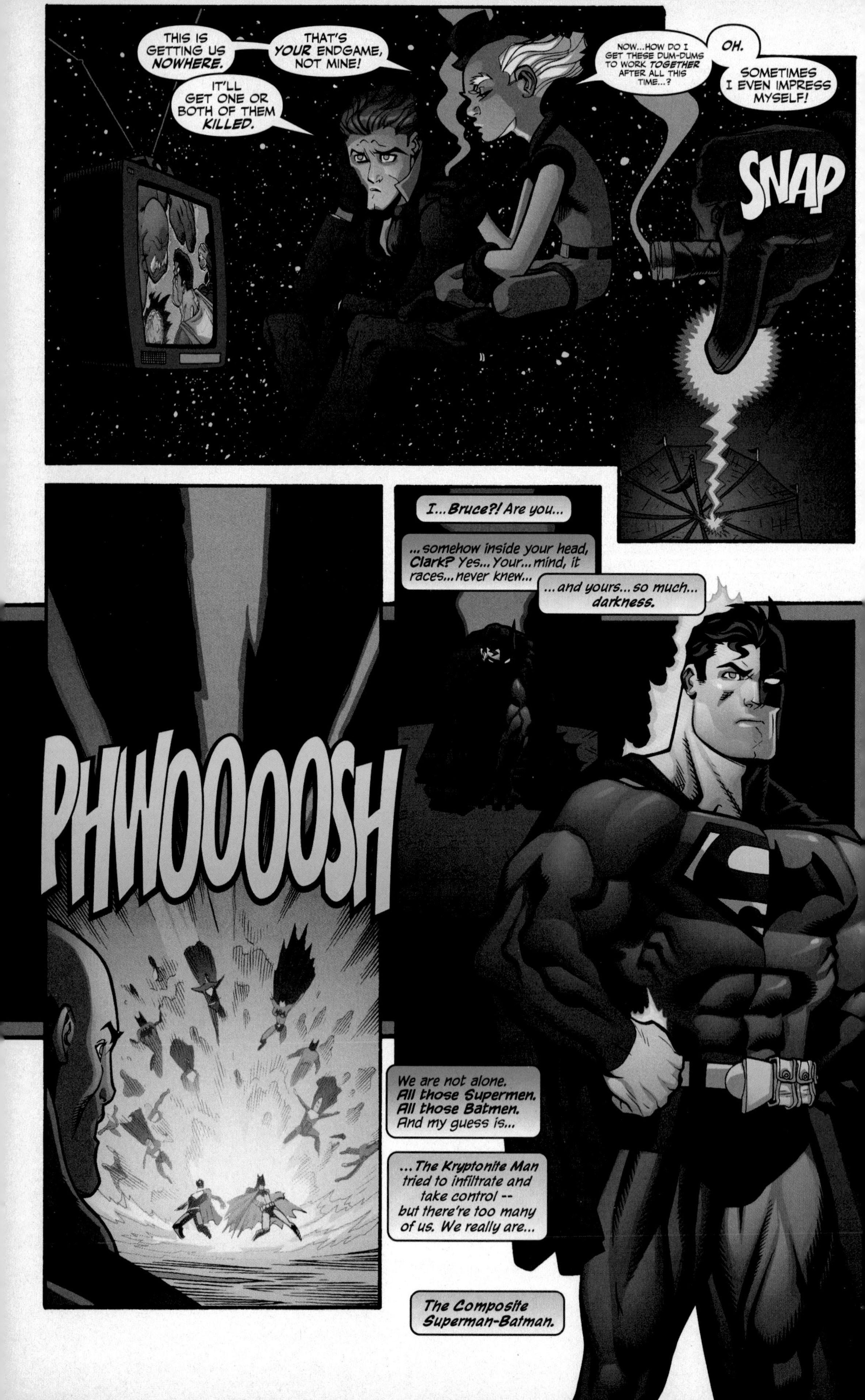

THIS IS GETTING US NOWHERE.
THAT'S YOUR ENDGAME, NOT MINE!
IT'LL GET ONE OR BOTH OF THEM KILLED.
NOW...HOW DO I GET THESE DUM-DUMS TO WORK TOGETHER AFTER ALL THIS TIME...?
OH.
SOMETIMES I EVEN IMPRESS MYSELF!
SNAP
PHWOOOOSH
I...Bruce?! Are you...
...somehow inside your head, Clark? Yes... Your... mind, it races... never knew...
...and yours... so much... darkness.
We are not alone. All those Supermen. All those Batmen. And my guess is...
...The Kryptonite Man tried to infiltrate and take control -- but there're too many of us. We really are...
The Composite Superman-Batman.

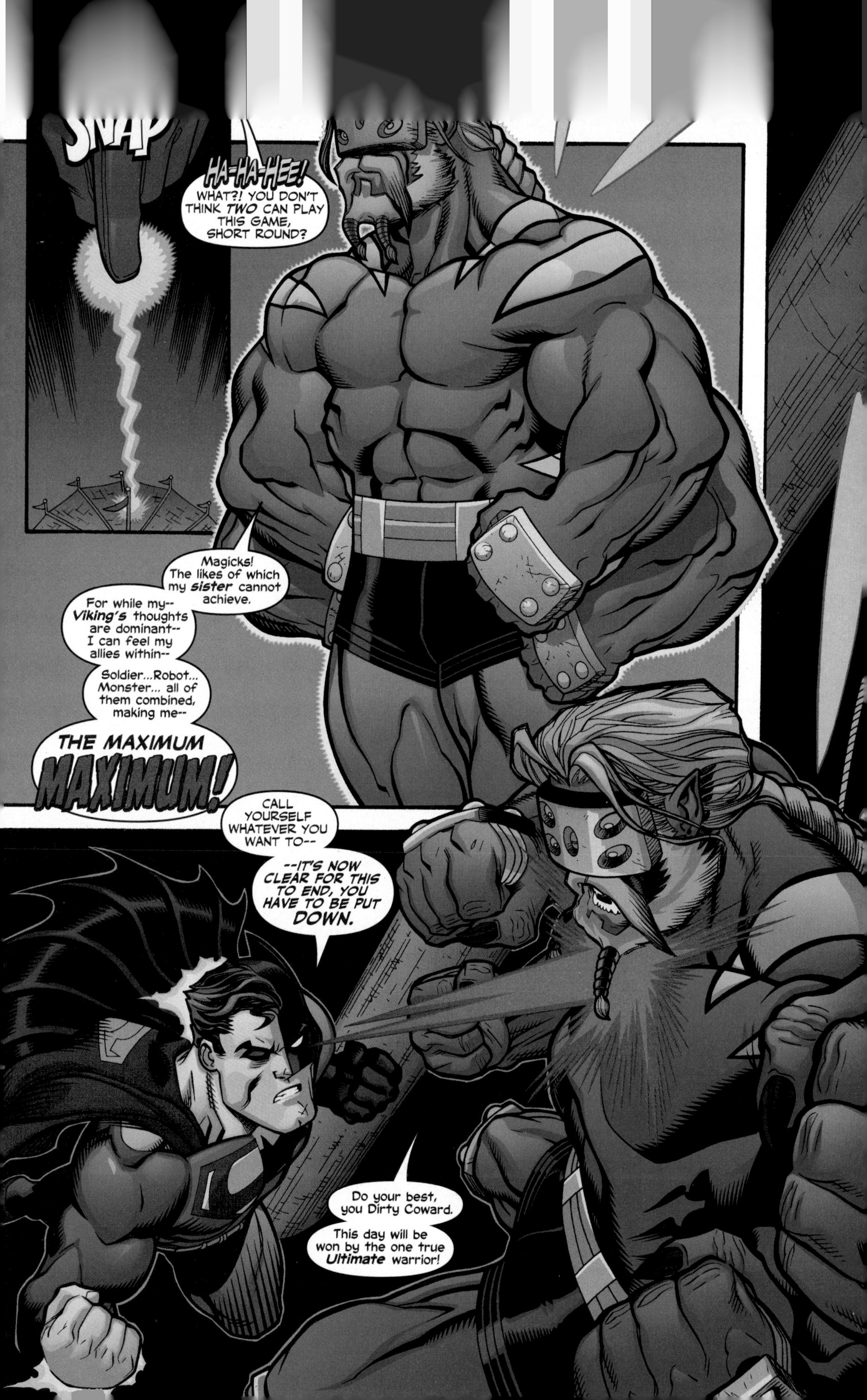
SNAP
HA-HA-HEE!
WHAT?! YOU DON'T THINK TWO CAN PLAY THIS GAME, SHORT ROUND?
Magicks! The likes of which my sister cannot achieve.
For while my-- Viking's thoughts are dominant-- I can feel my allies within--
Soldier...Robot... Monster... all of them combined, making me--
THE MAXIMUM MAXIMUM!
CALL YOURSELF WHATEVER YOU WANT TO--
--IT'S NOW CLEAR FOR THIS TO END, YOU HAVE TO BE PUT DOWN.
Do your best, you Dirty Coward.
This day will be won by the one true Ultimate warrior!

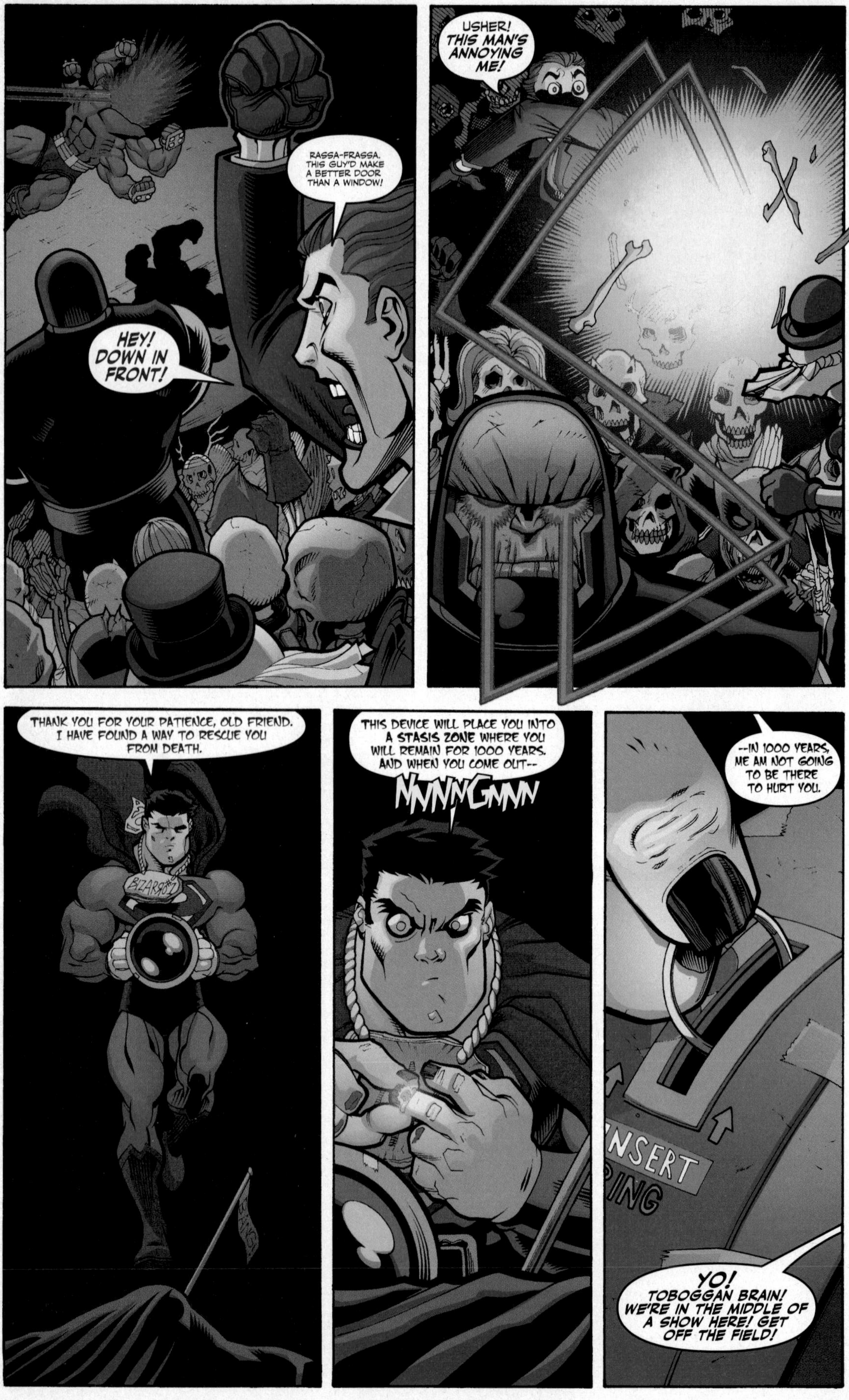
RASSA-FRASSA. THIS GUY'D MAKE A BETTER DOOR THAN A WINDOW!
HEY! DOWN IN FRONT!
USHER! THIS MAN'S ANNOYING ME!
THANK YOU FOR YOUR PATIENCE, OLD FRIEND. I HAVE FOUND A WAY TO RESCUE YOU FROM DEATH.
BIZARRO#1
THIS DEVICE WILL PLACE YOU INTO A STASIS ZONE WHERE YOU WILL REMAIN FOR 1000 YEARS. AND WHEN YOU COME OUT--
NNNNGNNN
--IN 1000 YEARS, ME AM NOT GOING TO BE THERE TO HURT YOU.
INSERT
RING
YO! TOBOGGAN BRAIN! WE'RE IN THE MIDDLE OF A SHOW HERE! GET OFF THE FIELD!

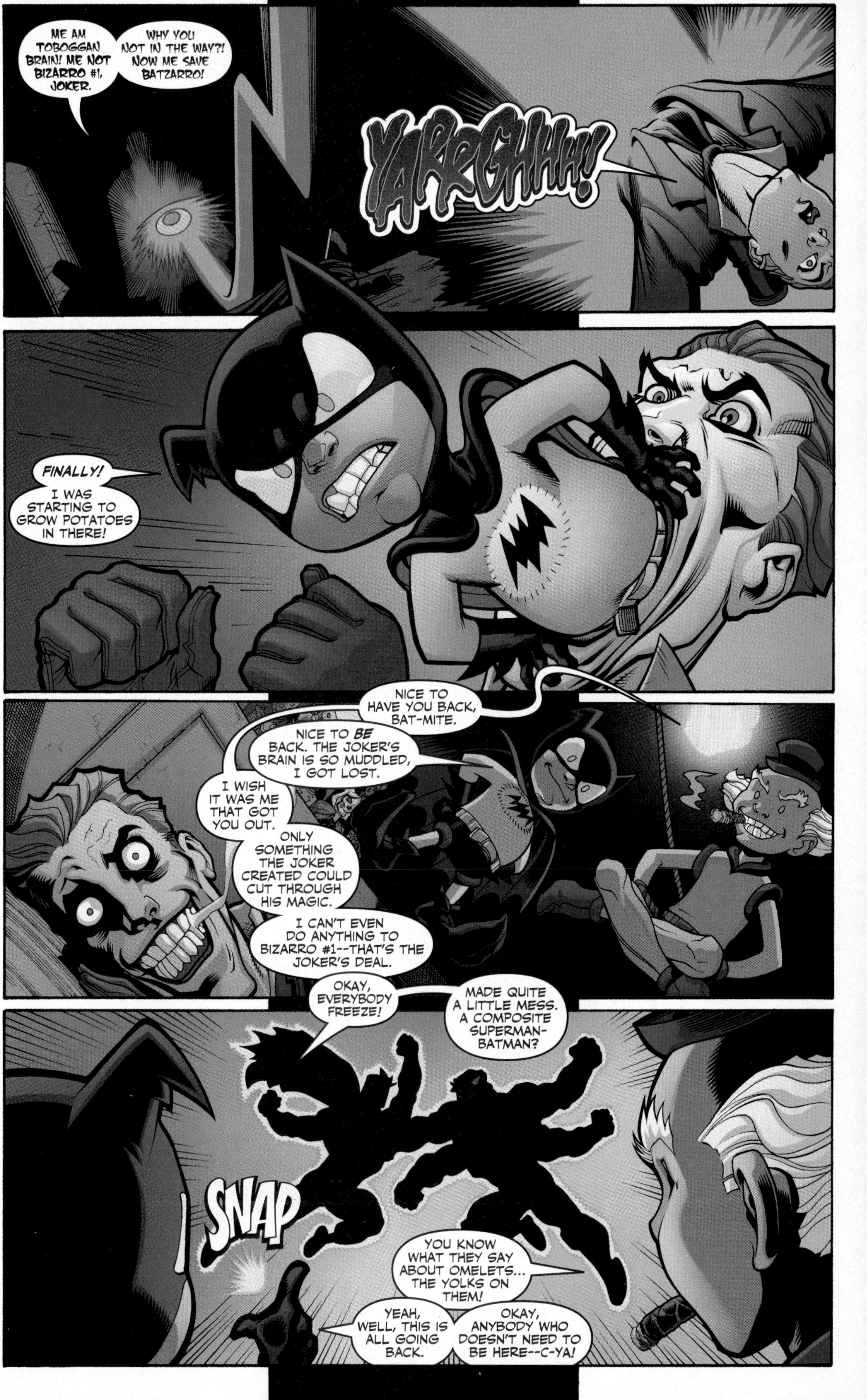
ME AM TOBOGGAN BRAIN! ME NOT BIZARRO #1, JOKER.
WHY YOU NOT IN THE WAY?! NOW ME SAVE BATZARRO!
YARRGHHH!
FINALLY! I WAS STARTING TO GROW POTATOES IN THERE!
NICE TO HAVE YOU BACK, BAT-MITE.
NICE TO BE BACK. THE JOKER'S BRAIN IS SO MUDDLED, I GOT LOST.
I WISH IT WAS ME THAT GOT YOU OUT.
ONLY SOMETHING THE JOKER CREATED COULD CUT THROUGH HIS MAGIC.
I CAN'T EVEN DO ANYTHING TO BIZARRO #1--THAT'S THE JOKER'S DEAL.
OKAY, EVERYBODY FREEZE!
MADE QUITE A LITTLE MESS. A COMPOSITE SUPERMAN-BATMAN?
SNAP
YOU KNOW WHAT THEY SAY ABOUT OMELETS... THE YOLKS ON THEM!
YEAH, WELL, THIS IS ALL GOING BACK.
OKAY, ANYBODY WHO DOESN'T NEED TO BE HERE--C-YA!

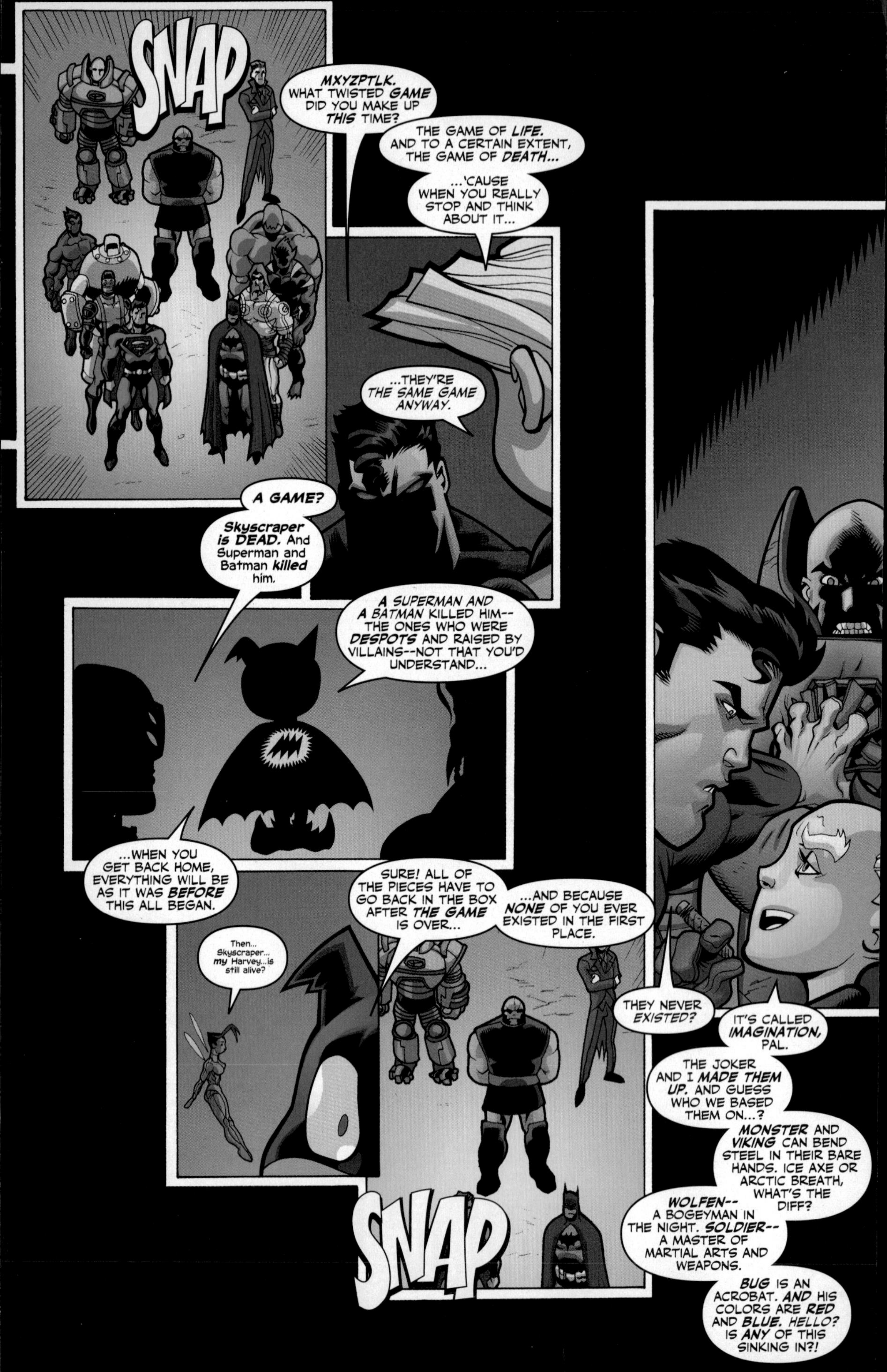
SNAP
MXYZPTLK. WHAT TWISTED GAME DID YOU MAKE UP THIS TIME?
THE GAME OF LIFE. AND TO A CERTAIN EXTENT, THE GAME OF DEATH...
...'CAUSE WHEN YOU REALLY STOP AND THINK ABOUT IT...
...THEY'RE THE SAME GAME ANYWAY.
A GAME?
Skyscraper is DEAD. And Superman and Batman killed him.
A SUPERMAN AND A BATMAN KILLED HIM-- THE ONES WHO WERE DESPOTS AND RAISED BY VILLAINS--NOT THAT YOU'D UNDERSTAND...
...WHEN YOU GET BACK HOME, EVERYTHING WILL BE AS IT WAS BEFORE THIS ALL BEGAN.
Then... Skyscraper... my Harvey...is still alive?
SURE! ALL OF THE PIECES HAVE TO GO BACK IN THE BOX AFTER THE GAME IS OVER...
...AND BECAUSE NONE OF YOU EVER EXISTED IN THE FIRST PLACE.
THEY NEVER EXISTED?
IT'S CALLED IMAGINATION, PAL.
THE JOKER AND I MADE THEM UP. AND GUESS WHO WE BASED THEM ON...?
MONSTER AND VIKING CAN BEND STEEL IN THEIR BARE HANDS. ICE AXE OR ARCTIC BREATH, WHAT'S THE DIFF?
WOLFEN-- A BOGEYMAN IN THE NIGHT. SOLDIER-- A MASTER OF MARTIAL ARTS AND WEAPONS.
BUG IS AN ACROBAT. AND HIS COLORS ARE RED AND BLUE. HELLO? IS ANY OF THIS SINKING IN?!
SNAP

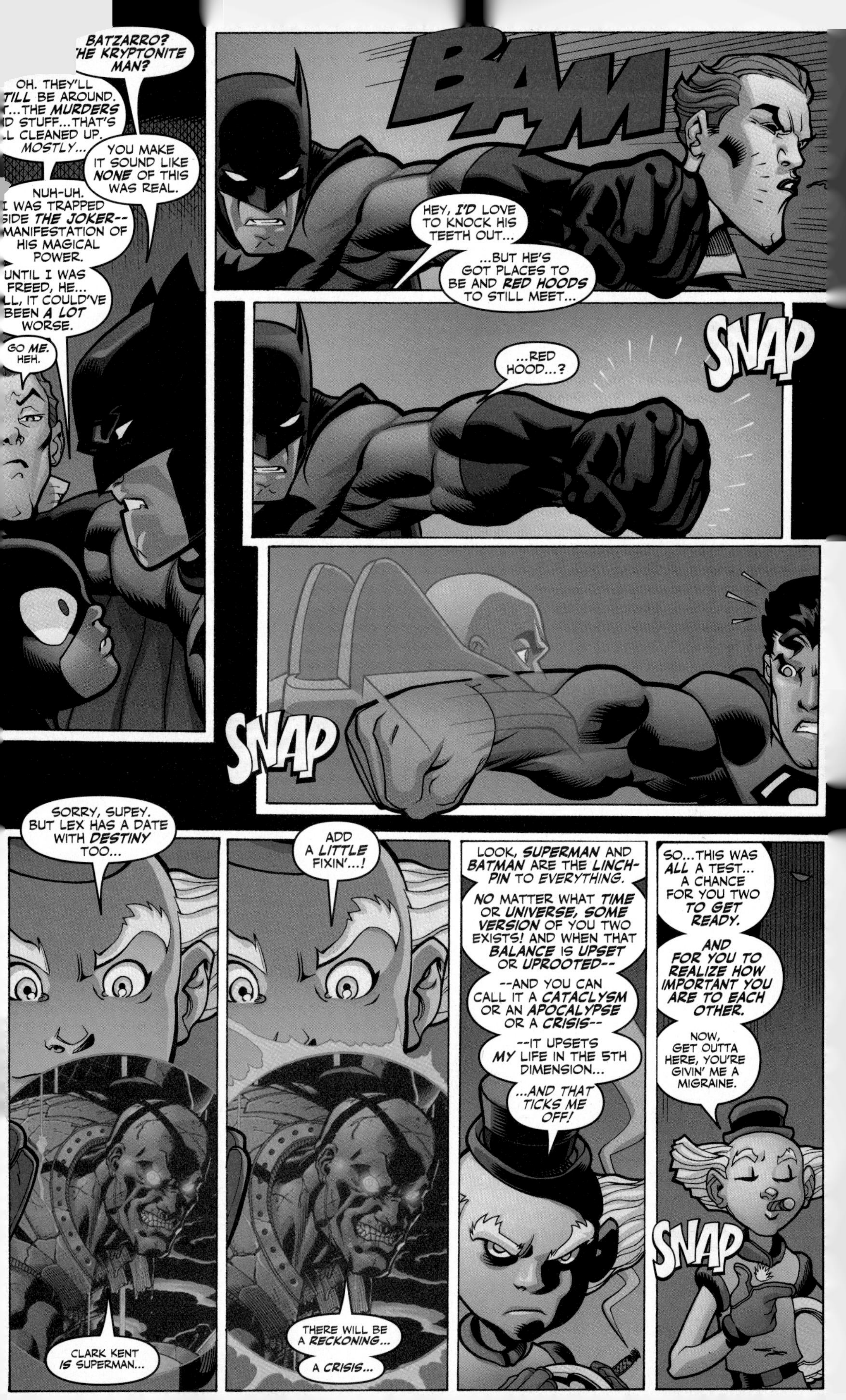

BATZARRO? HE KRYPTONITE MAN?
OH. THEY'LL TILL BE AROUND. T...THE MURDERS D STUFF...THAT'S L CLEANED UP. MOSTLY...
YOU MAKE IT SOUND LIKE NONE OF THIS WAS REAL.
NUH-UH. I WAS TRAPPED SIDE THE JOKER-- MANIFESTATION OF HIS MAGICAL POWER.
UNTIL I WAS FREED, HE... LL, IT COULD'VE BEEN A LOT WORSE.
GO ME. HEH.
BAM
HEY, I'D LOVE TO KNOCK HIS TEETH OUT...
...BUT HE'S GOT PLACES TO BE AND RED HOODS TO STILL MEET...
...RED HOOD...?
SNAP
SNAP
SORRY, SUPEY. BUT LEX HAS A DATE WITH DESTINY TOO...
CLARK KENT IS SUPERMAN...
ADD A LITTLE FIXIN'...!
THERE WILL BE A RECKONING...
A CRISIS...
LOOK, SUPERMAN AND BATMAN ARE THE LINCH-PIN TO EVERYTHING.
NO MATTER WHAT TIME OR UNIVERSE, SOME VERSION OF YOU TWO EXISTS! AND WHEN THAT BALANCE IS UPSET OR UPROOTED--
--AND YOU CAN CALL IT A CATACLYSM OR AN APOCALYPSE OR A CRISIS--
--IT UPSETS MY LIFE IN THE 5TH DIMENSION...
...AND THAT TICKS ME OFF!
SO...THIS WAS ALL A TEST... A CHANCE FOR YOU TWO TO GET READY.
AND FOR YOU TO REALIZE HOW IMPORTANT YOU ARE TO EACH OTHER.
NOW, GET OUTTA HERE, YOU'RE GIVIN' ME A MIGRAINE.
SNAP

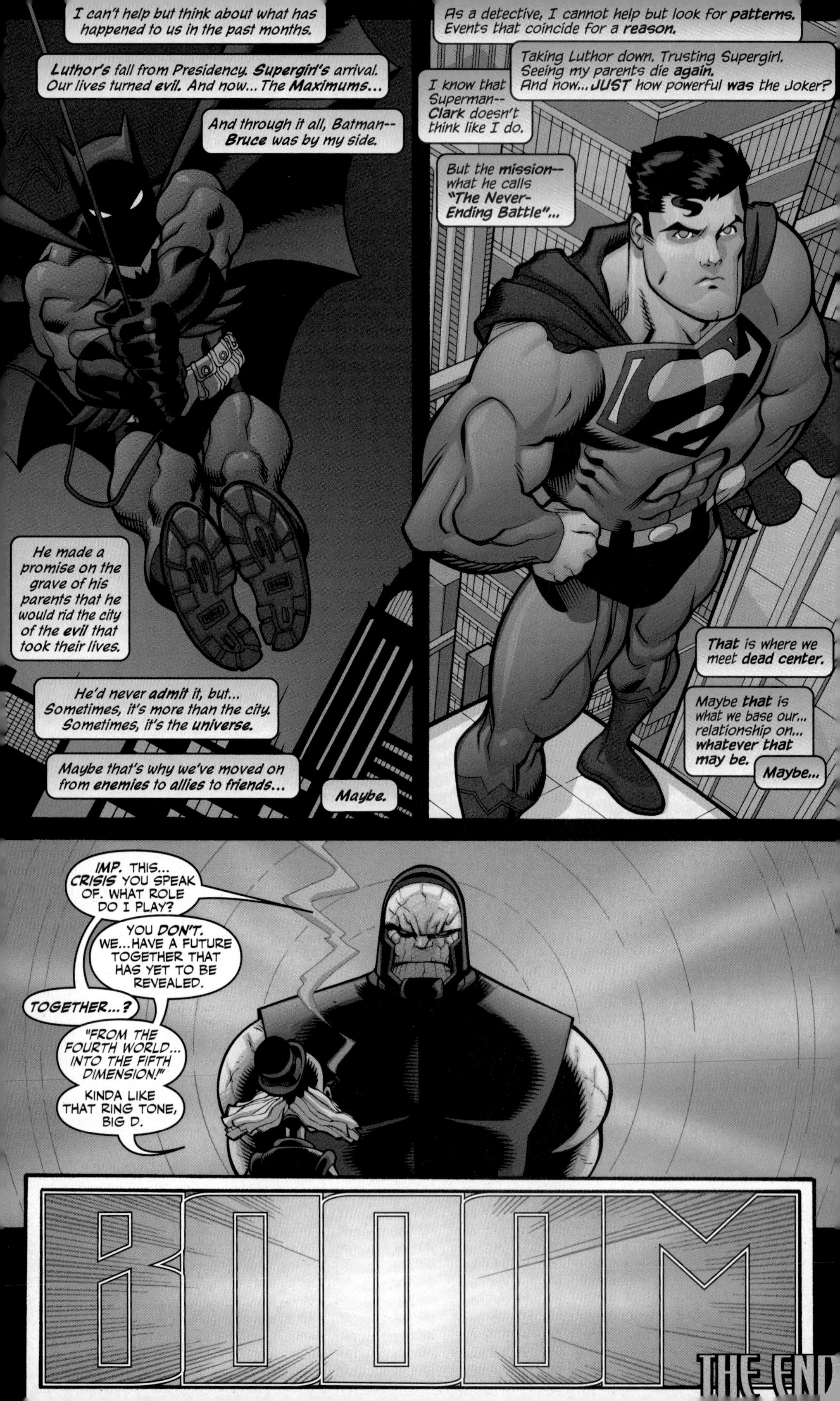

I can't help but think about what has happened to us in the past months.
Luthor's fall from Presidency. Supergirl's arrival. Our lives turned evil. And now... The Maximums...
And through it all, Batman-- Bruce was by my side.
He made a promise on the grave of his parents that he would rid the city of the evil that took their lives.
He'd never admit it, but... Sometimes, it's more than the city. Sometimes, it's the universe.
Maybe that's why we've moved on from enemies to allies to friends...
Maybe.
As a detective, I cannot help but look for patterns. Events that coincide for a reason.
Taking Luthor down. Trusting Supergirl. Seeing my parents die again. And now... JUST how powerful was the Joker?
I know that Superman-- Clark doesn't think like I do.
But the mission-- what he calls "The Never-Ending Battle"...
That is where we meet dead center.
Maybe that is what we base our... relationship on... whatever that may be.
Maybe...
IMP. THIS... CRISIS YOU SPEAK OF. WHAT ROLE DO I PLAY?
YOU DON'T. WE...HAVE A FUTURE TOGETHER THAT HAS YET TO BE REVEALED.
TOGETHER...?
"FROM THE FOURTH WORLD... INTO THE FIFTH DIMENSION!"
KINDA LIKE THAT RING TONE, BIG D.
BOOM
THE END

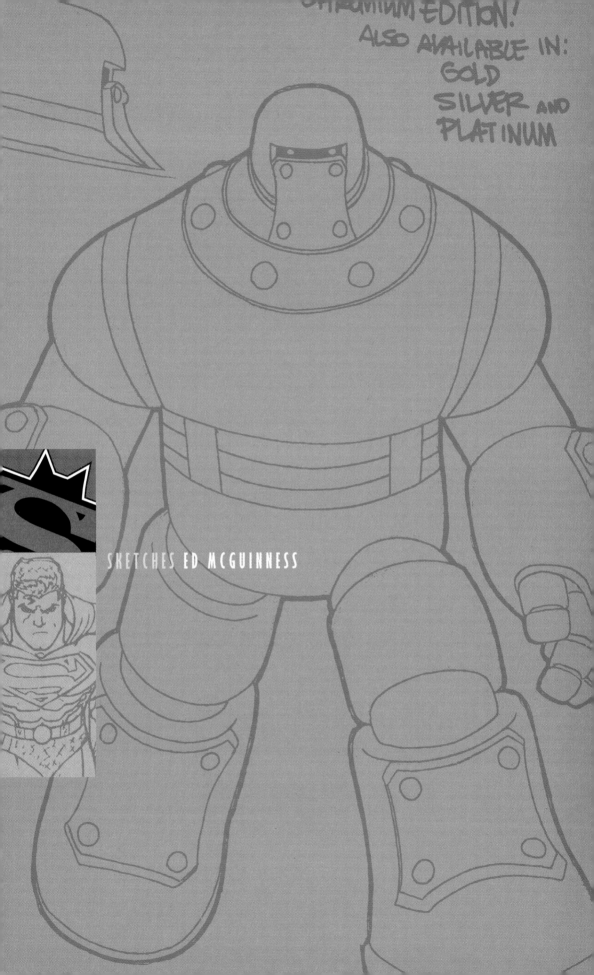

CHROMIUM EDITION!
ALSO AVAILABLE IN:
GOLD
SILVER AND
PLATINUM

SKETCHES ED MCGUINNESS

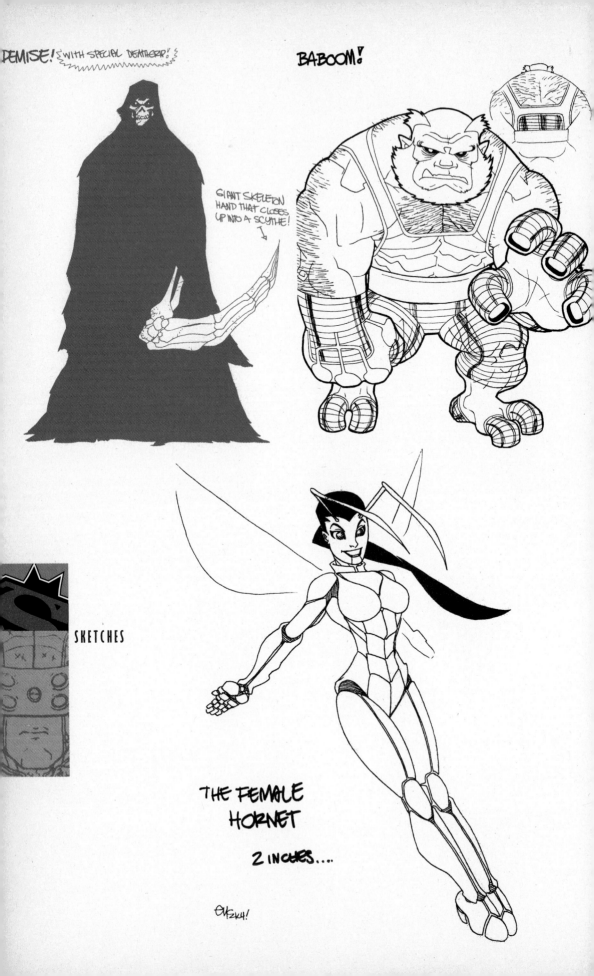

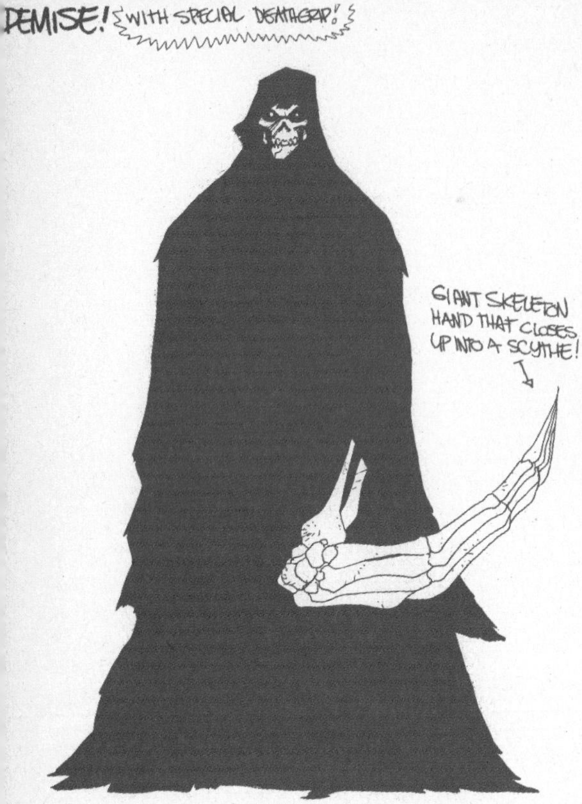
DEMISE!
WITH SPECIAL DEATHGRIP!
GIANT SKELETON HAND THAT CLOSES UP INTO A SCYTHE!

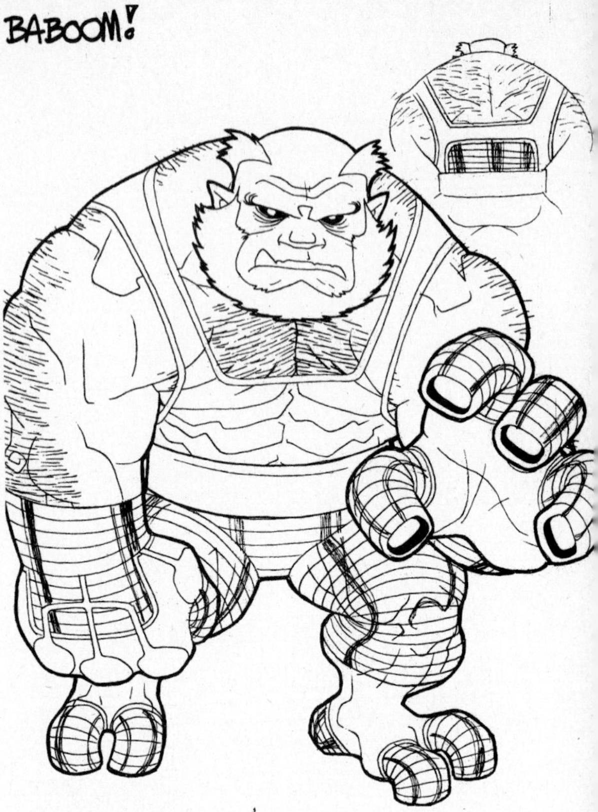
BABOOM!

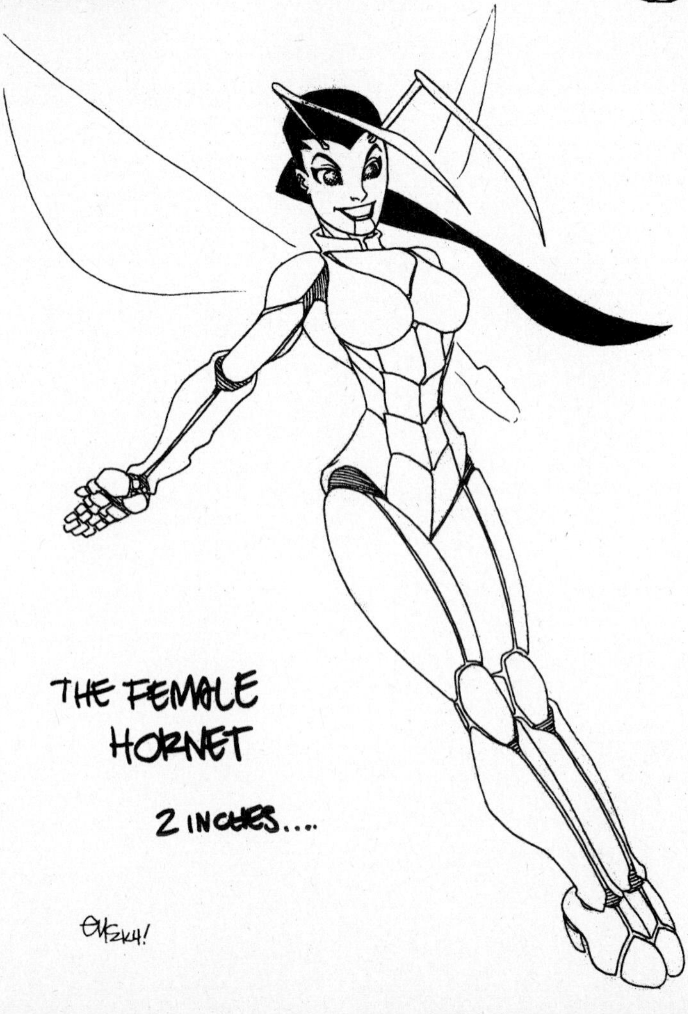
THE FEMALE HORNET
2 INCHES....

NEW MONSTER HEAD!

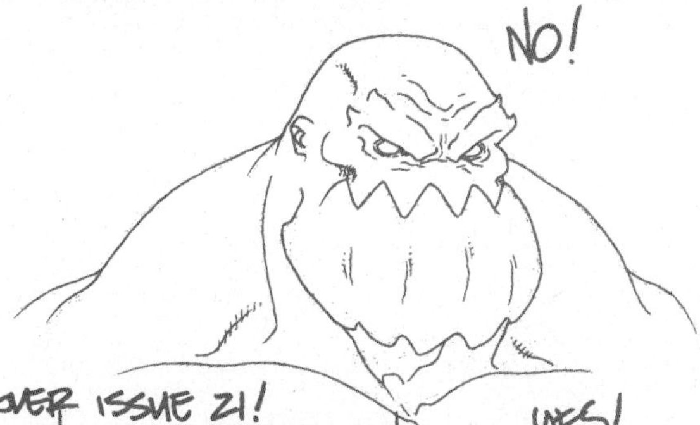
NO!

COVER ISSUE 21!

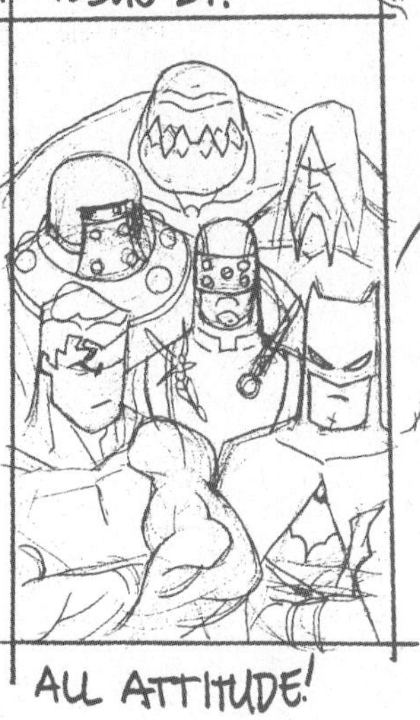

ALL ATTITUDE!

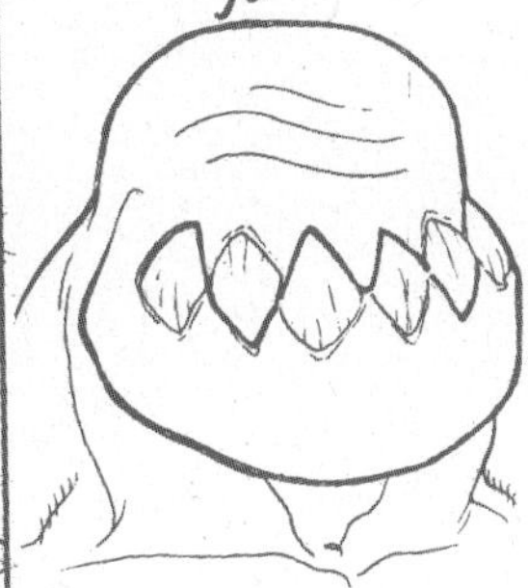
YES!

MONSTER!

THE PURPLE
THE LAVENDER
LOCOMOTIVE!

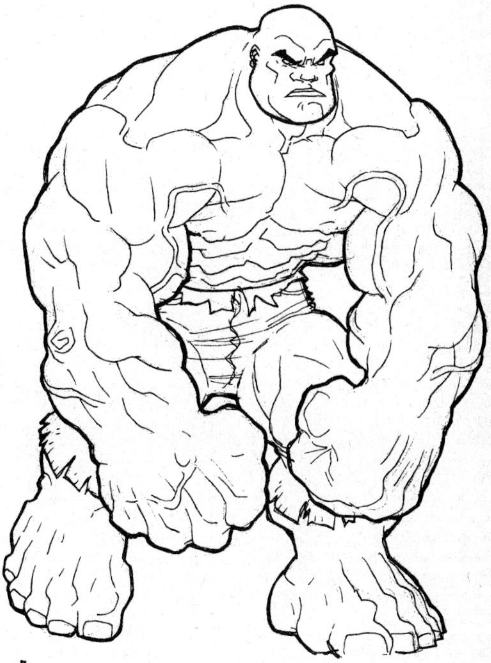

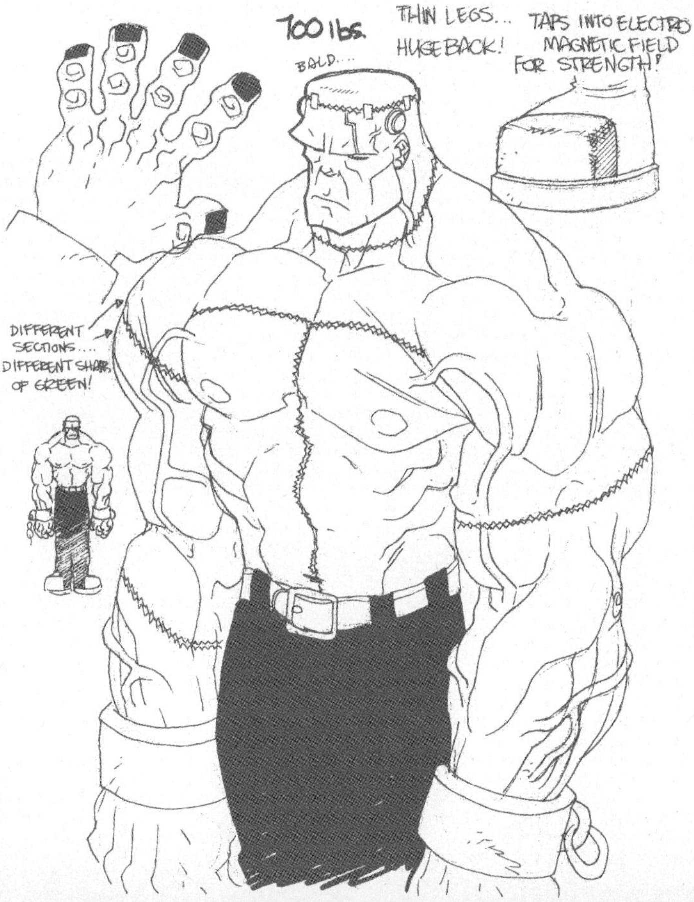
700 lbs.
BALD....
THIN LEGS...
HUGE BACK!
TAPS INTO ELECTRO
MAGNETIC FIELD
FOR STRENGTH!
DIFFERENT
SECTIONS....
DIFFERENT SHA
OF GREEN!

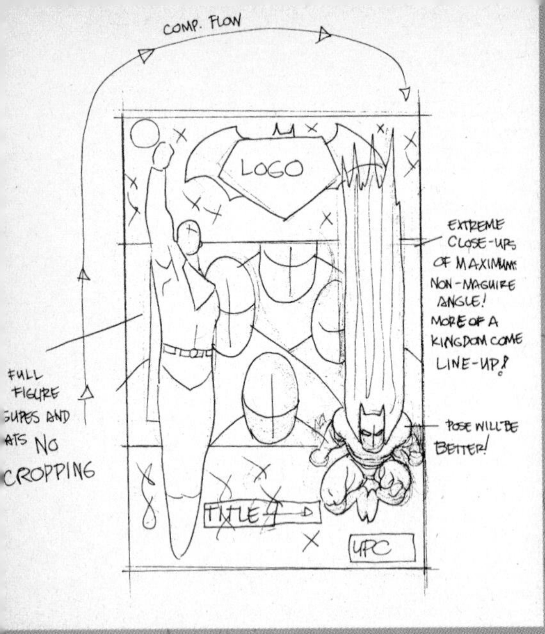
COMP. FLOW
LOGO
EXTREME CLOSE-UPS OF MAXIMUM NON-MAGUIRE ANGLE! MORE OF A KINGDOM COME LINE-UP!
POSE WILL BE BETTER!
FULL FIGURE
NO CROPPING
TITLE
UPC

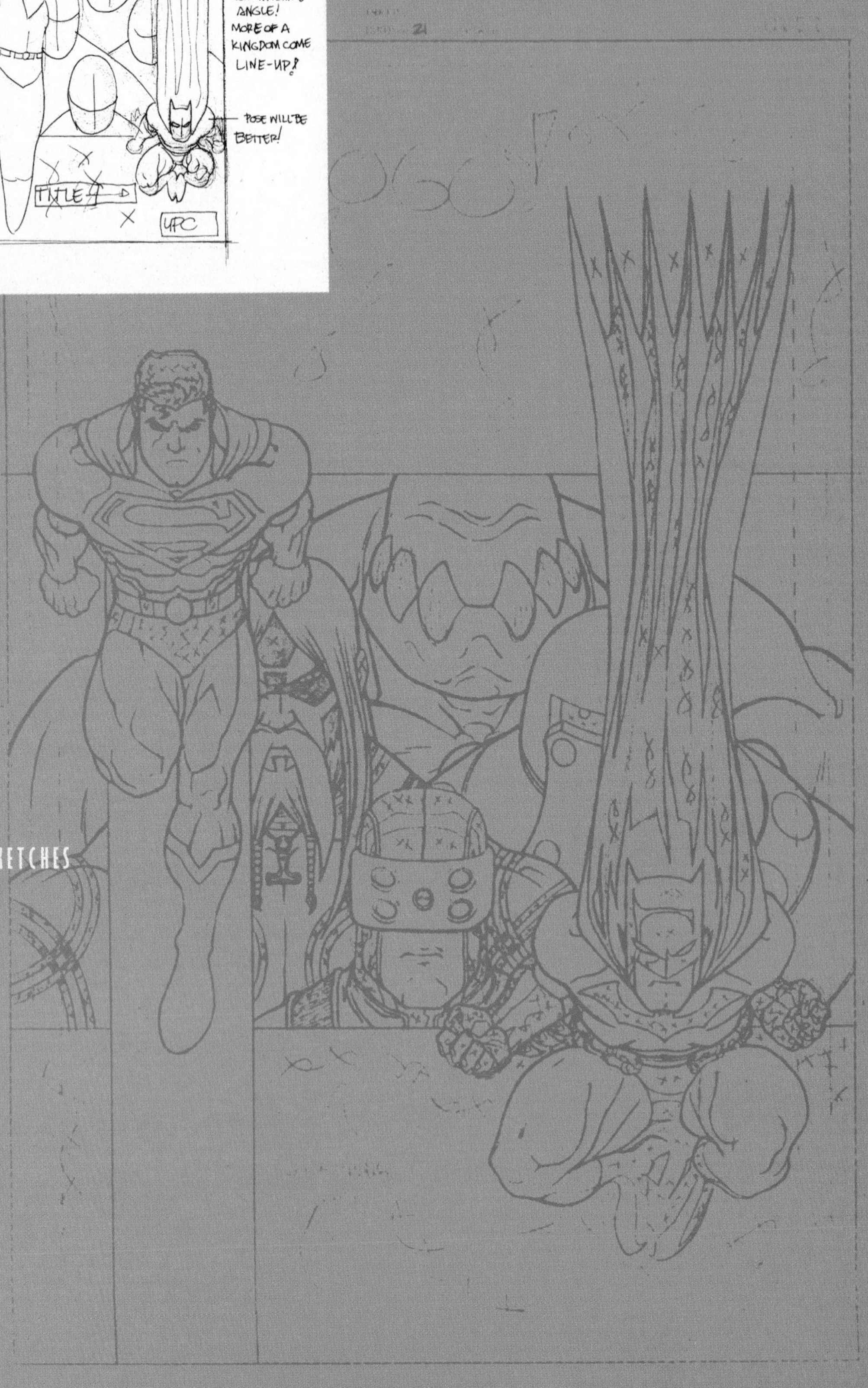

SKETCHES

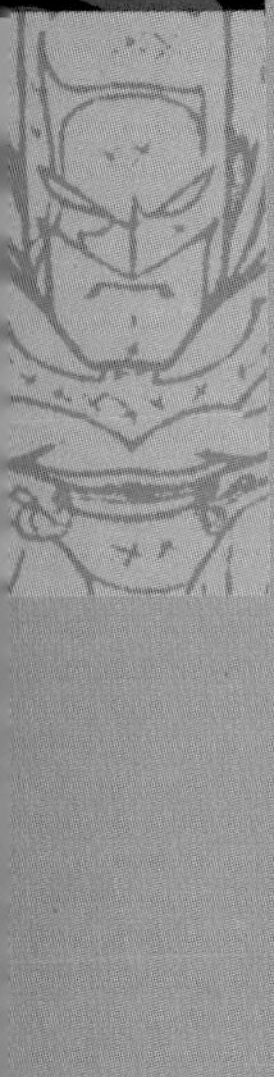

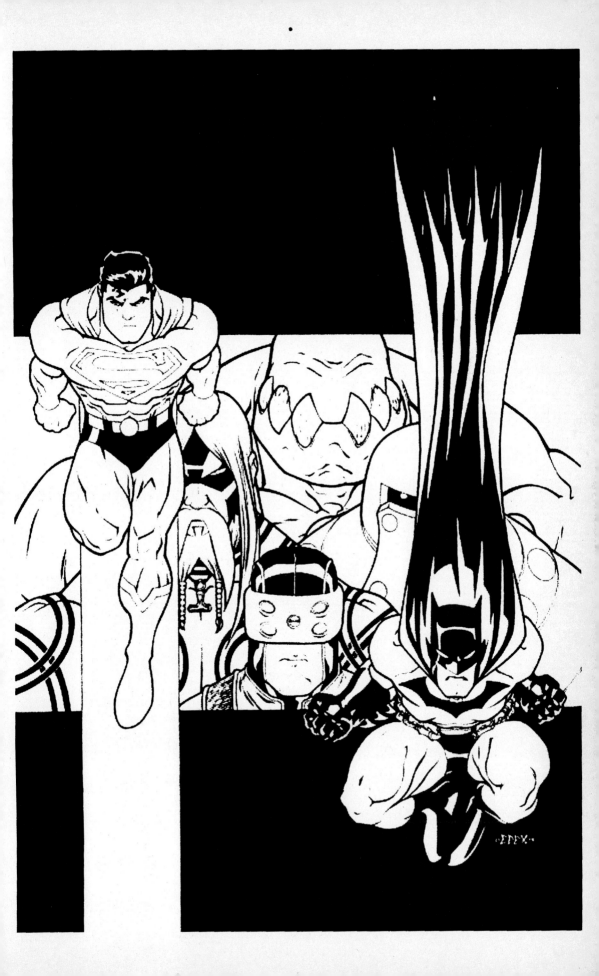

SOLDIER!

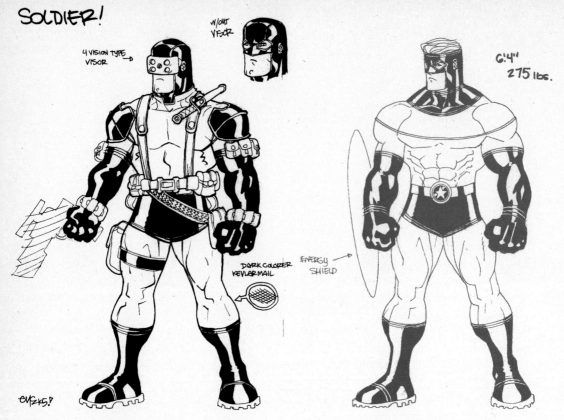

w/out VISOR

4 VISION TYPE VISOR

6'4" 275 lbs.

DARK COLORER KEVLAR MAIL

ENERGY SHIELD

evezk5!

SKYSKRAPER 25 STORIES

rapier

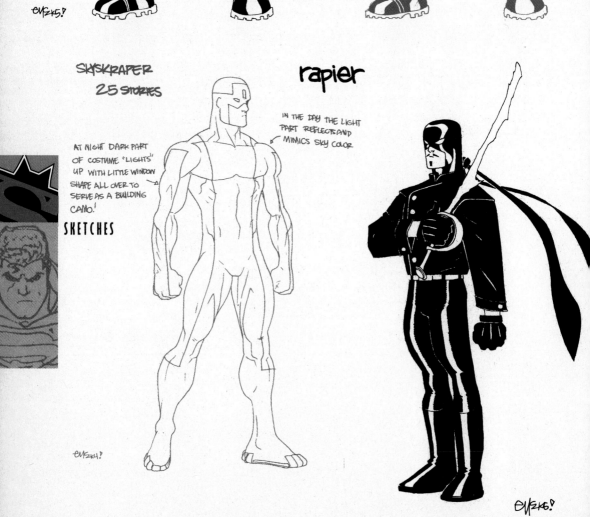

AT NIGHT DARK PART OF COSTUME "LIGHTS" UP WITH LITTLE WINDOW SHAPE ALL OVER TO SERVE AS A BUILDING CAMO!

IN THE DAY THE LIGHT PART REFLECTS AND MIMICS SKY COLOR

SKETCHES

evezk4!

evezk5!

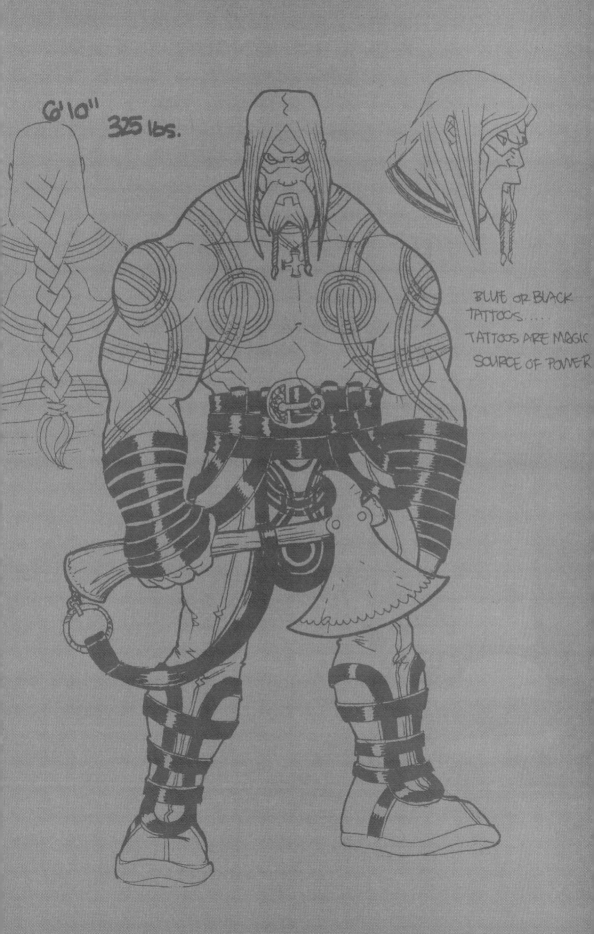

6'10" 325 lbs.

BLUE OR BLACK
TATTOOS...
TATTOOS ARE MAGIC
SOURCE OF POWER

BIOGRAPHIES

JEPH LOEB is the author of BATMAN: THE LONG HALLOWEEN, BATMAN: DARK VICTORY, SUPERMAN FOR ALL SEASONS, Spider-Man: Blue, Daredevil: Yellow and Hulk: Gray. A writer/producer living in Los Angeles, his credits include Teen Wolf, Commando, Smallville and Lost.

ED McGUINNESS first gained the notice of comic book fans with his work on Deadpool and Vampirella. His short run on WildStorm's MR. MAJESTIC landed him a gig on the monthly SUPERMAN title with Jeph Loeb, which led to the THUNDERCATS: RECLAIMING THUNDERA miniseries and arcs on SUPERMAN/BATMAN. He lives in Maine with his wife and four kids.

DEXTER VINES has been an inker in the comics industry for nearly a decade, having worked on numerous titles for various publishers, including Uncanny X-Men, Weapon X and Wolverine for Marvel Comics, Meridian for CrossGen Entertainment, and BATMAN: TENSES for DC.

DAVE STEWART began his career as an intern at Dark Horse Comics and then quickly moved into coloring comics. His credits include Fray, HUMAN TARGET: DIRECTOR'S CUT, SUPERMAN/BATMAN/ WONDER WOMAN: TRINITY, H-E-R-O and Hellboy: The Third Wish (for which he won an Eisner and Harvey Award). He lives in Portland, Oregon.

RICHARD STARKINGS is best known as the creator of the Comicraft studio, purveyors of unique design and fine lettering — and a copious catalogue of comic book fonts — since 1992. He is less well known as the creator and publisher of Hip Flask and his semi-autobiographical cartoon strip, Hedge Backwards. He never seems to get tired of reminding people that he lettered BATMAN: THE KILLING JOKE with a pen.

READ MORE OF THE
MAN OF STEEL'S
ADVENTURES IN
THESE COLLECTIONS
FROM DC COMICS:

SUPERMAN

SUPERMAN: FOR TOMORROW VOLUME 1

Brian Azzarello, Jim Lee and **Scott Williams** tell the epic tale of a cataclysmic event that strikes the Earth, affecting millions – including those closest to the Man of Steel.

"A BIG HERO NEEDS A BIG STORY, AND THIS TEAM DOESN'T DISAPPOINT."
— THE WASHINGTON POST

SUPERMAN: THE MAN OF STEEL VOLUME 1	SUPERMAN FOR ALL SEASONS	THE DEATH OF SUPERMAN

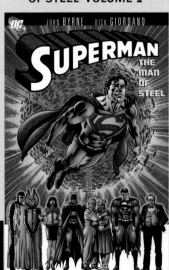 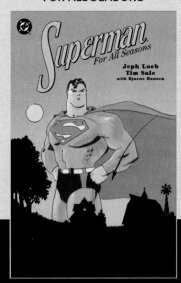 

JOHN BYRNE DICK GIORDANO	JEPH LOEB TIM SALE	DAN JURGENS JERRY ORDWAY JACKSON GUICE

SEARCH THE GRAPHIC NOVELS SECTION OF
www.DCCOMICS.com
FOR ART AND INFORMATION ON ALL OF OUR BOOKS!

READ MORE OF THE DARK KNIGHT
DETECTIVE'S ADVENTURES
IN THESE COLLECTIONS
FROM DC COMICS:

BATMAN

BATMAN: HUSH VOLUME 1

Jeph Loeb, Jim Lee and **Scott Williams** tell an epic tale of friendship, trust and betrayal, in the first volume of a tale that spans a lifetime of the Dark Knight.

"THE ACTION IS EXCITING AND THE DETAIL IS METICULOUS."
— CRITIQUES ON INFINITE EARTHS

BARTON PEVERIL
COLLEGE LIBRARY
EASTLEIGH SO50 5ZA

BATMAN:
THE DARK KNIGHT RETURNS

BATMAN:
THE LONG HALLOWEEN

BATMAN:
YEAR ONE

FRANK MILLER
KLAUS JANSON
LYNN VARLEY

JEPH LOEB
TIM SALE

FRANK MILLER
DAVID MAZZUCCHELLI

SEARCH THE GRAPHIC NOVELS SECTION OF
www.DCCOMICS.com
FOR ART AND INFORMATION ON ALL OF OUR BOOKS!